T0367704

Global Marketing Management System

SECOND EDITION

Global Marketing Management System

Basil Janavaras • Suresh George
Minnesota State University, USA   *Coventry University, UK*

World Scientific

NEW JERSEY · LONDON · SINGAPORE · BEIJING · SHANGHAI · HONG KONG · TAIPEI · CHENNAI · TOKYO

Published by

World Scientific Publishing Co. Pte. Ltd.

5 Toh Tuck Link, Singapore 596224

USA office: 27 Warren Street, Suite 401-402, Hackensack, NJ 07601

UK office: 57 Shelton Street, Covent Garden, London WC2H 9HE

Library of Congress Cataloging-in-Publication Data
Names: Janavaras, Basil J., 1943–   author. | George, Suresh, author.
Title: Global marketing management system / by Basil Janavaras,
    Minnesota State University, USA, Suresh George, Coventry University, UK.
Description: 2nd edition. | New Jersey : World Scientific, [2017] |
    Includes bibliographical references and index.
Identifiers: LCCN 2016052381 | ISBN 9789813201071 (hardcover)
Subjects: LCSH: Export marketing. | Business planning.
Classification: LCC HF1416 .J36 2017 | DDC 658.8/4--dc23
LC record available at https://lccn.loc.gov/2016052381

British Library Cataloguing-in-Publication Data
A catalogue record for this book is available from the British Library.

Desk Editor: Alisha Nguyen

Typeset by Stallion Press
Email: enquiries@stallionpress.com

Printed in Singapore

Endorsements

I have recently used GMMSO4 and have welcomed the improvements made to the earlier versions. These improvements enable users to save Money, Effort, Time and Stress (METS). The excellent graphical representations are also worth a mention as in previous versions users had to create their own. From a user's perspective it is extremely helpful to have these created for you.

When applied correctly, GMMSO4 provides decision makers with outcomes based on facts rather than guess work or gut feelings. I would recommend the GMMSO4 to senior executives as an essential part of their business toolkit as it integrates the functionalities of all departments in bringing their products to new global markets.

Amos Anderson
C.E.O. JAS Solutions for Business Ltd.
JASS

I have been using the GMMSO software for many years and it is with great delight that I see the 4th edition available. Based on our class experience with the GMMSO, I would not hesitate to recommend it to any lecturers who are willing to make their classes more practical, innovative, relevant and engaging, in order to prepare students capable to deliver real case project solutions to their future or current employers. In fact, The GMMSO software is so well structured and based on a very solid theoretical framework that we have to adopt and use it as the basis for our International Strategic Management course which is part of MBA and MSc in International Business programmes.

Dr. Emanuel Gomes
Senior Lecturer (Associate Professor)
in International Business and Strategy,
The Department of Strategy and International Business
University of Birmingham, U.K.

Having used GMMSO previously as a student and now as a practitioner, have seen it transform global potential to confidently executed strategy. It's a high quality tool that supports those seeking to make sense of the world's data and its opportunities. GMMSO bears particular importance to knowledge intensive situations and organizations including Universities and all key industries with an international outlook and gives peace of mind to erstwhile uncertain decision making processes.

Andrew Amayo
Lecturer in International Management and CMI Programme Director,
Birmingham City University, U.K

In the PRIMA program the students are taught the GMMSO simulation program which is an innovative tool for designing a business strategy for international markets. Through this simulation program, the students are able to create, plan, and test multiple business actions, with the option to change all the parameters in order to achieve the best possible outcome for the organization. Moreover GMMSO includes all the necessary parameters an international marketer must know, in order to act with success in the global business environment. I firmly believe that this software is indispensable to any company that plans to expand in foreign markets.

George J. Avlonitis
Professor and Director of MSc International Marketing;
Deputy Chairman of the Academic Council
Athens University of Economics and Business

GMMSO has contributed to the structure, effectiveness and student satisfaction of my IB course for six years. The project brings the real world into the classroom and encourages students not only to do academic research but to network with professionals. Students who want relevant and real learning enjoy the GMMSO journey.

Todd Friends
Assistant Professor of IB & Management
Whitworth University

GMMSO is used in courses of the Masters´ Program International Business — Central European Business Realities for more than 4 years, with a very positive feedback from students. Students learn through simulation that enable them to feel the real practice with real cases. They learn how to operate business, what parametres could be decisive for the best outcome and what solutions are brought by their decisions. GMMSO provides an application of the theoretical background on a completely different basis than other "like practical" courses and is a very useful and welcome step to a real business life. I do not hesitate to recommend it to other Universities and business schools.

Ludmila Sterbova
Vice-Dean & Director of International Business Program
University of Economics, Prague

GMMSO is an excellent support for my International Marketing course. I have been using it for two years and I will certainly use it in the future. It provides an excellent structure and valuable guidelines for students drafting a marketing plan for the first time. I would definitely recommend it to my colleagues.

Ernesto Tavoletti
Associate Professor of Economics and Management of Enterprise
Università di Macerata

The Powertrak MBA program at Saint Mary's University of Minnesota (www.smumn.edu/mba) requires use of GMMSO in our MBA capstone course and the EIMSO in our Trade Management course. Business in America needs more MBA grads that have learned to think through the process of developing a market. There is no better tool than GMMSO and EIMSO to make sure that process is thorough, based on data and is comparative.

Dr. Karen Gulliver
Professor and MBA Director
Saint Mary's University of Minnesota

I've been using GMMSO in my class of International Marketing since 2006. This interesting online software has remarkably evolved and I consider it as the right tool for applying strategic marketing decisions. One thing I am sure of is that students are learning something meaningful and applicable to life beyond the classroom.

Nizar Souiden
Professor
Laval University

The GMMSO is a very useful tool for any educator teaching international marketing or marketing strategy.

Dr. David Shani
MBA Program Director
Kean University

GMMSO gives my students a logical, step by step approach to international expansion, with recommendations that have been invaluable to businesses in our global business practicum.

Dr. Joseph McGill
Professor
Kean University

I would highly recommend this program for anyone teaching MBA's international marketing. My students stated in the course evaluations that the most beneficial aspect of the class was the GMMSO assignment. GMMSO lets the students personalize their learning experience by selecting the product/service and regions of the world they are interested in.

Dr. Barbara Wooldridge
Professor
Tampa University

I would like to recommend the JAI software (GMPSO, GMMSO, and EIMSO) to anyone who is a student of or a professional in International Marketing/Business Development. I used the software as a student and I continue to do so as a manager with international responsibility.

(Far East Regional Office, Waukesha Engine Dresser, Inc.).
Miguel Spada
Regional Manager

I used the GMMSO software in my International Marketing course. The software helped me understand the complexities of finding an international market and making sure it fits the company's long term vision and goals. While completing the different sections of the project, I was able to make better sense of my textbook content. I would recommend this software to all business students.

Kira Diner
Student
Minnesota State University, Mankato

The GMMSO4 course and software brings a unique approach towards market entry. It masterly combines qualitative as well as quantitative analysis of various factors that affect the market selection, entry or positioning strategy. I was impressed by GMSMO tool and I would like to use it for my personal purposes regarding my own business venture. I highly recommend this program.

Karel Kotoun
MSc International Economics University of Economics Prague

Having used GMMSO previously as a student and now as a practitioner, have seen it transform global potential to confidently executed strategy. It's a high quality tool that supports those seeking to make sense of the world's data and its opportunities. GMMSO bears particular importance to knowledge intensive situations and organizations including Universities and all key industries with an international outlook and gives peace of mind to erstwhile uncertain decision making processes.

Ioanna Bampali
Student of MSc in Marketing and Communication Specialized in
International Marketing (PR.I.MA.)
Athens University of Economics and Business

"There is only one good, knowledge, and one evil, ignorance."

— Socrates

To my family in the USA, Greece, prematurely deceased and beloved John and my friends and associates around the world.

Basil Janavaras

To those who matter! Maja and our daughters, Vanessa and Shifrah who live in a global world

Suresh George

Brief Table of Contents

Table of Contents

About the Authors

Dr. Basil Janavaras is Professor Emeritus of International Business at Minnesota State University, Mankato (MSU), MN, USA and President/CEO of JAI, Inc., a global marketing management training and consulting firm (www.janavaras.com). Dr. Janavaras spent more than 30 years assisting companies and academic institutions expand into global markets and establish their presence and success abroad. He helped company managers develop a global orientation toward international business, and integrate global dimensions into their strategic plans.

He has published a number of articles in several business journals. He has authored the *Global Marketing Management System* textbook (previously published by Pearson Education, Inc., 1998), and co-authored:

- Avlonitis, G, Lymperopoulos, K. & Janavaras, B., (2010), *Modern Marketing Strategies for Global Markets*, Athens, Greece, Rosili Publishing.
- Janavaras, B., Paladini, S., & George, S., (2013), *Going Global: A Practical Guide*, Pearson Education.
- Lymperopoulos, K, Janavaras, B., & Salamoura, M., (2015), Strategies *for International Marketing & Exporting*, Athens, Greece, Kallipos (National Metsovion University).
- A chapter in the *Palgrave Handbook of Experiential Learning in International Business*.

He has developed the **Global Marketing Management System Online (www.gmmso4.com)** software, and the **Export Import Management System Online (www.eimso2.com) software.** These software packages enable users to conduct global market research, identify high potential country markets, determine best entry mode strategies and develop their international marketing/exporting plans. His LinkedIn profile can be accessed at: https://www.linkedin.com/in/bjjanavaras

Dr. Suresh George is a Principal Lecturer in International Business at Coventry University and currently the course director for the MSc in International business management. He lectures on Global Strategy, Emerging Markets and Organizational Strategy. With over 21 years of experiencing business within an international context, Suresh has lived or worked across India, Kenya, Nigeria, Oman and the UK. He has published a number of articles in several business journals. He has co-authored with Basil Janavaras the *Going Global — a practical guide* textbook (published by Pearson Education, Inc., 2013) as well as a chapter in the well regarded *Palgrave Handbook of Experiential Learning in International Business.*

Suresh is also the creator of the GLOBESTRATEGY (http://globestrategy.net) learning resource for International Business He tweets as@sureshgeorge.

Preface

The *Global Marketing Management System* (GMMS) book (originally published in 1998) has been thoroughly revised and a new web-based software, *Global Marketing Management System Online* (GMMSO4), has been developed and added to the book. The GMMS approach (GMMS book + GMMSO4 software) provides a rigorous theoretical base and a comprehensive, systematic and integrative planning process designed to guide students and managers alike through the decision-making process of a company seeking global market opportunities.

This unique GMMS approach reflects the philosophy of the authors: Project Based Learning (PBL) using a strategic and applied oriented methodology to global business planning and strategy formulation in an increasingly interconnected world. It provides the platform, tools and a systematic step-by-step process designed to support users in their roles as managers and decision makers in a global setting. According to Shields (2005), PBL incorporates methods from problem-based learning, cooperative learning, constructive learning, active learning, and project management theory. Developing workplace know-how should be the main objective of any project-based learning. Shields identifies five competencies that projects should address: (a) the ability to identify, organize, plan, and allocate resources; (b) interpersonal skills; (c) the ability to acquire and use information; (d) the ability to understand complex interrelationships; and (e) the ability to work with a variety of technologies, (Janavaras, 2012).

The GMMS package is designed for and serves the needs of the following undergraduate and MBA/MSc courses:

- Global or International Business Strategy
- Global or International Marketing/Strategy
- International Management
- International Business (An Introductory course using part of the GMMSO4 software for the class project can be used)
- Entrepreneurship courses

The project-based learning style of the GMMS process helps to position the instructor as a facilitator and coach of learning outcomes. In addition, the GMMS approach gives an instructor the autonomy to customize for course objectives and exceed them. Combining international business theory and the authors' own teaching and hands-on business experiences, the GMMS process demonstrates the successful application of using web-based tools in teaching international business.

GMMS bridges the gap between theory and practice

The GMMS approach, addresses one of the most critical issues confronting business professors, that is, how to best bridge the gap between theory and practice. This package enables students to work online from anywhere in the world. Students, working individually or in groups, have an opportunity to integrate all functional business areas, assess the impact of environmental forces students and learn how to:

- Perform a situation analysis of a company in a global context.
- Research global markets for a product/service.
- Identify high potential country markets for company's product/ service.

- Conduct competitive analysis.
- Enter foreign markets.
- Develop international marketing/export plans and strategies.
- Use Internet resources and information effectively from any- where in the world.

In today's digital and globalized world there exists a compelling need for a book using the GMMS approach in developing interna- tional business plans and strategies according to the assessment of market opportunities combined with the firm's internal resources.

The GMMS approach facilitates interactive learning.

Interactive learning, made possible with the increasing influence of the Internet and online learning, has a lasting impact on a person's ability to retain and understand information as described by the classic study conducted by the National Training Laboratory's "Learning Pyramid" (DeKanter, 2005). As represented by the statis- tics on retention rates below, students will have a greater opportu- nity to learn and retain the information presented in the web based tools than by simply learning the material in a traditional way:

- Teach others/use immediately 90%
- Practice by doing 75%
- Discussion Group 50%
- See a demonstration 30%
- Learn from audio/visual 20%
- Reading 10%
- Lecture 5%

Several surveys have proven (Janavaras, 2007, Janavaras, Gomes. Young, 2008, Gomes, Janavaras, 2008) that GMMSO soft- ware is an excellent way for students to enhance their understand- ing of decision making in international management and bridge the gap between theory and practice.

The GMMS approach is grounded on sound and proven theoretical and empirical pillars.

The GMMS approach finds its theoretical and empirical justification from the international business and strategic management literature (Cavusgil, 1980; Ghoshal and Bartlett, 1991; Grosse and Behrman, 1992 and Holtbrugge, 1997). Regarding International Marketing Management literature, Kotabe and Helsen (2001, 578–580) mention that the content of global strategic marketing plan that guides the strategic and tactical marketing decisions usually covers four areas:

- Market situation analysis
- Objectives for each country
- Strategies and resource allocation
- Action plans (for each marketing mix element)

Hollensen (2007, 670–673) describes the stages in the development of a global marketing plan as follows:

- Deciding whether to internationalize
- Deciding which markets to enter
- Market entry strategies
- Designing the global marketing program — developing the international marketing mix
- Implementing and coordinating the global marketing program according to the allocation of marketing resources indicated in the marketing budget.

Special Features of the Approach

1. A practical and realistic format

The GMMS approach offers a unique step-by-step approach to decision-making in international business. Each Chapter of the book and each Module of the software provide the objectives, steps to be followed to achieve these objectives and examples from actual case studies. Students and managers begin each component of the international business planning process with a clear understanding of its purpose and its application to the company.

2. Illustrative models, concepts and case studies

The GMMS approach is not an attempt to write another textbook on international business. However, in an effort to bridge the gap between theory and practice and enhance global business understanding, we have included selected concepts and theories on each component part as it relates to globalization, global business planning and strategy, environmental assessments and country identification, analysis and evaluation among others. These theories can be emphasized or further enhanced at the discretion of the student, manager, or instructor. Real world case studies have been included to demonstrate how the process works and facilitate the completion of the project.

3. GMMS online resources and additional sources of international business information

In order to facilitate the research process and enhance global business understanding a list of targeted resources are provided for each component of the GMMS process. Great effort has been taken to provide multiple sources for determining foreign market opportunities. Students and managers will find these sources to be of great assistance to them in securing the most current data with the minimum amount of effort, time and cost.

4. Company profile and product/marketing questionnaire

A GMMS company profile and product/marketing questionnaires have been provided. Users have the option to make use of these questionnaires to help them gather pertinent information in order to complete their projects.

5. Glossary of terms

The definition of terms specific to GMMS process have been provided along with other terms used in international business and trade.

6. Instructor's manual and user guide

A comprehensive Instructor's Manual, a PP presentation explaining the GMMS process, Video and Student User Guide are available by accessing the GMMSO4 software, http://www.book.gmmso4.com.

The Global Marketing Management System(GMMS)
Second Edition

PART A
Chapter 1 Globalization and Global Business Education

- Theorectial basis
  Globalization and Trade
  Economic indicators of globalization
  Globalization and the need for a global business education
- Project based learning and Online teaching tools in IB
- The need for the GMMSO software approach

Chapter 2 Understanding the firm's Strategic Position

- Information Scanning
- Performing a Firm level strategic analysis
- Product/Service Analysis
- Target market profiling
- Global Involvement
- Internal Environment Analysis
- External Enviornment Analysis
- SWOT strategies
- GLOBAL readiness scoring
- Additional reading
- Online support resources for Chapter 2

Chapter 3 The Search for Global Markets

- A preliminary screening of markets
- The process of screening countries using three separate screening matrices; The ranking and clustering of countries/markets for further in-depth analysis.
- Competitive analysis of the top two countries/markets.
- Identification of market and firm sales potential
- Analyzing market /country specific competitive analysis
- Identification of country entry conditions for the firm
- Analysis of financial and market entry conditions
- Identifying the best entry mode for a specific market
- Additional reading
- Online support resources for Chapter 3

Chapter 4 Creating an Entry Strategy into a Selected Market

- Selecting an entry mode based on the firm's capabilities and objectives
- Evaluating the business environment of the selected market
- Creating a marketing plan with its firm specific goals and objectives Developing a Product Strategy Developing a Pricing Strategy
- Creation of a promotional strategy
- Developing of a Distribution strategy
- Creation of a financial strategy
- Creating the organizational structure for the new market
- Understanding possible exit strategies and scenarios
- Additional reading
- Online support resources for Chapter 4

PART B
The GMMSO4 Software System

- Background to the development of the online version of the GMMS method
- Learning Outcomes
- The GMMSO4 Layout
- Outline of each module
- Correlation between GMMSO and International Business Topics
- Teaching with the GMMSO4 software
- Using the Software

PART C

- A Case Study created using the GMMS approach and GMMSO4 software

Appendices
A: Company Profile Questionnaire
B: Product/Marketing Questionnaire
C: Bibliography
E: Subject Index
F: Endorsements

7. Sample Course Outlines

Course outlines using the GMMS approach in their international business courses are provided. These are actual outlines provided by Instructors who have used the GMMSO4 software for their class projects at both the undergraduate and MBA level.

GMMS

Global Marketing Management System Online

GMMSO4 is a web-based global marketing management research and strategic planning program. **As a bonus, each student who purchases the second edition of** *Global Marketing Management System* **will receive a complimentary registration code that will provide access to the software.** This practical, realistic program guides students through the systematic and integrative process of gathering, evaluating, and using certain types of information to help them to determine which markets to enter with a particular product/service and to create a marketing plan for the country with the optimal market environment for penetration. It is both interactive and experiential. More specifically, the program enables students to:

o Perform a situation analysis of a company in a global context.
o Research global markets.
o Identify high potential country markets for selected products/ services.
o Conduct in-depth market and competitive analysis.
o Determine best entry mode strategies.
o Develop international marketing plans and strategies.

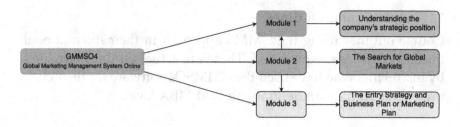

Support Materials

o A Student Guide.
o Glossary.
o Targeted Web-based resources.
o Actual sample student projects as models to guide first-time users through the GMMSO process.
o An Instructor's Manual is also available to those who use the GMMSO software.
o Frequently asked questions/answers/suggestions.
o Power Point presentation of the entire GMMSO for instructional purposes.
o Video resources

Since this is a web-based product, there is no administrative work for the instructor.

Additional benefits for Instructors:

o Ability to monitor student progress and review completed projects online.
o Allows you to integrate knowledge from this and other courses.
o Bridges the gap between theory and the real world of business.
o Practical and realistic.
o Obtain technical support
o Can be used from anywhere in the world!

If you are interested in using the GMMSO for your class project, register online: ⑨ http://www.book.gmmso4.com or contact your local (company name) representative for details at: sales@wspc. com.sg

Background

The GMMSO software is based on the Global Marketing Management System (GMMS) book originally published in 1998 by Basil Janavaras and has been revised four times since. It's the result of 30 years of teaching international business courses, research, consulting and actual business experiences on the part of the author. Many instructors and students from universities around the world have used the software in international business, management and marketing courses. Company executives, international business practitioners and consultants have been involved in the development of this software and have effectively used the system.

Finally, we are delighted that we can share with you this book and software and wish you to learn from it and enjoy use it. We would also like to learn from all those who use our book and software. We welcome your comments, suggestions and questions.

Basil Janavaras and Suresh George

Acknowledgements

We are indebted and would like to thank the many individuals such as instructors, students, and international business executives/trade professionals from around the world who have contributed to and used the GMSM approach. They all believed in international business education, research and strategic thinking and problem solving. They were driven by the desire to make a contribution toward bridging the gap between international business theory and practice and enhance global business understanding. However, this edition of the of the Global Marketing Management (GMMS) book along with the approach that is being used would have not be possible without the invaluable contribution made by my co-author and friend Dr. Suresh George and our research assistant (and Marketing Director of JAI), Christos Zoumpos.

The first author would like to express his sincere gratitude to the following special individuals who contributed immensely to the GMMS process:

- Dr. Emanuel Gomes, *University of Birmingham, UK*
- Dr. Turgut Guvenli, *Minnesota State University, Mankato, USA*
- Dr. Frederick Hoyt, *Illinois Wesleyan University, USA*
- Dr. Todd Friends, *Whitworth University, USA*
- Nizar Souiden, *Laval University, Canada*

- Mr. Christos Zoumpos for his valuable contribution to and excellent work on the Lafkiotis Winery case study using the GMMSO4 software.
- My wife, Linda for her invaluable support, advice and patience.
- Finally and most importantly, I would like to thank all the Instructors, professionals and my students at Minnesota State University, Athens University of Economics and Business (MSc PRIMA) and the University of Economics Prague (MBA/MSc) who have used the GMMS process over the last several years.

The second author would like to thank:

- The MBA and MSc students at Coventry University who have contributed to the GMMS pedagogy and practice for the last decade.
- Mr. Amos Anderson, FRSA, CEO of JASS Solutions
- My wife, Maja for being supportive and patient with this book

As we indicated in the Preface, would we welcome to hear from you, our valued customers, and encourage you to continue contributing to and using the GMMS book and software, www.book.gmmso4.com. Thank you all, indeed!

Part A

The Global Marketing Management System

Introduction

To realize that you do not understand is a virtue; not to realize that you do not understand is a defect

— Lao Tzu

Imagine that you could build a time machine and go back in time to look at the world of trade and international business. If one were to go back a mere three decades, you would see that transport and communication were key barriers to international trade. The division of the world into political blocs had created distinctive spheres of economic activity, some of which were artificially constrained by state managed enterprises and others by what we now call "free trade". Drastic decrease in the cost of transport and communication brought about by the increasing use of technology as well as geopolitical changes have dramatically increased the volume of international trade to over a 7% increase every year since 1970.[a] From 1980 onwards, developing economies increased their share of international trade to almost 42% of global trade with Asia emerging as a fulcrum of these so-called "emerging markets".

We attribute this drastic economic growth to an economic phenomenon called Globalization — the interconnectedness of markets, states, culture, products, and innovation into a constant moment of goods and services across the globe. Globalization is not a recent phenomenon having been around for centuries, with the colonization of different parts of the world by early hunting

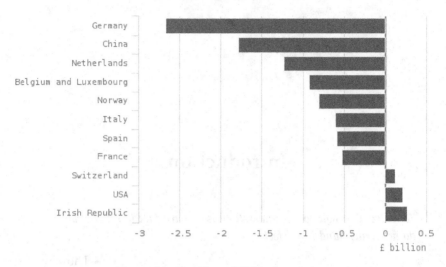

Figure 1: Significant UK Trade partners.

Source: ONS.

tribes, to the formation of societies leading onto the creation of nations. With the advent of new agriculture techniques, production and distribution networks were developed that help transfer food surpluses. The easier movement of trade across borders, declining communication and logistic costs, and the rise of new technologies, has allowed anyone, anywhere to become consumers of global goods and services. We call this integration "globalization" and this has been responsible for the fast rise in global trade. The academic debate around this has been divided with some arguing that globalization has been positive and others focusing on the negative consequences of globalization. Perhaps, the world is not connected as it seems as we see in the argument by Pankak Ghemwat[1] 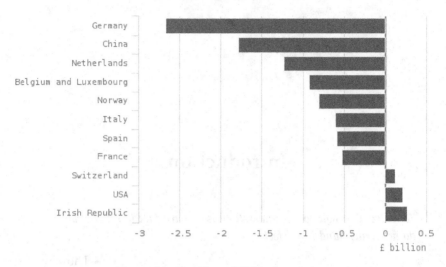. Another aspect of globalization has been freeing or liberalization of trade within the political debate that has divided academic theory on how best markets can be liberalized in order to balance the interests of local and non-local actors and institutions[b].

---

[1] http://www.ted.com/talks/pankaj_ghemawat_actually_the_world_isn_t_flat.

All of these phenomena rely on the world of International Business to facilitate the movement of these goods and services seamlessly and efficiently across national borders. But international business is an all-encompassing term that has for the most been dependent on the response of organizations to shifts within the global economy. The rise of the emerging markets as a powerful competitor to many developed economies with an attendant shift in the political landscape has thrown in newer dimensions of global competition for many firms. In the global economy, transnational companies rely on both developing and developed countries to successfully complete their ultimate goal: that of maximizing profits while minimizing costs.[c]

The nature of consumer behavior is constantly changing and firms need to constantly adapt and serve new segments in new

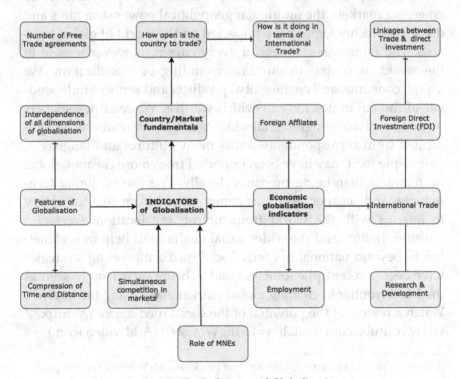

Figure 2: The Indicators of Globalization

geographies. Firms want to locate in large markets, close to customers, to reduce trade costs.[d] The nature of doing business is changing in a dynamic global environment and firms entering new markets often have to manage different challenges. The case of Coca-Cola facing challenges in the Iranian market is a key example of this dynamism and can be seen in the case study by Koc & Koc (2014).[e] Coca-Cola has faced challenges that range from geopolitical issues to religious and social cultural attitudes of drinking soft drinks.

For the business analyst quiz looking at expanding a product or service into new market, the attendant attributes of globalization, specifically the economic indicators of globalization,[2] are a useful tool to understand the impacts of globalization.

In 2016, global trade dynamics are markedly different from those in the past. The rise of new political actors specifically from emerging markets, the multipolar geopolitical power structures and disruptive technologies have impacted on the world of global business. The interconnectedness of every citizen, however remote in the world, is central to our understanding of globalization. We aspire, consume, and create global products and services independent of the cultural setting in which we live. We read newspapers owned by global conglomerates like *NewsCorp* or read articles syndicated from correspondents across many cultures and languages. Our staple food may have been imported from more cheaper global destinations than being produced locally. The rise of digital technologies and cheaper electronic components has created the ability to interact with the world from almost any location. *Facebook* , *Linkedin, Twitter*, and the wider social media tools help us seek networks beyond national borders. Social media marketing strategies have been a recent phenomenon and is being increasingly seen as the latest frontier in creating global market entry using the internet. Watch a review of the potential of the social media here (🔊 http://www.youtube.com/watch?v=knIEgWcGsb0) (Add video icon.)

---

[2]Data from the EU economic indicators can be viewed at 🔊 http://ec.europa.eu/eurostat/web/economic-globalisation-indicators/indicators.

The discussion of globalization, its attendant benefits, disadvantages and advantages, as well as the nature of the markets in which globalization occurs is not the remit of this book. For the interested reader, Ian Goldin and Kenneth Reinert's 2007[f] book is a useful primer on Globalization policies on equal market competition amongst and within countries. A wealth of information around the topic is also hosted on the globalization website[3] at Emory University. The 2013 Davos Summit focused on the challenges of emerging markets and you can watch the debate in its entirety online.[4]

This book focuses on the resultant impact of globalization on business education. The education of a new generation of students who are digital natives and demand more from the business curriculum. Using a new approach, we introduce a more contemporary methodology of teaching and learning.

1.1. Globalization and the Need for a Global Business Education

In spite of advances in management theory, the core of international business theory still revolves around the firm and its management of the business environment. For many firms, the expansion into new markets is becoming closely intertwined with gaining competitive advantage in an era of globalization. Companies seek new markets to either increase sales, increase profits or even to ensure greater efficiencies or reduce vulnerability from dependence on a single market. But *Verbeke and Kano*[5] believe that the "dominant paradigm" in international business today is the new internalization theory that depends on analyzing the strategies of multinationals based in emerging-economy home countries

---

[3] http://sociology.emory.edu/faculty/globalization/.
[4] http://www.youtube.com/watch?v=aZEz99ToAaw.
[5] Wilkins, M. (2015), 'the history of multinationals: A 2015 view', Business History Review, 89(3), 405–414, Academic Search Complete, EBSCOhost.

To this end, companies need to create and execute the best possible, yet practical market entry strategies. Companies need to understand the intricacies of regions and manage the challenges of individual markets. Business school students are now increasingly expected to be able to address the challenges of creating market entry strategies almost as soon as they graduate. This therefore lends itself to the challenge faced by most business schools in providing up-to-date, realistic, and pedagogical sound knowledge.

The challenge of educating a new generation of learners has been aptly described by Mironov-Duret, Cîmpeanu, Mărgărit & Pîrju[g] (2011) as follows:

1. *"The development of business in nowadays world takes place in an economic, social and political environment, being centered on one hand on a set of coordinates at a national/international level and on the other hand on the cultural dimension which leads to a progressive enlargement of the internationalization and globalization process of the socio-economic life.*

2. *Business internationalization represents an objective process of enhancing the involvement of companies in international transactions, which implies the existence of a global business environment of market economy.*

3. *The challenges of globalization are diverse, business internationalization having long exceeded the initial export–import stage of goods and services between states.*

4. *The elaboration of market strategy entrance and the development of the company on the foreign market is an important attribute of company management with an international vocation. This implies to take into consideration the development of the global framework and the potential of the company, in order to determine the objectives of internationalization and the forms of internationalization.*

5. *The objectives of internationalization can have in view several elements such as turnover growth, profitability enhancement, acceleration of company rate of growth by stimulating internal development, increased share of international activities across the company's*

business by exploiting economies of scale and the possibilities of production differentiation. Among proactive motivations there are the advantages in the achievement of profit, single producer status, technological advantage, exclusive information, managerial involvement, tax advantages, and economies of scale. Among reactive motivations the following aspects can be mentioned: competition pressure decreased domestic sales, excess capacity, saturation of domestic markets, approaching clients and partners. The advantages of active exporters are, for example: expanding sales markets, increasing profit by seizing market opportunities, such as favourable comparative costs, economies of mass production, multiplying effects, better use of production capacity by expanding customers' data base, providing greater long term profitability by capitalizing on the sustainable benefits offered by the external market. improvement of marketing potential by direct confrontation with international competition, the desire to strengthen credibility, the reducing of commercial risks by their dissemination in multiple markets and by diversifying types of products and operations. International scale activities inspires confidence, is a guarantee of quality and dynamism and it creates a favourable perception of the company, which is mirrored upon the activities it carries at internal level.

6. *On the other hand, entering external markets implies a series of costs and risks which must be balanced with the estimated benefits"*

In this book, we attempt to offer a practical solution to students, business owners, and anyone with interest in internationalizing their products or services for the new global consumer base.

1.2. Project-based Learning and GMMSO

The global marketing management system online (GMMSO) software is a management tool designed to help companies enter or expand their presence in foreign markets. This system helps address one of the key issues in teaching: how to enable students to engage with knowledge provided by higher education institutions. In a review of entrepreneurship programs, Mwasalwiba (2010) has indicated that this is a key issue in business education. Enabling the student to immerse himself or herself within knowledge is to a create a unique learning experience through the contextual provision[h] of solutions to real life business scenarios and problems.

Based on problem-based learning, the GMMSO4 system offers an innovative solution to teaching realism in international business, marketing, entrepreneurship, and global strategy. The philosophy of the GMMSO4 system revolves around a problem-based enquiry and learning pedagogical structure that is modular in delivery. The modular approach lends itself to developing a case study around the learning topic. Using critical analysis, real scenarios, company information, and market profiling, problem situations are developed which provide students with opportunities for interpretation, analysis, inquiry, and problem solving.[i] Using this approach, students are able to link understanding of these problems to the theoretical knowledge gained from the classroom.

With its origins in healthcare education, problem-based learning helps the student to challenge existing scenarios and *'engages the learner at a much deeper level, tapping on both the cognitive and behavioral responses*[i]. It generally involves small groups of students working with the facilitator to stimulate intellectual and interactive discussions around a set of problems which, often through the process of brainstorming, lead to resource in innovative solutions. Using this process, students increasingly become effective and self-directed individuals who can take charge of their own learning and become more globally employable [j].

Instructors, students, and stakeholders in businesses can use the GMMSO4 software to systematically identify global market opportunities or high potential markets and develop international marketing plans and strategies around the opportunities or markets.

Some of the underlying questions that the system addresses are:

- Can I go global with my existing product or service?
- What are the key attributes of my existing value chain that can be deployed into a new market?

- What are the high potential markets for my product or services?
- What markets should be entered first and why?
- What is the most effective marketing strategy for each selected or potential target market?
- What is the nature of competition both domestic as well as global?
- What is the nature of market entry strategy into a selected market?

Endnotes

[a]Trends in international trade, World trade report (2013). ⑤ https://www.wto.org/english/res_e/booksp_e/wtr13-2b_e.pdf.

[b]Silver, C., Jae-Hyup, L., & Jeeyoon, P. (2015). What firms want: investigating globalization's influence on the market for lawyers in Korea. *Columbia Journal of Asian Law*, 28(1), 1–40. Academic Search Complete, EBSCOhost.

[c]Trinidad R. A., Soriano-Miras, R., Rodríguez, B. F., Kopinak, K., & Hennebry, J. (2015). The localized global economy in Northern Morocco. *Revista Española De Investigaciones Sociologicas*, 152, 121–140.

[d]Damijan, J. P., & Konings, J. (2011). Agglomeration economies, globalization and productivity: Firm level evidence for Slovenia. Federal Reserve Bank of St. Louis, St. Louis.

[e]⑤ http://www.econjournals.com/index.php/irmm/article/view/852/pdf.

[f]Ian, G., & Reinert, K. (2007). *Globalization for Development: Trade, Finance, Aid, Migration, and Policy*, Revised Edition. Washington, DC: World Bank and Palgrave Macmillan. © World Bank. ⑤ https://openknowledge.worldbank.org/handle/10986/6618 License: Creative Commons Attribution CC BY 3.0 IGO.

[g]Mironov.-Duret, G., Cîmpeanu, A., Mărgărit, A., & Pîrju, S. (2011). The internationalization and globalization of business mechanisms and motivations. *Proceedings of the Scientific Conference AFASES*, pp. 85–90.

[h]Middleton, K. W., & Donnellon. A. (2014). Personalizing entrepreneurial learning: A pedagogy for facilitating the know why. *Entrepreneurship Research Journal*, 4(2), 167–204.

[i]Anderson, T., & Rourke, L. (2002). Using web-based, group communication systems to support case study learning at a distance. *The International Review of Research in Open and Distributed Learning*, 3(2). ⑤ http://www.irrodl.org/index.php/irrodl/article/view/107/186.

[j]Yeo, R. K. (2007). Problem-based learning: A viable approach in leadership development? *Journal of Management Development*, 26(9), 874–894.

Chapter 1

Understanding the Firm's Strategic Position

Customer needs are continually growing and changing in excessive competitive environment. Firms should sense and respond to these changes much more quickly than competitors to create competitive advantage.[1]

One of the key aspects of internationalizing a firm lies in understanding the capabilities and resources of the firm, more specifically its weakness and the firm's ability in managing opportunities in the global business environment. Management teams will need to conduct a structured analysis in understanding the strategic position of the firm. Not only does this assist in creating a more effective and targeted global strategy, but it also helps management to redefine their business within the framework of the global marketing imperative. Some small firms use a process of internationalization to obtain access to finance, technical knowledge, as well as to overcome competitive pressures in the local market.

The Purpose of a current situational or (positional) analysis is the first stage of the GMMS methodology, before embarking on global expansion strategy(ies) and provides a snapshot of issues/problems

---

[1] Roberts, N. & Grover, V. (2012). Investigating firm's customer agility and firm performance: The importance of aligning sense and respond capabilities. *Journal of Business Research*, 65(5), 579–585.

around the firm.[a] Some of the key questions that have to be asked in a firm's position analysis before deciding on its global strategy are:

- Who owns and/or controls the firm?
- What has been the recent history of the firm?
- What business or businesses is the firm in?
- What are the firm's products in each business segment?
- What are the customer segments in each business?
- What are is the structure and dynamics of the industry in which the firm competes? How competitive is the firm?
- What changes are taking place in the industry or allied industry that will affect the firm specifically of the industry in general?
- How does the firm compete at the product or business level?
- What are the firm's internal sources of competitive advantage/ disadvantage?
- What is the firm's current strategy?
- How well is the firm performing from a financial perspective?

Additional information on the key issues at the firm-level strategic analysis can be read from the article by Boardman, Shapiro and Vining (2004).[2]

Within the GMMS methodology, the following steps are suggested in the analysis of the firm:

1. Establish a relationship with a well-informed contact person at the firm (or contact persons) and identify the company's principal product or service.
2. Conduct an internal analysis of the company.
3. Using relevant data classification systems (SIC, HS, and NAIC), classify the firm's product in domestic, international, and regional markets to facilitate the marketing research process.

---

[2]Boardman, A. E., Shapiro, D. M. & Vining, A. R. (2004). A framework for comprehensive strategic analysis. *Journal of Strategic Management Education*, 1(2), 1–36.

4. Review the firm's philosophy, mission, vision, and product strategy (both past and present).
5. Examine the firm's competitive advantages, disadvantages, international marketing experience, and asset capability base for a possible global expansion.
6. Conduct a product/service/marketing analysis for the firm's principal product or service. This should help identify the product/service attributes for each product or service.
7. Create a target market profiling for the end-user/buyer of the firm and determine whether it is best suited for developed, newly industrialized, less-developed (LDC)[3] or big emerging markets (BEMs).[4]
8. Analyze and evaluate the firm's current pricing, promotion, and distribution strategies.
9. Conduct an external analysis of the global environment in which the company operates.
10. Examine product/marketing strategy relative to the competition over the past 3 years and review product placement within the product life-cycle theory (PLC) and the international trade product life-cycle theory (ITPLC).
11. Review the economic, demographic, technology, social cultural and political/legal history of the industry with industry trends over the past 5 years.
12. Begin to identify or contact domestic, foreign, and international organizations that are unique to the firm's product and markets.
13. Review if the firm is fully exploiting its global market opportunities and fully addressing all of its threats of constraints.

In this chapter, each of this sub-processes is discussed.

---

[3]The list of LDC states by the UN in 2016 can be found on http://www.un.org/en/development/desa/policy/cdp/ldc/ldc_list.pdf.
[4]Some authors may argue that the BEMs are becoming obsolete. However, an article on the *Financial Times* "Emerging markets: Redrawing the global map" can a useful commentary on this term. It can be read on https://www.ft.com/content/4a915716-39dc-11e5-8613-07d16aad2152.

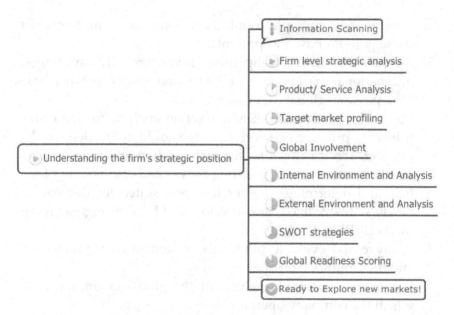

Figure 1:   The Firm's Strategic Position

1. Information Scanning

The first process of understanding the firm's position begins with information scanning. Information scanning can be considered as the identification of domestic and international organizations unique to the firm's products and markets. Research on some of these organizations can assist with market research or data collection providing information that is directly relevant in determining global market opportunities.

If you are not using your own firm for internationalization, you will need to choose an industry and a company within the selected industry. For background information, external analysis of the industry would be the first port of call. A useful place to begin can be the GLOBALEDGE[5] industry profiles. For research on the financial details of existing firms, the OPENCORPORATE[6] database is useful and contains a the list of companies across several territories.

---

[5] http://globaledge.msu.edu/global-insights.
[6] https://opencorporates.com/.

Public vs. Private Companies — typically, public companies are easier to research than private companies. However, many public companies are already well established internationally. If you choose a public company which is already involved internationally, later in the project, you may need to select countries or markets with countries in which the company does not have presence.

Fictional Companies — Those who would like to create their own companies or decide to use fictional companies will need permission from their instructors, keeping in mind, financial data will need to be projected for fictional companies.

2. Performing a Firm-Level Strategic Analysis

Once a firm has been chosen for analysis, the next step is to perform a *company strategic analysis*, analyze the *internal strategic capability* of the company and determine the nature of the firm's *international involvement*. This will involve sitting down with key stakeholders in the firm to look at several key aspects of the firm or in other words, a strategic analysis at the firm level.

The globalized nature of today's business environment creates several questions for forms seeking to expand. Some of these questions according to Ireland and Webb[b] (2007) are:

- In what market should we compete?
- Should we offer standardized products across all markets or should we modify our products for local preferences?
- How much risk are we willing to accept to compete in markets with which we are not familiar?
- What kind of skill sets shall be developed in order to become more innovative?

2.1. *Company background*

The firm-level analysis should start with an understanding of the background, followed by an analysis of its internal and external capabilities, threats, industry-level disruptive trends, and the nature of its international involvement.

2.2. *Nature of the company*

The first step is to ask the following questions:

- Is the company an independent company or part of a group of companies?
- If part of a group, name the group and analyze the impact of the group's brand equity on the internationalization of your chosen firm.

2.2.1. *Organizational purposes*

You will need to research on the firm's objectives, its mission statement, vision[7], and the values it represents.

2.2.2. *Company mission statement*

Not all companies have a clear mission statement. If this is the case, check out the company's website. Look for any clues about the goals of the company.

Values

What are the company's values?

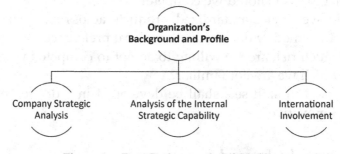

Figure 2:   Firm Background and Profiling

---

[7]Readers might want to watch a video "How Vision — and Persistence — Built Bangladesh's GrameenPhone." ⑤ http://knowledge.wharton.upenn.edu/article/how-iqbal-quadir-built-grameenphone/for a better understanding of the importance of a firm's vision.

Figure 3: Firm-Level Analysis

Figure 3 shows the GMMS logic that is used in the strategic analysis of the firm

Analysis of the company background should answer the following questions:

1) How did the company begin?
2) Who started the company? When?
3) What does the company do?
4) Where is the company's headquarters located? What are other company locations?
5) How has the company expanded since it began? You may wish to use a timeline here to describe how the company has expanded and changed over time.

A company profile questionnaire worksheet may be used to structure the market research and information scanning around the firm. Please see an example of the company profile questionnaire in the appendices.

2.2.3. *Financial analysis*

An important part of information scanning of the firm lies in the ability to understand its financial affairs. Financial information needs to provide the following characteristics[c]:

- Relevance of the financial information — this has the ability to make a difference in the decision-making process.
- Faithful representation of facts and figures that is complete, neutral, and free from error.
- Comparability across years — tells users of the information provided and can be compared with businesses utilize similar accounting practices.
- Verifiability — information provided researched should represent the economic activities of the business.
- Timeliness — needs to available to decision makers in time to be useful.
- Understandability — It is clear and concise.

There are three financial statements used commonly:

1. The income statement,
2. Balance sheet, and
3. Statement of cash flow.

A brief description of each of the financial statements is given below[8]:

The *income statement* gives an account of what the company sold and spent in the year (revenues and expenses)

---

[8]*Source*: Boundless (2016, 26 May). "Liquidity Ratios." *Boundless Business.* Ⓕ https://www.boundless.com/business/textbooks/boundless-business-textbook/financial-statements-18/ratio-analysis-and-statement-evaluation-108/liquidity-ratios-506-3529/.

The *balance sheet* is a financial snapshot of the company's assets and liabilities, and informs shareholders about its financial health.

The *cash flow statement* shows what came into and went out of the company in cash. It gives a better idea than the other two financial statements about how well the company can meet its cash obligations.

An example of a financial analysis is shown below:

Income Statement

	Current year	Last year	Previous year
Net sales			
Cost of goods sold			
Calculate gross profit (Loss)*			
Operating income (Loss)			
Net profit (Loss) after taxes			

*Gross Profit (Loss) = [Net Sales] — [Cost of Goods Sold]

Balance Sheet

Cash			
Marketable securities			
Accounts receivables			
Inventory			
Long-term assets			
Total assets			
Current liabilities			
Non-current liabilities			
Preferred stock			
Total common equity			
Calculate total liabilities and equity			

Liquidity Ratios[9]

Current = ([Cash + Market. Sec. + Accounts Rec. + Inventory]/
Current Liabilities)

Quick = ([Cash + Market. Sec. + Accoutns Rec.]/Current Liabilities)

LEVERAGE

Debt/Equity = ([Curent Liabilities + Non Curent Liabilities]/Total
Common Equity)

Activity

Reciev. Turn. = (Sales/Avg. accounts. Rec.)
Inv. Turn. = (Cost of Goods Sold/Aver.Inv)
Asset Turn. = (Sales/Avg. Total Asset)

PROFITABILITY

Net Profit Margin = (NIAT/Sales)
ROE = (NIAT/Avg. Total Common Equity)
ROA = (NIAT/Avg. Total Asset)

*Further information on these financial statements can be read from Henry
Dauderis & David Annand's book on financial accounting or section on
liquidity ratios in the Boundless book on business.*

2.2.4. *Capital resource analysis*

Understanding the financial statements of the firm is key to
performing a capital resource analysis that will help in the capital
budgeting decision for internationalization activities. The

---

[9]Table contributed by Harry Thiewes, Professor of Finance Minnesota State
University, Mankato.

process of capital budgeting is vital as decisions on long-term investments have to be based on the returns which these investments will make. Often, it is important for the management team of the firm to understand what the present value of this future investment is, how long it will take to offer returns, and how profitable this investment will be in relation to an alternative investment.

Many firms limit use of a technique of capital rationing in which a determined amount of funds are available to capital projects including expansion into new international markets. Unless the internationalization strategy can offer to add value and maximize return on investments, many international expansion strategies lose out on other competing capital projects within the firm. The use of financial ratios can be a general guide in marketing decision making and planning; helping the global project team feel more (or less) confident about the firm's financial readiness to expand into foreign markets.

The three popular decision-making techniques using capital budgeting decisions are:

- Payback Period,
- Net Present Value (NPV), and
- Internal rate of return (IRR)

Before committing to the exploration of new markets for the firm, it might be wise to start with senior management and their capital budgeting decision to understand if financial resources can be dedicated to market expansion.

Dun and Bradstreet compile industry benchmarks compiled from their database of public and private companies, featuring 14 key business ratios for public and private companies in 800 lines of business. It may be accessed from your local institutional library or by access through the company's website. FORBES also publishes a list of the top 15 industries and profit margins every year on their website. In addition, many governments[d] publish sectorial profitability ratios. For most UK higher education institutions, and firms, the FAME database from Bureau van dijk can be used to find industry profitability ratios, SIC code analysis, peer group analysis, as well as M&A activities in the industry.

Moving on from the financial analysis of the firm is the understanding of its corporate-level strategies.

2.2.5. *Corporate-level strategies*

A corporate-level strategy is the direction an organization takes with the objective of achieving business success in the long term. The corporate-level strategy should answer the following questions:

- What are the levels of diversification — low, moderate, or high?
- What are the reasons for diversification — resources, incentives, and/or managerial motives?
- How can the firm create value through a set of choices and actions at its corporate-level strategy?
- How can it capture this value and sustain it across new markets?

Another key driver of corporate-level strategy that finds relevance in internationalization is the *strategic intent* of organizations. Why do firms for example move across borders? Is it to acquire specific capabilities, leverage unique ownership-level advantages, or to take advantage of institutional benefits? A detailed understanding of the strategic intent at the corporate level can be seen in George Yip's article.[e]

At this stage, the reader may wish to briefly describe the company's scope, diversification of products, and the markets for those products and global involvement strategies before moving to the product and strategic business unit analysis.

2.2.6. *Product line or strategic business unit*

The seminal article of Prahalad and Hamel (1990)[10] made the concept of business units within a firm particularly interesting to understand the choices that could be made. The importance of analyzing the product line of the firm comes from its role in the firm's competitiveness. Understanding these product-level competences can help management to consolidate corporate wide skill sets and advantages into core competences that can help the business to adapt to changing external pressure.

2.2.7. *Business-level strategies*

A business-level strategy is a long-term approach to implementing a firm's business plans to achieve its business objectives. It can also be linked to understanding how the competitive advantage of each business is created and sustained over time.

The business-level strategy analysis can be a window into choices *that a firm can make in relation to its long-term objectives, its value proposition of the market and how it intends to build and sustain a competitive business system.*[f]

Analysis of any firm should answer the following fundamental questions:

1) Who will the product/service serve?
2) What kind of needs will the product/service satisfy?
3) How will the product/service satisfy those needs?

---

[10]Prahalad, C. K. & Hamel, G. (2001). The core competence of the corporation. *Harvard Business Review*.

Differences in business strategies at the firm level originate from the way firms create and define their product–market domains. In an earlier framework[11] that tried to understand business strategy at the firm level, four types of firms were identified. *Prospectors* are firms that seek to locate and exploit new product and market opportunities, while *defenders* tried to create and defend a specific portion of the total market by creating a stable product of customers and products. The analyser tried to seek and exploit new markets while defending their traditional product market domains. The last type of a firm in this typology, the *reactor* was considered to be less innovative. It might be useful to understand what frame of reference the target firm fits in during the process of company strategic analysis.

Porter (1980)[g] proposed that business strategy should be viewed as a product of how the firm creates *value* (i.e., differentiation or low cost) and how it defines its scope of market coverage (i.e., focused or market-wide. Most companies employ one of the five generic business-level strategies. The five generic business-level strategies are:

1) Overall low-cost provider
2) Broad differentiation
3) Best cost provider
4) Focused low-cost
5) Focused differentiation

Porter's framework is useful to explain the profitability of the business as explained in Figure 4.

---

[11]Miles, R. & Snow, C. (1978). *Organizational Strategy, Structure, and Process*. New York: McGraw-Hill.

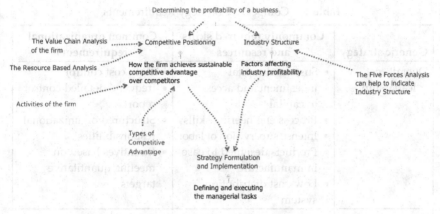

Figure 4: Determining the Profitability of a Business

Using the above structure, you may wish to ask the following:

1) What is your company's business-level strategy (Cost Leadership — low price, product/service differentiation, focused differentiation — niche, or other?)
2) How can you add value to your existing business by moving into new markets?

Determining the business strategy of the firm can help in determining how the firm can be positioned. Does a firm have strategy that depends on a specific position in the industry or is its strategy based on focusing on specific customer segments?

The competitive strategy for the firm's principal product or service should conform to its mission and philosophy and be consistent with company capabilities and resources. Table 1 depicts Porter's generic competitive strategies and commonly associated skills, resources, and organizational requirements. A clear understanding of company strategy will contribute greatly to the development of global marketing objectives, market opportunity criteria, and the creation of marketing mix strategies.

Table 1:   Competitive Strategy Requirements

Generic strategy	Commonly required skills and resources	Common organizational requirements
Overall cost leadership	• Sustained capital investment and access to capital • Process engineering skills • Intense supervision of labor • Products designed to ease in manufacture • Low-cost distribution system	• Tight cost control • frequent, detailed control reports • Structured organizational responsibilities • Incentives based on meeting quantitative targets
Differentiation	• Strong marketing abilities • Product engineering • Creative flair • Strong capability in research and development • Corporate reputation for quality or technological leadership • Long tradition in the industry or a unique combination of skills drawn from other business • Strong cooperation from channels	• Strong coordination among functions in R&D, product development and marketing • Subjective measurement and incentives instead of quantitative measures • Capabilities to attract highly skilled labor, scientist creative personnel
Focus	• A combination of the above policies specifically directed at a strategic target	• Combination of the above policies directed at the particular strategic target

Using this approach, you may wish to describe the firm's strategy for its principal product/service:

The next step is to define what the firm's competitive advantages and disadvantages are:

Another framework that can help to conceptualize business strategy in terms of actionable milestones is a concept of the balanced scorecard by Kaplan and Norton.[12] The balanced scorecard approach looks at the business strategy of the firm from four different perspectives.

1. The Customer Perspective — How do we look to our customers?
2. The Financial Perspective — How does a firm appear to its shareholders?
3. Business Processes — What business processes are the value drivers and create the most profit for the firm?
4. Organization Learning — Can the firm sustain innovation, change & improvement?

Additional reading on the balanced scorecard can be seen in the open lectures[13] by Rohan Sahani and Arnoldo Hax.

2.2.8. *Product strategy and analysis*

The first step in analyzing the product line of any target firm is to identify relevant data classification systems for the firm's product,

---

[12]Kaplan, R. S. & D., P. (1992). The balanced scorecard-measures that drive performances. *Harvard Business Review*, Norton.
[13]🕯 http://ocw.mit.edu/courses/sloan-school-of-management/15-902-strategic-management-i-fall-2006/lecture-notes/bud_aggmet.pdf.

complimentary product(s), alternative product(s), and if applicable the industrial buyer or consumer for these products.

Product classification codes and definitions are necessary to make enquiries and collect statistical data or information (for example, in the earlier section we have discussed understanding financial ratios. This can be obtained from statistical data and information of the industry in which the firm operates).

Product classification codes are useful in

1. analyzing the firm's current marketing strategy,
2. analyzing export/import statistics to identify global marketing opportunities, identifying potential distributors, and planning global marketing strategies for the primary target markets.

It is also useful to classify products using product codes to understand any value-added tax, duties, levies due under both domestic and overseas tax regimes.

In order to find the correct code for your product, it needs to be described accurately. Each component of the code includes:

- the duty and tax components
- any specific measures
- regulations
- conditions of use
- and special notes

The major classification systems used are:

- The **Combined Nomenclature** (CN)[14] which is EU "owned";
- Standard International Trade Classification (SITC) which is owned by the United Nations Statistical Division. The SITC is

---

[14]For more information on the CN system, please visit (🌐) http://ec.europa.eu/taxation_customs/customs/customs_duties/tariff_aspects/combined_nomenclature/index_en.htm.

a classification of goods used to classify the exports and imports of a country to enable comparing different countries and years.

- The **Harmonized Commodity Description and Coding System**, also known as the Harmonized System (HS) of tariff nomenclature, is an internationally standardized system of names and numbers to classify traded products.
- **Standard Industrial Classification (SIC)**[15] for use in classifying business establishments and other statistical units by the type of economic activity in which they are engaged.
- **North American Industry Classification System,**[16] version used in the United States of America. The NAICS system provides common industry definitions for Canada, Mexico, and the United States to facilitate economic analyses that cover the economies of the three North American countries.
- SIC for Japan.[17]
- **International Standard Industrial Classification** (ISIC)[18] of All Economic Activities, Revision 4 (draft).

The number of digits of the commodity code you should use depends on what level you need:

Level	Number of digits to use
HS	6
CN	8
EU TARIC (TARiff Integre Communautaire)	10

---

[15]For more information on the SIC code, please visit 🌐 http://www.ons.gov.uk/ons/guide-method/classifications/current-standard-classifications/standard-industrial-classification/index.html.

[16]For more information on the NAICS, please visit 🌐 http://www.census.gov/eos/www/naics/.

[17]For more information on the Japan classification, please visit 🌐 http://www.stat.go.jp/english/info/index.htm.

[18]For more information on the ISIC code, please visit 🌐 http://unstats.un.org/unsd/cr/registry/isic-4.asp.

UK Firms can use an online tool.[19]

Product/ Service	Classification code	Complimentary product/Service	Alternative product/ service(s)	Industrial buyer/ consumer
1				
2				
3				
4				
5				
6				

Once the product code has been identified, a process of product analysis can begin using the following spreadsheet.

2.2.9. *Target market profiling*

The purpose of product/marketing analysis is to assess current target markets, product attributes, and the strategies being used to bring the firm's product to the market. This analysis is helpful as an evaluation of the consistency of firm goals and objectives with operations.

Specifically, the target market profile along with product analysis will prove useful in developing a screening criteria for target markets with a need/desire from the product and adequate market size.

The worksheet below can help in determining the target market profile.

---

[19] https://www.gov.uk/trade-tariff) to search for import and export commodity codes.

	Home market	Foreign market
Describe the end-user and/or buyer of the company's principal product		
What is your target market and the needs of your customers? How are you fulfilling these needs?		
Is the buyer/consumer Industrial buyer/ consumer?		
Who is the end consumer		
Customer profile		
Create a customer profile describing your customer as clearly as you can.		
What is the geographical location of your customers?		
Online profile		
Are your customers online?		
What kind of websites do your customers use to buy similar products?		
What kind of payment methods are used online?		
How does the delivery of online sales contribute to your sales?		
Based on the analysis of the end-user/buyer and product attributes, determine which market the firm's product or service is best suited for.		

2.2.10. *Product analysis*

The analyst needs to identify the attributes of the firm's principal product (service) and assess the intended and perceived benefits of these attributes in current target markets. This assessment, indicating the firm's success in meeting the needs and wants of the buyer/ consumer relative to the competition, will be useful in evaluating foreign marketing opportunities once a target country is selected.

It is also useful in estimating sales potential in a new market and in developing a product strategy for that market.

A simple exercise in product analysis can be done using the worksheet below:

Product attributes	Product benefits (Real and perceived)
Technology level (high technology to low technology)	
Needs that are satisfied	
Functions of the product	
Features of the product	
Operational attributes (conditions of use, restrictions on use)	
Skills required for operation	
Size of the product (dimensions, weight)	
Taste, color, shape and style	
Material/ingredients	
Packaging	
After sales requirement (service, parts)	
Religious implications	
Complimentary or related products	
Patents, trademarks, copyrights	
Research and development	

Following on from the analysis of the product, the analyst should now move towards pricing. Please refer to the Product/ Marketing Questionnaire in the appendices for an example of the how this analysis can be done with the firm.

2.2.11. *Pricing analysis*

"Prices" are essentially promotional instruments set to maximize the firm's total profits. By analyzing and evaluating current pricing objectives and strategies, the analyst can make better informed decisions about pricing strategies in new markets.

Traditional pricing strategies are based around the 3C strategy or *a set of constraints that pricing strategies must overcome to succeed*[h]:

- Costs
- Customer
- Competition

A more recent update of the 3C pricing strategy model has been around the creation of value in pricing strategy, or the 4C model. This is structured around:

- The ability of the pricing strategy to create value
- The calibration of these value in the strategy
- The ability to communicate value
- The ability to capture value

Some key questions to be asked at pricing analysis are:

1. What are the firm's current pricing objectives?

- Target return on investment
- Target market share
- Maximize long/short run profits
- Growth
- Stability
- Other

2. What is the firm's current pricing strategy (market skimming, penetration pricing or market holding pricing) and why?

Domestic market	Overseas market

3. **What pricing strategies does the firm currently uses to determine its products price in international markets?**

- Cost-plus pricing
- Customer-based pricing
- Competition-based pricing
- Trade/end user discount
- Marginal cost pricing
- Market oriented pricing
- Others

The theoretical aspects of pricing strategies are discussed below have been extracted from the lecture notes of Catherine Tucker at MIT Sloan. [20]

2.2.12. *Defining cost-based pricing*

Cost-based pricing — This pricing is calculated on the basis of what it costs you to make the product. Cost-based pricing involves setting a price such that

$$Price = (1 + percent \ markup) \ (Unit \ Variable \ Cost + Average \ Fixed \ Cost)$$

Some practical issues in implementing cost-based pricing are:

a. You have to know costs.
b. Costs are a function of sales which are in turn a function of prices. This makes such calculations circular.

---

[20] https://ocw.mit.edu/courses/sloan-school-of-management/15-818-pricing-spring-2010/lecture-notes/

c. Cost-based pricing is misplaced in industries where there are high fixed costs and near-zero marginal costs. Distributing fixed costs is hard.
d. Ignoring the value you create leads to under pricing.

2.2.13. *Defining customer-based pricing*

Customer-based pricing is allowing your customers to dictate your pricing policy. Some examples are allowing purchasing agents to dictate their prices or giving away a valuable product or add-on for free.

Some practical issues in implementing customer-based pricing are:

a. Customers do not reveal how much they value the product.
b. Customers need to be educated about the value of the product.
c. When customers are used to being in control of a firm's pricing, they revolt at any price changes.

2.2.14. *Defining competition-based pricing*

Competition-based pricing describes the situation where a firm does not have a pricing policy that relates to its product, but instead a pricing policy that reflects its competitors' pricing decisions.

Some practical issues in implementing this strategy are:

a. It encourages firms to ignore their unique value proposition
b. It can lead to price wars
c. Focusing on market share does not necessarily lead to maximum profits

4. Using current pricing methods in terms of sale, calculate the price of the selected product. Please see the example spreadsheet below to calculate the price of the selected product

Cost head	Home country	Country 1	Country 2	Country 3	Country 4	Country 5	Country 6
Manufacturing cost							
Taxes							
Selling Price							

5. What are the firm's trade discounts to its channel members?

A specific channel or avenue that a firm uses to make its products and services available to the end customer is called marketing channel. Marketing channel pricing decisions are important as the features and prices of the product itself. Channel members often can act to continuously provide an outlet for the sales of a firm's goods and services. Sometimes products and services have to pass through multiple marketing channels are what are called intermediaries. Intermediaries have capabilities that many firms may lack and can provide them with contact with the right customers, the right marketing expertise, distribution capabilities, and also the ability to offer credit.

In order to retain its channel members, firms need to understand pricing strategies in terms of discounts to its channel members.

Some practical strategies[21] can be:

1. Plot the price paid against the number of units bought by the customer. Often it becomes evident that your best

---

[21] From Tucker, C. *15.818 Pricing, Spring 2010.* Massachusetts Institute of Technology: MIT OpenCourseWare. ⓢ http://ocw.mit.edu. License: Creative Commons BY-NC-SA.

(high-volume) customers are paying more per unit than your less profitable customers.

2. Construct a "price waterfall" chart. This allows you to work out the true net price for each customer.

    a. Start with "transaction price"
    b. Net rebate
    c. Net allowance
    d. Net discount
    e. Calculate final "pocket price"

3. Establish economic value before discussing price. Be the first person to bring up price: If you don't talk price, your customer will.

4. Establish consistent, transparent criteria for discounting

    a. Fixed prices
    b. Flexible offers
    c. Never give ad hoc discounts to repeat customers
    d. Reward loyalty and trial, not sheer volume

5. Be firm with the price

6. Ban phrases like:

    a. Regular, normal, list, book, lowest, best, reduced, basic, usual price
    b. The best I can do
    c. We can work a little on this price
    d. Our price is lower than anyone else
    e. Our price is less than a bag of chips per widget
    f. How does US $100 sound to you? Am I in the ballpark?
    g. Tell me where I need to be
    h. What do I have to do to get your business?

You also wish to research on the cost/pricing structure of competitor products/channels in potential markets.

2.2.15. *Analysis of the international involvement of the firm*

The objective here is to understand the state of internationalization of the firm. The GMMS method uses a logical approach using the following questions.

A. Is the company involved internationally?

Yes — If the company is already involved internationally, you will need to asses it's method of international involvement, its organization of the export function, and the length of its international experience. You will need to do the same assessment for the company's competitors.

No — If the company has no international involvement, then assess the international involvement of its competitors.

B. Who are the firm's domestic competitors as well its global competitors?
Research the company's top three competitors. Don't just guess!

2.2.16. *Methods of international involvement*

You may find the worksheet below useful in defining the methods of international involvement. It may be difficult to find out which methods competitors are using. Make sure to check competitors' websites to help you. Company annual Reports are also helpful in finding out competitive information.

Once this exercise is complete, the resulting matrix should provide more clarity on how the firm can manage its competitive advantage even across national borders

Method of Involvement	The firm	Competitor-1	Competitor-2	Competitor-3
In direct exporting	☐	☐	☐	☐
Direct exporting	☐	☐	☐	☐
Overseas sales subsidiary	☐	☐	☐	☐
Overseas marketing subsidiary	☐	☐	☐	☐
Joint venture (manufacturing)	☐	☐	☐	☐
Joint venture (marketing)	☐	☐	☐	☐
Whollyowned manufacturingsubsidiary	☐	☐	☐	☐
Contract manufacturing	☐	☐	☐	☐
Management contract	☐	☐	☐	☐
Licensing	☐	☐	☐	☐
Franchising	☐	☐	☐	☐
Company-owned retail store	☐	☐	☐	☐
E-Commerce	☐	☐	☐	☐
Importing (Final product)	☐	☐	☐	☐
Importing (Importing component parts)	☐	☐	☐	☐
Offshore call centers	☐	☐	☐	☐
Foreign retailer acquisitions	☐	☐	☐	☐
Currently not involved internationally	☐	☐	☐	☐

Figure 5:   A Grid for International Involvement of the Firm

Once the level of international involvement of the firm has been determined, the next step is to analyze the internal environment of the firm, its capabilities and resources in pursuing new markets.

2.2.17. *Organization of international function*

If at the end of the above analysis, the analyst finds out that the target firm is involved in international markets, then the question that needs to be asked is the level of its corporate globality.[22]

A very good framework to define how global a company can be comes from the work of Gupta, Govindarajan and Wang

---

[22]The process of globality is considered to be instead of globalization, in which barriers are no longer present and was used for the first time in 1998 by Daniel Yergin in his book — Commanding Heights — The Battle for the World Economy.

(2008).[i] They define a global company in terms of four key dimensions:

1. The *globalization of its market presence* — or in other words, the extent to which a firm has global a market presence and customer base.
2. The *globalization of suppliers* — the extent to which the supply chain of the firm is located in different parts of the world.
3. The *globalization of its capital base* — the sources of international finance that a firm can access in order to fund further developmental needs.
4. The *globalization of the firm's corporate mindset* — or the ability of senior management to deal with cultural and transnational issues.

Although in the introduction chapter, the effect of globalization on international trade and business has been discussed with particular reference to the role of technology in shrinking the world of today, countries are still distant from each other. A useful framework in analyzing the distance between countries and regions is the CAGE framework of Ghemawat[j] which looks at differences between markets in terms of four key dimensions:

1. The *cultural* dimension — The notion that differences in religious belief, race, social norms, and language can create barriers that create distance in the way firms do business overseas.
2. *Administrative* or political distance — This is created by differences in the legal environment, the institutional environment and international relations between countries.
3. The *geographic* distance — This includes attributes like the physical size of the country, average distances to borders to access waterways and ports, the countries transportation and

communication infrastructure, and how this contribute or directly influence distribution and transportation costs.

4. The *economic* distance or in other words the level of economic development of markets and how it influences consumer behavior.

The CAGE dimensions are useful in analyzing how the current international organization of the firm can negate the risk of entering a new market. It can help analyze at this stage how the impact of distance can affect profitability of entering new markets with existing products and organizational structure. Some of the key attributes of the framework are explained in Figure 6 and is useful to the analyst in defining the current international organizational structure of the firm and how it might be modified or adapted during the process of entering new markets.

	Cultural Distance	Administrative Distance	Geographic Distance	Economic Distance
attributes creating distance	different languages	absence of colonial ties	physical remoteness	differences in consumer incomes
	different ethnicities; lack of connective ethnic or social networks	absence of shared monetary or political association	lack of a common border	differences in costs and quality of:
			lack of sea or river access	• natural resources
	different religions	political hostility	size of country	• financial resources
				• human resources
	different social norms	government policies	weak transportation or communication links	• infrastructure
		institutional weakness		• intermediate inputs
			differences in climates	• information or knowledge
industries or products affected by distance	products have high linguistic content (TV)	government involvement is high in industries that are:	products have a low value-to-weight or bulk ratio (cement)	nature of demand varies with income level (cars)
	products affect cultural or national identity of consumers (foods)	• producers of staple goods (electricity)	products are fragile or perishable (glass, fruit)	economies of standardization or scale are important (mobile phones)
		• producers of other "entitlements" (drugs)		
		• large employers (farming)		
	product features vary in terms of:	• large suppliers to government (mass transportation)	communications and connectivity are important (financial services)	labor and other factor cost differences are salient (garments)
	• size (cars)	• national champions (aerospace)		
	• standards (electrical appliances)	• vital to national security (telecommunications)	local supervision and operational requirements are high (many services)	distribution or business systems are different (insurance)
	• packaging	• exploiters of natural resources (oil, mining)		
	products carry country-specific quality associations (wines)	• subject to high sunk costs (infrastructure)		companies need to be responsive and agile (home appliances)

Figure 6: The CAGE Framework from Ghemawat (2001)

With these frameworks in mind, the analyst must look at the target firm and how its international function is organized. You might want to define the international function of the target firm in relation to its nearest competitors using the following example.

Organization of international function	Firm being analyzed	Competitor 1	Competitor 2	Competitor 3
Within sales/marketing team				
Separate International division				
Separate import/export department				
International logistics team				
Global structure by-product				
Global structure by-area				
Global structure by-function[19]				
Matrix structure[20]				

2.2.18. *Determining the internal environment of the selected company*

The objective here is to understand the capability of the firm to internationalize. Does it have resources to sustain its competitive

[23] A (*functional organization*) is a common type of organizational structure in which the organization is divided into smaller (*groups*) based on specialized functional areas, such as IT, finance, or marketing.
Source: Boundless (2016, 27 June). "Functional Structure." *Boundless Management*. Retrieved from 🖲 https://www.boundless.com/management/textbooks/boundless-management-textbook/organizational-structure-2/common-organizational-structures-25/functional-structure-146-3979/.

[24] Matrix organizations assign employees to two reporting lines, each with a boss representing a different hierarchy. One hierarchy is functional and assures that experts in the organization are well-trained and assessed by bosses who are highly qualified in the same areas of expertize. The other hierarchy is executive and works to ensure the experts bring specific projects to completion. Matrix organizations are by far the most complex and are more common in large corporations.
Source: Boundless (2016, 31 May). "Basic Types of Organizations". *Boundless Management*. Retrieved from 🖲 https://www.boundless.com/management/textbooks/boundless-management-textbook/organizational-structure-2/defining-organization-23/basic-types-of-organizations-142-1383/.

advantage across borders? A comprehensive set of lecture notes on creating competitive advantage may be downloaded for free from the MIT Sloan open course by Charles Fine and Donald Rosenfield.

You need to perform both a resource audit analysis as well as the value chain analysis here.

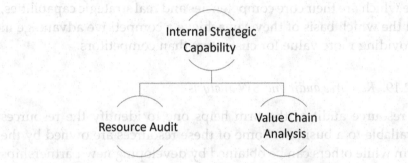

Figure 7: Determining the Internal Capability

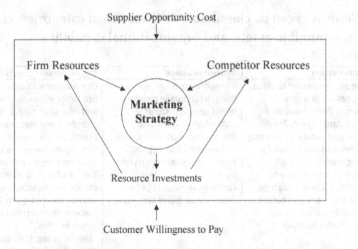

Figure 8: Creating Competitive Advantage from Wernerfelt (2003)

In order to determine the internal environment of the selected company, the GMMS methodology has simplified the process into two steps:

First, a resource audit is performed along with a value chain analysis. Secondly, an SW analysis of the strengths and weakness of the company is carried out.

A resource audit can help determine the organization's unique resources and a value chain Analysis will help identify the organization's core competencies. This will enable organizations to evaluate which are their core competencies and real strategic capabilities, on the which basis of they can achieve a competitive advantage in providing more value for customers than competitors.

2.2.19. *Resource audit and SW analysis*

A resource audit of the firm helps one to identify the resources available to a business. Some of these resources are owned by the firm while others can be obtained by developing new partnerships and alliances with other businesses operating in the same industry or from allied industries.

Resources can be classified into three broad categories; tangible assets, intangible assets, and organizational capabilities.

Tangible assets	Intangible assets	Organizational capabilities
These are the easiest to value, and often are the only resources that appear on a firm's balance sheet. They include real estate, production facilities, and raw materials, among others. Although tangible resources may be essential to a firm's strategy, due to their standard nature, they rarely are a source of competitive advantage.	Intangible assets include such things as company reputations, brand names, cultures, technological knowledge, patents and trademarks, and accumulated learning and experience. These assets often lay an important role in competitive advantage (or disadvantage), and firm value.	Organizational capabilities are not factor inputs like tangible and intangible assets; they are complex combinations of assets, people, and processes that organizations use to transform inputs into outputs. The list of organizational capabilities includes a set of abilities describing efficiency and effectiveness: low cost structure, "lean" manufacturing, high quality production, fast product development

Figure 9:   Classifying Firm Resources[k]

A resource audit can be approached by simply listing each of the key resources available to a firm and determining if it is a strength or weakness to the firm. Using the worksheet below, the resource audit can be used to create a list of internal factors that can be used later in the SWOT analysis.

Type of resource	Description	Strength/Weakness
Financial resources		
Physical resources		
Intangible resources		
Human resources		
Organizational capabilities		
Any other resource		

The resource audit is normally performed in conjunction with the value chain analysis. A value chain identifies the supporting activities (employee skills, technology, infrastructure, etc.) and the primary activities (acquiring inputs, operations, distribution, sales, etc.) that can potentially create profit. Figure 10 shows an example of the structure of the value chain.

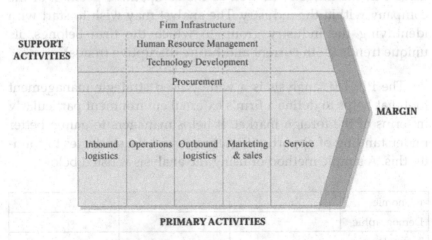

Figure 10:   The Value Chain Analysis[k]

Secondly, an SW analysis of the strengths and weakness of the company is carried out.

For business strategies to be effective, the company must exploit and expand on its strengths, as well as reduce or eliminate its weaknesses creating or improving its competitive advantage, in order to achieve profitability.

Some of the key questions to be determined by business in internal analysis can be:

1. What business are we in?
2. What business do we want to be in?
3. Do we have the resources and/or capabilities to move into a new business direction, possibly in a different market?

2.2.20. *Determining the external environment of a company*

The external environment of a company is often complex, but dynamic as it constantly changes and increasingly is becoming global. A company's external environment has two major parts: Its macro-environment and the industry context in which it operates. The analyst is expected to research on the key trends and drivers in the industry as well as the competitive position of the company within the industry. The analyst may wish to start with identifying the industry group to which the firm belongs, its unique trends (both current and future disruptive trends).

The PESTEL analysis is a widely used strategic management tool that helps to define a firm's external environment particularly in terms of the foreign market. It helps managers to gain a better understanding of opportunities, threats and the strategies to counter this. A simple method of using the analysis is listed below.

Economic			
Demographic			
Technological			
Socio-cultural			
Legal/political			

2.2.21. *The microenvironment*

The analyst also needs to understand the micro-environment of the firm in which it operates. The micro-environment includes elements within the firm's immediate area of operations. Such elements can affect its performance and decision-making freedom and can include the role of competitiveness, customers, distribution channels, suppliers, and other stakeholders. A commonly used approach in understanding the micro-environment is the 5C analysis.[25]

2.2.22. *Industry analysis*

The history of the industry and trends over time can provide the analyst of a firm with additional information about opportunities and threats in the global marketplace. Using Porter's Five Forces framework, assess the following forces. Make sure to include how each force will impact competition, profit potential, and demand.

For example, if the threat of new entrants is high, competition will increase because the company will be competing with many other companies. If competition is high, profit potential usually decreases because demand decreases. Video Icon A short introduction video to industry analysis that discusses the difference between an industry and a market, consumer information, and industry classifications is available at ⑨ https://www.youtube.com/watch?v=5DFd-ZNbNX4.

Industry associations are also useful sources of information for the analyst. In the U.K., the trade association forum (⑨ http://www.

---

[25]A explanation of the 5C analysis can be seen at ⑨ https://www.boundless.com/marketing/textbooks/boundless-marketing-textbook/marketing-strategies-and-planning-2/steps-to-creating-a-marketing-plan-28/conducting-a-situational-analysis-151-7221/.

taforum.org/Members) is a useful starting point. The American national standards Institute (🌐 http://www.standardsportal.org/usa_en/resources/trade_associations.aspx) is also useful as a source of information for American companies.

2.2.23. *S.W.O.T analysis*

Once both the SW and OT analysis has been carried out, these can be combined into a SWOT analysis. Some aspects of determining the strengths and weakness of a firm can be in relation to its competition.

Some useful questions to be asked at this stage can be:

- What is the nature of competitive advantage of your biggest competitor?
- Does your competition have a uniqueness in terms of product, specific expertize or geographical/product dominance?
- What kind of promotional strengths does the competition have?
- Is the strength of your competitor's promotional strategy key to their competitive advantage?
- How innovative is the competition? Is there a new pipeline of products that they are developing?

Determining the weakness of competition can also be done in the SWOT analysis by asking appropriate questions.

- Is the competition underserving or missing a specific market segment or a geographical location?
- What do the competitor's customers dislike in terms of the product offering?
- Is there a weakness in the competitor's business strategy that you can use to your advantage?

- Can you innovate across your value chain to deliver a competitive advantage that can address the weakness of the competitors?

Once the SWOT analysis is complete with the list of strengths, weaknesses, threats, and opportunities, the analyst is better placed to use the TOWS matrix to create strategies to counter or complement the SWOT analysis. The TOWS matrix is an externally focused tool that emphasises the external environment and helps you understand the strategic choices that the firm can make. The TOWS Matrix was first introduced in 1982 by Heinz Weihrich.[26] These strategies can include:

- *WT Strategy* — a defensive strategy that can minimize a firm's weakness and avoid the identified threats.
- *WO Strategy* — this strategy can help minimize the weakness of the firm by utilizing its opportunities.
- *ST Strategy* — this strategy utilizes the strength of the firm to reduce or minimize its perceived threats from the external environment.
- *SO Strategy* — are strategies that combine the firm's strengths with the identified opportunities in the best fit matrix.

In order to avoid a static analysis of the strategies, the analyst could extrapolate these strategies over time in order to cater to the future dimension of this analysis. A good example of using tool in identifying market opportunities can be seen in the work of Pholpuntin Serirat, Anuwichanont and Mechinda (2014).[1]

2.2.24. *Global readiness*

At this stage, the analysis should indicate from the strategic position of the firm whether it can internationalize. The GMMS

---

[26]An understanding of using the TOWS matrix in a practical setting can seen on the blog of Bruce Brunger ⑤ https://brungerblog.wordpress.com/2016/03/20/tows-matrix-for-marketing-brainstorming/

methodology now uses a series of *global readiness questions* to determine its ability to move into new markets.

The following questions are designed to assist:

1) A domestic company (one with no international involvement) to determine whether it is ready to expand abroad and to suggest an Entry Mode strategy.
2) An international company to compare and evaluate its present entry strategy with the one suggested by Global Readiness. If there is a difference between the two, the company may want to re-evaluate its strategy.

Directions: Rank each question on a scale from 1–5, 1 being least favorable and 5 being most favorable to globalization.

1) Is the foreign market similar to the domestic market? (The more similar the market the more favorable.)
2) Is the End User of the product in the foreign market the same as in the domestic market? (The more similar the End User the more favorable.)
3) Is the product successful in the domestic market? (The more successful the more favorable.)
4) Is the product unique? (The more unique the product the more favorable.)
5) Does the product perform the same function in the foreign market as it does in the domestic market? (If yes, the more favorable.)
6) Are the product use conditions the same in the foreign market as they are in the domestic market? (If yes, the more favorable.)
7) Does the product need modifications to meet the needs of the customers in the foreign market? (High level of modification will make it less favorable.)
8) What is the stage of the product's life cycle in the home market? (Early stage is more favorable.)
9) What is the stage of the product's life cycle in the international market? (Early stages are more favorable.)

10) Does the product require after-sales service? (If yes, the less favorable.)

11) Is the company in a position to provide after sales-service to its customers in the foreign market? (If yes, the more favorable.)

12) Would export orders hurt domestic sales? (If yes, the less favorable.)

13) Does the company have the financial resources necessary for export? (If yes, the more favorable.)

14) Does the company have in-house personnel with export related knowledge/experience? (If yes, the more favorable.)

15) Is international/global participation part of the Mission Statement of your company? (If yes, the more favorable.)

16) Is international expansion a part of the strategic business plan of the company? (If yes, the more favorable.)

17) Would the company be willing to investigate export market opportunities? (If yes, the more favorable.)

18) Would the company be willing to attend and/or participate in Trade Shows abroad?(If yes, the more favorable.)

19) Is the company willing to translate company literature into one or more foreign languages? (If yes, the more favorable.)

20) Are the company's top competitors involved internationally? (If yes, less favorable but this could also serve as one of the key reasons to internationalize.)

21) Is the industry highly regulated? (If yes, the less favorable.)

22) Is the company certified ISO 9000 or other certification? (If yes, the more favorable.)

Global readiness results

At the end of the exercise, please add up the total score for the firm and the following logic should provide you with a suggested entry mode.

---

[27]An Excellent article on how to find and use an Export Management Company can be read at 🌐 http://fita.org/aotm/0499.html.

[28]Information on how to use export agents for international trade can be found on 🌐 https://www.gov.uk/export-agents.

Score Range	Suggested Entry Mode
0–19	Not ready to export
20–29	E-commerce
30–39	Indirect export: → Export management company[22] → Export agent[23] → Piggyback marketing → Export trading company → Offshore call centers
40–49	Contractual arrangements: → Contract manufacturing → Management contract → Licensing or franchising
50–69	Direct exporting: → Foreign based agents → Foreign based distributors → Foreign sales representatives → Foreign retailer → Direct sales to end user
70–89	Foreign marketing presence: → Foreign sales branch → Foreign sales/marketing subsidiary → Company owned retail store(s)
90–100	Foreign manufacturing: → Joint venture → Wholly owned (100%) manufacturing subsidiary

3. Summary

At the end of this Chapter, you would have analyzed the selected firm and obtained an understanding of its position. Based on your findings and with the global readiness score for your firm, you will be in a position to recommend specific actions the firm should take in terms of global expansion.

In practice, firms that may wish to expand their business operations to new markets consider a number of strategic decisions to be taken. These include defining the product that wants to market, the country market it wants to enter, the timing of entry and the entry mode to be used in the market. Firms may also wish to address new market segments including perhaps non-profit and the third sector segments. The analyst interested in exploring areas other of potential expansion like corporate social responsibility strategies may wish read the article by Husted and Allen (2012).

The next chapter will concentrate on the search for global markets for the firm's selected product or service.

Endnotes

[a] Mahoney, J. T., & Chi. T. (2001). Business strategies in transition economies. *Academy of Management Review*, 26(2), 311–313.

[b] Ireland, R. D., & Webb, J. W. (2007). Strategic entrepreneurship: Creating competitive advantage through streams of innovation. *Business Horizons*, 50(1), 49–59.

[c] Dauderis, H., & Annand, D. (2014). Introduction to financial accounting. Lyrx. com. ⑤ http://lifa1.lyryx.com/textbooks/ANNAND_1/base2014/Dauderis Annand-IntroFinAcct-2014A.pdf.

[d] The UK government office of National statistics (ONS) publishes the profitability of UK Companies Statistical bulletins online at. ⑤ http://www.ons.gov.uk/economy/nationalaccounts/uksectoraccounts/bulletins/profitabilityofuk-companies/previousReleases .

[e] Rui, H., & Yip, G. S., (2008). Foreign acquisitions by Chinese firms: A strategic intent perspective. *Journal of World Business*, 43(2), 213–226.

[f] Lasserre, P., (2012). *Global Strategic Management*. Palgrave Macmillan.

[g] Porter, M. E. (1980). *Competitive Strategy*. Free Press.

[h] Tucker, C. (2010). *15.818 Pricing*, Massachusetts Institute of Technology: MIT OpenCourseWare. ⑤ http://ocw.mit.edu. License: Creative Commons BY-NC-SA.

[i] Gupta, A. K., Govindarajan, V., & Wang, H., (2008). *The Quest for Global Dominance: Transforming Global Presence into Global Competitive Advantage*. John Wiley & Sons.

[j] Ghemawat, P. (2001). Distance still matters. *Harvard Business Review*, 79(8), 137–147.

[k] Rohan Sahani, and Arnoldo Hax (2006). *15.902 Strategic Management I*. Massachusetts Institute of Technology: MIT OpenCourseWare. ⑤ http://ocw.mit.edu. License: Creative Commons BY-NC-SA.

[l] Pholpuntin, S., Serirat, S., Anuwichanont, J., & Mechinda, P. (2014). The analysis of TOWS matrix for promoting Thai kitchens into ASEAN Markets of Lao people's democratic republic and socialist kingdom of Cambodia. *Universal Journal of Industrial and Business Management*, 2(7), 182–187.

Additional Reading

1. A comprehensive set of lecture notes on creating competitive advantage may be downloaded for free from the MIT Sloan open course by Charles Fine, and Donald Rosenfield (2010). *15.769 Operations Strategy,* Massachusetts Institute of Technology: MIT OpenCourseWare. ⑤ ocw.mit.edu. License: Creative Commons BY-NC-SA.

2. A comprehensive set of lecture notes, on marketing strategy along with course assignments, may be downloaded for free from the MIT Sloan open course. ⑤ ocw.mit.edu/courses/sloan-school-of-management/15-834-marketing-strategy-spring-2003/.

3. A course on how to price goods and services by providing a framework for understanding pricing strategies and tactics. ⑤ ocw.mit.edu/courses/sloan-school-of-management/15-818-pricing-spring-2010/.

4. Boardman, A. E., Shapiro, D. M., & Vining A. R. (2004). A framework for comprehensive strategic analysis. *Journal of Strategic Management Education, 1*(2), 1–36.

5. *Global managers: how to obtain them in organizations.* An MBA thesis that provides insights into creating global management talent. ⑤ dspace.mit.edu/handle/1721.1/43612.

6. *Globalization at NTT DoCoMo: Implementing global business management strategies.* This thesis introduces the key elements and appropriate procedures for decision making in global business from top management's point of view. ⑤ dspace.mit.edu/handle/1721.1/17889.

7. Husted, B. W., Allen, D. B., & Kock, N., (2015). Value creation through social strategy. *Business & Society, 54*(2), 147–186.

8. Lessard, D. (2003). Frameworks for global strategic analysis. *Journal of Strategic Management Education 1,* 19–37.

9. Liquidity Ratios (2016, 26 May). *Boundless Business.* Boundless. ⑤ https://www.boundless.com/business/textbooks/boundless-business-textbook/financial-statements-18/ratio-analysis-and-statement-evaluation-108/liquidity-ratios-506-3529/.

10. Weihrich, H. (1982). The TOWS matrix — A tool for situational analysis. *Long Range Planning, 15*(2), 54–66.

Additional Information

- For a quick web search of UK listed companies, try using the ⑤ https://beta.companieshouse.gov.uk/portal.
- A list of registered (limited liability) companies can also be viewed at ⑤ http://index.okfn.org/dataset/companies/.

Online Resources

1. **Annual Reports** — 🌐 tinyurl.com/gwmhr4t.
2. **Bloomberg** — 🌐 www.bloomberg.com/.
3. **Business.com** — 🌐 tinyurl.com/gletwel.
4. **Businessballs** — 🌐 tinyurl.com/hkk2w6z.
5. **Center for Business Planning** — 🌐 www.businessplans.org/topic60.html.
6. **CNN Money** — 🌐 money.cnn.com/.
7. **Company Insights From Bloomberg** — 🌐 tinyurl.com/co4jpas.
8. **Company Spotlight** — 🌐 http://www.companyspotlight.com/.
9. **Connecting Industry** — 🌐 www.thomasnet.com/.
10. **Corporate Information** — 🌐 www.corporateinformation.com.
11. **Current Industrial Reports (CIR)** — 🌐 www.census.gov/cir/www/.
12. **Deloitte** — 🌐 tinyurl.com/7svfa4j.
13. **Economist Intelligence Unit** — 🌐 www.eiu.com.
14. **eCrat.com: Bringing Together Resources for Addressing Today's Business, Social Enterprise and Intern** — 🌐 www.ecrat.com/home.html.
15. **EDGAR–US company information and filings** — 🌐 tinyurl.com/4px4l.
16. **Entrepreneur** — 🌐 tinyurl.com/685twn.
17. **European Business Directory (Business to Business)** — 🌐 www.europages.co.uk.
18. **Federal Statistics** — 🌐 www.fedstats.gov.
19. **Financial Times** — 🌐 www.ft.com.
20. **Fortune 500 List of Global Companies** — 🌐 tinyurl.com/zjaolym.
21. **Gapminder Desktop** — 🌐 www.gapminder.org/.
22. **Global Information Network for SMEs** — 🌐 www.gin.sme.ne.jp.
23. **Hemscott (Financial information on UK and Irish listed companies)** — 🌐 www.hemscott.com/companies.do.
24. **Hoovers Company Search** — 🌐 tinyurl.com/pxfkgsg.
25. **How to Define Your Target Market** — 🌐 tinyurl.com/2vonccc.
26. **IBS Global Consulting** — 🌐 www.ibsglobalconsulting.com/.
27. **Industry Canada** — 🌐 www.ic.gc.ca/epic/site/ic1.nsf/en/home.
28. **Industry Research Desk** — 🌐 www.virtualpet.com/industry/.
29. **London Evening Standard** — 🌐 www.thisislondon.co.uk/standard-business/.
30. **Porter`s Five Forces** — 🌐 www.quickmba.com/strategy/porter.shtml.
31. **Porter`s Generic Strategies** — 🌐 www.quickmba.com/strategy/generic.shtml.
32. **Principal Business Activities–UK** — 🌐 tinyurl.com/yctmtdq.
33. **RESEARCHANDMARKETS** — 🌐 www.researchandmarkets.com/index.asp.
34. **Standard Industrial Classification–UK** — 🌐 tinyurl.com/3pekej8.
35. **Steps to Identify Your Target Market** — 🌐 tinyurl.com/zz9n96x.
36. **SWOT Analysis** — 🌐 www.quickmba.com/strategy/swot/.
37. **Tariff and Import Fees** — 🌐 www.export.gov/regulation/index.asp.

38. **The World Bank** — 🌀 www.worldbank.org/.
39. **Thomas Global** — 🌀 tinyurl.com/jdva4zk.
40. **ThomasNET** — 🌀 www.thomasnet.com/.
41. **U.S. Department of Labor Occupational Safety & Health Administration** — 🌀 www.osha.gov/.
42. **U.S. Food and Drug Administration** — 🌀 www.fda.gov/default.htm.
43. **UK Companies** — 🌀 tinyurl.com/yctmtdq.
44. **US International Trade Commission** — 🌀 www.dataweb.usitc.gov/.
45. **Vault Search for Companies** — 🌀 www.vault.com/rankings-reviews/find-a-company.aspx.
46. **World Industry Reporter** — 🌀 http://www.worldindustrialreporter.com/solusource/.
47. **Yahoo Finance** — 🌀 finance.yahoo.com/.
48. **Yellow Pages** — 🌀 www.yellowpages.com/.

Chapter 2

The Search for Global Markets

We are like the dwarfs seated on the shoulders of giants. We see more things than the ancients and things more distant, but this is due neither to the sharpness of our own sight, not the greatness of our own stature, but because we are raised and borne aloft on that giant mass.

— Saint Bernard of Clairvaux

Following on from the previous chapter, where the capabilities and resources available to the firm have been identified, we now move on to the process of internationalization — specifically the process of seeking new markets for the selected firm.

At this stage, top management would have been informed of the suitability of the firm as a candidate for internationalization and a decision-making process needs to be set in motion to seek markets for the firm. In other words, the process of the global market opportunity[1] assessment would begin for a selected product/service or product line.

---

[1]Opportunity is desirable but uncertain situations are present in foreign markets, which allows firms to benefit from engaging in new cross-border business activities that provide economic value for the firm (Holm, Johanson, & Kao, 2015).

1. The Decision Making Process

For the senior management team to make a decision about expanding into international markets, a number of decisions[a] have to be taken. A seminal work is the Uppasala[b] model of internationalizing the firm.

These include:

1. The first decision that needs to be taken is why the firm has to be involved in international business.
2. The product the company wants to market (WHAT). A key question that must be asked by the analyst at this stage is what are the distinctive features of the product or service in terms of price, quality, and other characteristics? Are these unique characteristics in non-domestic markets as well? What is the global product lifecycle of the selected product or service? Is there a scope to adapt the product or service to foreign market? What are the costs involved in adaptation?
3. The country or market it wants to enter (WHERE).[2] What are the target market segments to which the firm's product or services can be offered?
4. The timing of entry[3] (WHEN) and
5. The entry mode (HOW).
6. Does the firm have business relationship with other firms[4] in a specific foreign market? How can these opportunities be recognized and exploited within the context of the firm's current strategic position?

---

[2]A description of researching markets can be read on the ICAEW directors briefing. 🖱 http://www.icaew.com/~/media/corporate/files/library/collections/online%20resources/briefings/directors%20briefings/ei2resea.ashx.

[3]A review of the existing academic theory around "Timing of entry" can be read in Zachary, M. A., Gianiodis, P. T., Payne, G. T. & Markman, G. D., (2014). Entry timing enduring lessons and future directions. *Journal of Management*, *41*, 1388–1415.

[4]Holm, D. B., Johanson, M. & Kao, P. T., (2015). From outsider to insider: Opportunity development in foreign market networks. *Journal of International Entrepreneurship*, *13*(3), 337–359.

Once the management of the firm has decided on searching for new markets, the next process the screening of the global marketplace. Although several forms of market selection models are available in the literature, most of these agree that the process of assessing overseas markets lies within three separate stages:

1. The preliminary screening that identifies prospective target markets for subsequent in-depth analysis,
2. in-depth screening and
3. selection of the final market.

In the Global Marketing Management System (GMMS) methodology, the process of searching for markets is structured as follows:

1. A preliminary screening of markets.
2. The process of screening countries using three separate screening matrices.
3. The ranking and clustering of countries/markets for further in-depth analysis.
4. Competitive analysis of the top two countries/markets.
5. Identification of market and firm sales potential.
6. Analyzing market/country specific competitive analysis.
7. Identification of country entry conditions for the firm.
8. Analysis of financial and market entry conditions.
9. Identifying the best entry mode for a specific market.

2. Preliminary Screening of Markets[5]

The purpose of the preliminary screening is to segment the market using *macro*, *micro*, and *accessibility* criteria. A firm must choose its target markets from a broad selection of available markets based on several criteria. One of the great debates among economists and

---

[5]Please note that in the GMMSO4 software, preliminary screening is carried out by the system using its databases and suggested countries/markets are automatically suggested.

policymakers concerns how best to approach liberalizing markets[c] in order to balance the interests of local and non-local actors and institutions.

The global marketplace may be first divided into all-inclusive regions of the world. Breaking down market research into unique geographic or economic areas facilitates the analyst in eliminating low potential and/or high-risk markets. A good database for preliminary screening of markets on the basis of their ease of doing business is the DOING BUSINESS[6] guide from the World Bank. Economies are ranked around the ease of doing business on a rank of 1–189, where the higher rank indicates an environment that is more conducive to setting up of the local business. Based on the distance to frontier[7] scoring methodology, this ranking can be the first port of call for macro-level market screening. From these the analyst can include high potential and low-risk markets as prospective markets for entry.

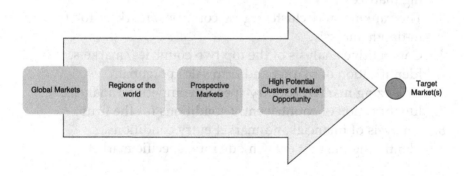

Global markets differ in terms of market size, income, and level of development, language, culture, religion, political and economic stability, social aspects and complexity of doing business. The COFACE online resource listed at the end of this chapter can help

---

[6] ⟲ http://www.doingbusiness.org/rankings.

[7] The distance to frontier score captures the gap between an economy's performance and a measure of best practice across the entire sample of 36 indicators for 10 Doing Business topics in the database.

in this research. Most firms are able to recognize opportunities within their current area of operations and often fail to seek opportunities beyond their comfort zone. Thus, selection of market is one of the most complex processes in the process of global market expansion. Several seminal works on the process of screening markets are available in the literature. At the end of this chapter, the authors have collated some essential additional reading material that can help understanding of the theoretical background.

During preliminary screening of markets, the analyst needs to be aware of two possible errors[8] that can creep in:

1. Ignoring markets or countries that can offer good prospects due to lack of sufficient market research or information.
2. Minimizing the risk of spending too much time investigating countries that are poor prospects.

The general assumption is that preliminary screening should identify promising target countries on markets disregarding the possible entry mode. But some scholars like Koch (2001)[d] have suggested that preliminary screening should be combined with entry mode analysis. In reality, many firms do not perform a strategic analysis but rather start the international expansion by entering neighboring countries, perhaps in response to unsolicited orders and gradually increasing its involvement in geographically and culturally close markets. This could be perhaps because of the limited experience of managers at these firms, the difficulties in collecting market research and the huge diversity of the global marketplace. Another method, the Overall Market Opportunity Index (OMOI)[9]

---

[8]Górecka, D., & Szałucka, M. (2013). *Country market selection in international expansion using multicriteria decision aiding methods.* International Workshop On Multiple Criteria Decision Making, 31–55. Academic Search Complete, EBSCOhost.
[9]Read more about this tool on Cavusgil, S. T. (1997). Measuring the potential of emerging markets: An indexing approach. *Business Horizons, 40*(1), 87–91.

tool first quantifies and ranks market potential based on fundamental economic, political, and social measures including size of the middle class, political risk, economic freedom, telecommunications, and physical infrastructure.

3. The Process of Screening Countries Using Three Separate Screening Matrices

During the process of decision making described in the first section of this chapter, senior management would have used a preliminary form of criteria with which to screen markets. The processess of screening within the GMMS philosophy are designed to identify the best market(s) for the firm's product or service by eliminating markets that fail to achieve an acceptable assessment of

a. a need/desire from the product,
b. market size and growth,
c. the ability of its population to purchase a product/service,
d. and finally the ability of the firm to enter this specific market.

Those markets that do not meet the firm's minimum requirement for market potential, economic growth, political risk, and available labor or natural resources should be eliminated by the analyst.

As shown in Figure 1, the GMMS methodology is based around the use of *Macro-level* criteria, *Micro-level* criteria, and *Accessibility criteria* to further screen markets. These criteria must be weighted by the analyst for effective screening to take place.

3.1. *Country screening and selection*

To identify best market for entry purposes, companies are normally expected to engage in an extensive evaluation of countries' attractiveness process (Figure 2). Lascu (2015)[e] suggests that countries are submitted to the following screening process to ensure that

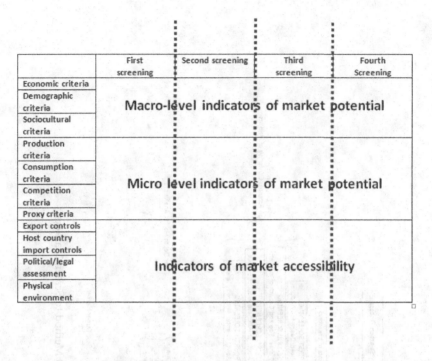

	First screening	Second screening	Third screening	Fourth Screening
Economic criteria				
Demographic criteria	Macro-level indicators of market potential			
Sociocultural criteria				
Production criteria				
Consumption criteria	Micro level indicators of market potential			
Competition criteria				
Proxy criteria				
Export controls				
Host country import controls				
Political/legal assessment	Indicators of market accessibility			
Physical environment				

Figure 1: Country Screening Matrix

companies segment and select markets with the highest market potential in light of each company's specific goals and resources:

- Selecting important *criteria* (these criteria, in turn, are used in the screening process to select and target the countries that present the highest potential to the company).
- Assigning an importance *score* to country screening criteria.
- Evaluating *country performance* on each of the screening criteria.
- Calculating the *country attractiveness* score.

3.2. Selection and the process of using criteria (or criterion) in market screening

3.2.1. Data collection strategies for selected criteria

It is most important that the collection of single factor and/or multiple factor indices (especially between different regions of

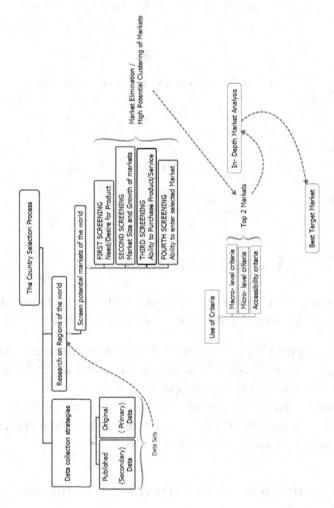

Figure 2: The GMMSO Method to Screen Markets

the world) ensures compatibility and consistency of measurement units, definitions of variables measured and the time period under analysis. The analyst may use a worksheet to record the definitions of the selected criteria, criteria purpose and its relative importance (weight) and data sources for the collected data (Figure 3).

General economic indicators are widely available from most government statistical organizations as well as international sources like the United Nations or the International Monetary Fund. Trade data may be gleaned from trade associations and trade journals. Some published sources may provide composite indicators. For example, the Economist intelligence unit (EIU) provides and publishes a series of indicators including one of market size which measures the relative size of each national market as a percentage of a regional market (e.g., The UK in Europe). These are based on an average of nine underlying indicators. A market intensity composite measures the degree of concentrated purchasing power based on various per capita and ownership levels. These underlining indicators are available annually in the Economist databases.

Select appropriate criteria! For example, if the product/service is intended for adults over 65 years old, you should select the age distribution criterion; determine how many adults are over 65 years old in a particular country. The company's target market is the most important indicator of which criteria to choose.

1. Macro-level criteria
2. Micro-level criteria
3. Accessibility criteria
4. Market entry strategy criteria.

3.3. *Weighting the criteria*

There is generally no clear agreement on how to assign weights to criteria in order to reflect their importance. Some scholars have

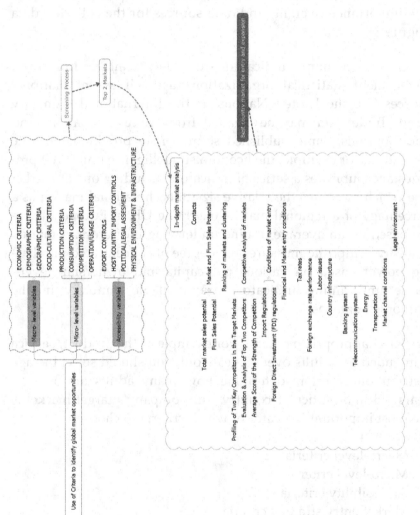

Figure 3:   The Use of Criteria to Screen Markets

suggested that all criteria should be weighted equally while others think there are differences. What we would suggest is that the analyst's perception of the importance of the weight of the criteria relative to the product line and company objectives is the key.

3.4. *Macro-level variables*

During preliminary screening, the analyst may have already used sets of macro-level indicators to eliminate countries that do not meet specific firm level objectives. In selecting the macro-level criteria for preliminary screening, the analyst should understand that these criteria should be directly related to the objectives and goals of the firm. It should also be dependent on the exact motives behind the firm's involvement in international business. According to Dunning (1993), these motives can be *"market seeking, resource seeking, efficiency seeking, strategic asset seeking motives"*. The macro-level variables would also change depending on the preliminary type of entry strategy that the firm is planning to use in a new market (Figures 4 and 5).

Some of the general macro-level variables used[10] are:

- market size
- level of economic development
- importance of endowment factors (factors of production)
- market growth rate
- market intensity
- commercial/physical infrastructure
- economic freedom
- market receptivity
- country risk
- political stability
- geographic distance

---

[10]Górecka., D, & Szałucka, M. (2013). *Country market selection in international expansion using multicriteria decision aiding methods*. International Workshop On Multiple Criteria Decision Making, 31–55. Academic Search Complete, EBSCOhost.

Macro Criteria	(+ve/-ve)	Measuring Units	Weight (%)
Population	+ ve	Million	24
Ease of Doing Business Rank	+ ve	Unit	15
Population Growth	+ ve	%	14
Unemployement	+ ve	%	10
Urban vs Rural	+ ve	%	10
Tariffs on Product in Local market	- ve	unit	10
Imports of your product	+ ve	Mn	10
GDP growth	+ ve	annual %	5
Population ages 0-14	+ ve	% of total	2
		Total Weight:	100 (%)

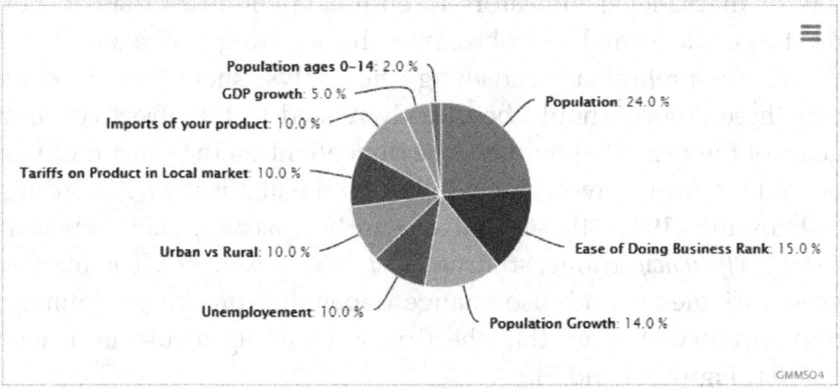

Figure 4:   The Screening of Macro-level Variables in the GMMSO4 Software

- cultural distance
- language differences
- religious differences
- government attitude to Foreign Direct Investment (FDI)
- Trade barriers.

The purpose of selecting macro-level variables is to identify the country with the highest market potential for the company's product/service. Table 1 is designed to guide the analyst in the selection of marketing the product or service in foreign markets. Some of the variables may not need analysis. Other necessary variables may not have been included in this list. For example, multifactor indexes may prove to be useful as indicators of proxy variables of market potential.

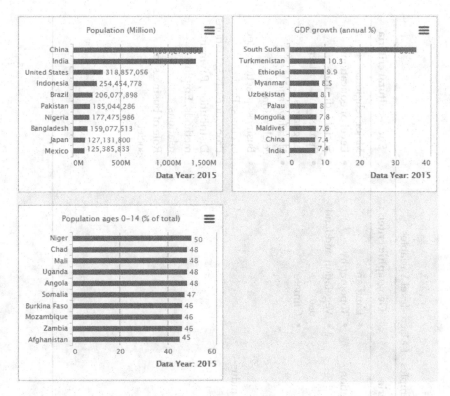

Figure 5: GMMSO4 Software Showing List of Countries after Screening

3.5. *Micro-level variables of market accessibility*

Although all the chosen criteria should be product/market specific, micro-level variables are specific to the attributes and benefits of the firm's principal product/service. Because the
developed micro-level variables will be entirely unique to each
company, Table 2 of criteria is only a suggestion. Note that both
direct and proxy variables can be used as micro-level indicators
(Figures 6 and 7).

3.6. *Market access indicators*

Access to market is just as important as market potential. Even
though they are quick to change, accessibility criteria play an

Table 1: Examples of Macro-level Variables

Economic criteria	Demographic criteria	Geographic criteria	Socio-cultural criteria
• Level of economic development (IC, NIC, LDC, BEM) • Gross national product • Income per capita • Interest rates • Exchange rate performance • Availability of hard currency • National health spending • Disposable income • Distribution of wealth • Housing starts • Banking system • Economic affiliations (EEC, EFTA, ANCOM) • Major industries • Energy consumption	• Population • Average age of population • Age distribution • Life stage • Population growth • Population density • Urban vs. rural • Male vs. female • Labor distribution by industry or profession • Labor unions	• Land area • Topography • Vegetation and land use • Climate	• Major religions • Level of education • Social indicators • Spoken and written languages • Holidays and celebrations • Business practices: Code of ethics, Pricing, Promotions, Negotiations, Distribution, Payment methods, Employee relations • Role of business in society

Table 2:   Examples of Micro-level Variables

Production criteria	Consumption criteria	Competition criteria	Operation/usage criteria
• Exports (complimentary, alternative, and company product(s))	• Imports (complimentary, alternative, and company product(s))	• Local competitors	• Ideal, expected, and/or necessary conditions for product/service usage
• Production of raw materials	• Product/Service consumption	• International competitors	• Operation conditions
• Production of complimentary product(s)	• Complimentary product/service consumption	• Competition Intensity	• Operation restrictions
• Production of alternative product(s)	• Alternative product/service consumption	• Nature of competition (price, non-price)	• Skills required for operation
• Processing Plants			• Living standards

Micro Criteria	(+ve/-ve)	Measuring Units	Weight (%)
International competitors	+ ve		40
Local competitors	+ ve		35
Production of raw materials	+ ve		10
Competition Intensity	+ ve		5
Alternative product/service consumption	+ ve		5
Ideal, expected, and/or necessary conditions for product/service usage	+ ve		5
		Total Weight:	100 (%)

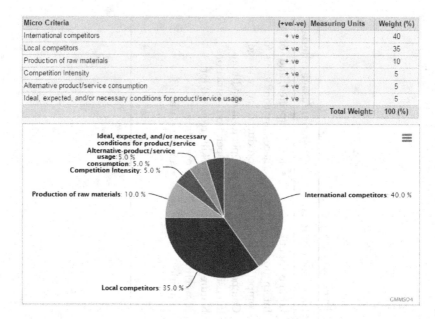

Figure 6: The Screening of Micro-level Variables in the GMMSO4 Software

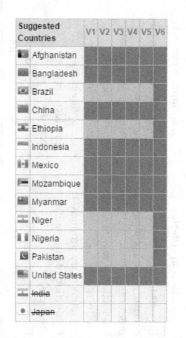

Figure 7: Suggested List of Countries after Micro-level Screening on the GMMSO4 Software

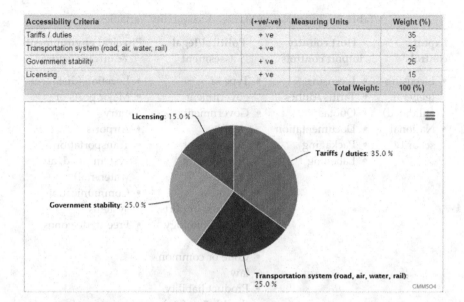

Accessibility Criteria	(+ve/-ve)	Measuring Units	Weight (%)
Tariffs / duties	+ ve		35
Transportation system (road, air, water, rail)	+ ve		25
Government stability	+ ve		25
Licensing	+ ve		15
		Total Weight:	100 (%)

Figure 8: The Screening of Micro-level Variables in the GMMSO4 Software

integral part in determining the success of entering foreign markets (Figure 8). Again, Table 3 is not exhaustive and is only meant as a guide for the analyst in developing product/service/market specific criteria.

3.7. *Country scoring process*

Against each selected criteria, research and input the values on the grid. You will need to include the year the information was collected, the unit of measure, the weight, and the value. The weight should vary from criterion to criterion. Some criteria are more important, assign a higher weight to those criteria. Make sure that the weights add up to 100% of the total selected criteria and sub criteria. Negative relationships will be assigned lower scores, while positive relationships will be assigned higher scores.

For example, if you have assigned a positive relationship to the population criteria and are evaluating China and the United States, China will rank #1 and the United States #2 because China has a

Table 3:   Examples of Market Accessibility Variables

Export controls	Host country import controls	Political/legal assesment	Physical environment & infrastructure
• Licensing (general, validated) • National security	• Licensing • Tariffs/duties • Quotas • Documentation • Packaging • Labelling	• Type of government • Government stability • Government procurement policies • Attitudes towards: Imports, FDI, Technology transfer • Code or common law • Product liability (health & safety) • Contractual requirements • Patents/ trademarks/ copyrights • Legislative process	• Location (distance) • Major ports of entry • Airports • Transportation system (road, air, water, rail) • Communication systems • Free-trade zones

larger population. An example of a negative relationship and the ranking is the measure of corruption. More corruption in a country is negative; this is why there is a negative relationship between the criteria and the value. The 2015 Transparency International Corruption Perceptions Index[11] lists China as having a corruption score of 37; the U.S. has a corruption score of 76. You will need to rank China #2 and the U.S. as #1 because the US has less corruption.

Once the grid is completed and the values inputted against each country, the grid should show a cluster of countries with the best potential for your product/service. The analyst will have to choose the top 2 markets from this cluster for further analysis (Figure 9).

---

[11] 🌐 http://www.transparency.org/cpi2015

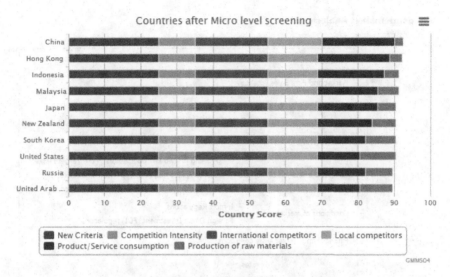

Figure 9: Country Screening on the GMMSO4 Software

4. Performing an in-depth Market Analysis of the Two Best Markets

When it has been established, from preliminary screening of global markets that market opportunities exist for the firm being analyzed, an in-depth market analysis and estimate of sales potential is have to be applied to each of the identified target market countries (Figure 10). The objective of this section is to identify the best Target Market country for the company and its products/services by using the following procedure:

Select the top 2 countries based on the country ranks in the previous section.

- Identify business contacts who are familiar with the Target Market countries: Agents/Distributors/Government agencies, Trade associations and organizations/Bank.
- Determine the Market Potential along with the company's sales potential in each country.
- Develop a profile for the top two (2) competitors in each country. For each competitor include an assessment of Product Attributes

In depth market Analysis

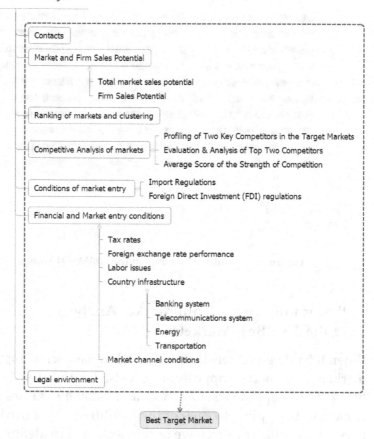

Figure 10:   In-depth Market Analysis

and benefits, Market Share, sales, Market Positioning, and competitor strengths and weaknesses.

- Analyze in detail the current market-entry conditions for each country.
- Analyze the existing financial and market conditions in each country to determine whether they are favorable for your particular product/service.

Select the market with the highest potential by ranking each country using the following five categories:

- Quality and strength of your contacts in each country.
- Degree and level of market competition in each country.
- Highest market and company sales potential (CSP) in each country.
- Most favorable market entry conditions in each country.
- Most favorable financial and market conditions in each country.

Some key questions that the analyst should be asking while performing in-depth analysis of the two best markets are:

- Who can help us bring our product/service to the selected market(s)? Do we have contact with any agents/distributors? Is there any government contact that can be exploited? What about industry-level associations? Is there a mechanism to send letters of enquiry to potential contacts in this market?
- What is a market structure and sales potential of our product/ service in the selected market(s)?
- What is the competitive environment in the selected market?
- What are the other market-entry conditions?
- What is the channel structure for the firm's selected product or service?

4.1. *Qualifying contacts*

In-depth market analysis and estimates of sales potential in any one country market would be difficult, to say the least, without making contact with those who are more familiar with the target market(s). Potential agents and/or distributors, foreign government bodies including commercial attaches at embassies and consulates, associations, and organizations can be helpful in this specialized networking activity. Research and sales letters of enquiry can provide in-depth market research and possibly establish relationships that may facilitate bringing the firm's product or service to the marketplace.

Before proceeding with the market analysis, first establish contact with those most familiar with the countries' target market. Research potential agents, distributors, foreign governments, associations, and organizations that can help the company establish itself in the new countries. In the column on the right, select the strongest contacts by clicking on the bubbles corresponding to the strongest contacts. Think about which contacts may be most useful and helpful.

Evaluate each contact's quality and strength on a scale of 1–5, 1 being least favorable and 5 being most favorable.

Country	Name of contact	Organization	Address	Phone	E-mail	Strength of contacts on a scale of 1-5
Country 1						1 2 3 4 5
						1 2 3 4 5
						1 2 3 4 5
						1 2 3 4 5
						1 2 3 4 5
						1 2 3 4 5
Country 2						1 2 3 4 5
						1 2 3 4 5
						1 2 3 4 5
						1 2 3 4 5
						1 2 3 4 5
						1 2 3 4 5

5. Market and Company Sales Potential

As a final country screening for global market opportunity, the analyst must first identify the target market(s) with the greatest potential for sales. Analysis of market conditions including demand analysis, competitive analysis, basic consumer purchase motivation, and available channels of distribution need to be addressed. The competitor profiles in each target market enable the selection of the best primary target market country for the firm and its product. It also helps in the development of an effective marketing strategy. While proprietary information may be inaccessible, industry/annual reports, competitors, clients, channel members, and company literature can in many cases, provide a wealth of competitor information.

In the GMMS methodology, we suggest that the market potential can be obtained by the following process.

5.1. *(a) Total market potential (TMP)*

Estimate the TMP in both selected top country for your product by using the formula:

$$TMP = a \times b \times c,$$

where,

a is the Number of potential (eligible/qualified) consumers,
b is the Frequency of purchase on an annual basis, and
c is the Selling price of the product.

For "*a*," don't input the population or age distribution. Only some of those people will be qualified consumers of the product. It's important to be consistent throughout the analysis.

The values of both "*b*" and "*c*." will have been addressed in the chapter on analyzing the position of the firm.

However, keep in mind the differences between the two countries as well, it is possible that the selling price and frequency of purchase will vary from country to country. The following work-book from the GMMS[12] methodology may be useful here.

	Country 1	Country 2
a = Number of potential (eligible/ qualified) consumers		
b = Frequency of purchase on an annual basis		
c = Selling price of the product		
TMP		

Table 2: An Example of Workbook Showing the Market Structure of a Target Market

	Market share (realized and unrealized)	Sales(for the past three years)	Market positioning	Strength/ weakness
Total market	100%	Estimated total sales potential		
Competitor A				
Competitor B				
Competitor C				
Competitor D				
Additional competitors				
Unrealized market potential				

	1	2	3	4	5	1	2	3	4	5
Evaluation of the TMP on a scale of 1–5										

---

[12]Note that this is done automatically in the GMMSO4 software.

Enter the numbers and calculate the TMP for each market. Then, rate the TMP for each country on a scale of 1–5, 1 being least favorable and 5 being most favorable. You will need to access each market and its TMP on the basis of your ability to enter and exploit the market from earlier analysis.

5.2. (b) CSP

It is unrealistic to aim for the TMP. Most companies set goals by trying to achieve a percentage of the TMP, also known as the CSP. The CSP is determined based on the company's history, pattern of growth, and degree of competition. Again, keep in mind that the CSP may vary for both countries.

The next step is to find a desired market share for each TMP and calculate the CSP as shown below:

Estimate CSP for the product: CSP =TMP × Desired Market Share %		
	Country 1	Country 2
TMP		
Desired Market Share (%)		
CSP= TMP × desired market share		

Now, rate the CSP for each country on a scale of 1–5, 1 being least favorable and 5 being most favorable.

Evaluation of the CSP on a scale of 1–5	1	2	3	4	5	1	2	3	4	5

5.3. *Market structure of the target market*

Publicly available reports like UNIDO Statistical Country Briefs[13] can provide details about the industry profile of a target market.

---

[13] 🌐 https://www.unido.org/resources/statistics/statistical-country-briefs.html

In addition, market research organizations[14] may be available to help with an assessment of the current market structure of each target market. The market structure is a strong determining factor for market entry.

In addition to the preliminary screening for market access ability, in-depth analysis of the conditions of market entry further as the feasibility and cost-effectiveness of entering any one target market. It is important to note that countries with the best market-entry conditions may not always be the ones with the greatest potential for sales.

6. Analyzing Market /Country Specific Competitive Analysis

Competitor profiles in each target market enable the selection of the best primary target market country for the company and its product, as well as the development of an effective marketing program. While proprietary information may be inaccessible, industry/ annual reports, competitor's clients, channel members and company literature can, in many cases, provide a wealth of competitor information.

Choose the top two competitors that the company will have to compete with in each country. They can be local or international competitors. More than likely, the top two competitors will both be international competitors. It may be helpful to choose one international competitor and one local competitor. Again, consider the company's current history and pattern of reacting to competitors.

---

[14]The GreenBook Directory helps you find marketing research suppliers, facilities, and consultants as well as providers of related services and is available on: 🌐 http://www.greenbook.org/.

Before choosing the competitors, ask the following questions:

1. Will local or international competitors be a bigger threat to the company's success?
2. Do consumers in the specific countries favor local companies over international companies?

After choosing the top two competitors for both countries, analyze them using the table provided. Compare them side-by-side. Don't forget to repeat the process for the second country.

Country market X	Competitor 1	Competitor 2
Competitor Name:		
Product/Service Name:		
Location of Headquarters (country):		
Total Sales (countrywide):		
Total Sales (worldwide):		
Number of Employees.		
Profile		
Distribution E-Commerce:		
Pricing Strategy:		
Product Attributes and Benefits:		
Promotion Strategy		
Quality:		
Service:		
Target Market Profile:		

Now, rate the two countries threat of competition on a scale of 1–5, 1 being the biggest threat and 5 being the less threatening.

Once the exercise has been completed for both markets, evaluate the degree and level of market competition in each market on a scale of 1–15.

Evaluation Criteria	Country 1					Country 2				
Degree and level of market competition in each country	1	2	3	4	5	1	2	3	4	5

7. Identification of Country-entry Conditions for the Firm

7.1. *Import regulations*

Each country has a different set of regulations regarding the importation of goods.

Use the matrix below to explain what types of regulations are present in each country.

Regulations	Country 1					Country 2				
Administrative Barriers	1	2	3	4	5	1	2	3	4	5
Import Licensing Requirements										
Quotas										
Tariffs										
Any additional regulations										
Explanation for each of the regulations and your perception of its impact on your product										

Score the import regulations on a scale of 1–5, 1 being least favorable and 5 being most favorable. If the company chosen provides a service, there may be no licensing requirements, quotas, or tariffs. If this is the case, rate those import regulations with a 5.

Find out if there are any regulations for international companies providing a service. You may wish to add additional regulations. Your research may be used to explain the regulations required to provide a service.

You should also explain the reason for the particular rates given.

7.2. *FDI regulations*

Much like with import regulations, countries have regulations on FDI. Restrictions on FDI vary from country to country. The world bank publishes indicators of FDI across borders on its INVESTING ACROSS BORDERS database.[15]

Use this matrix below to score the different regulations as they pertain to the company and its country of origin; 1 is least favorable and 5 is most favorable. Explain the reason for the rates given. You may wish to add additional FDI regulations.

FDI regulations	Country 1					Country 2				
	1	2	3	4	5	1	2	3	4	5
Are foreign based companies allowed 100% Equity ownership of domestic firms?										
Are foreign companies allowed to establish their own retail establishments?										
Can foreign companies borrow locally?										
Does the government restrict the amount or type of investment?										
Does the government restrict the Repatriation of Earnings?										
Any additional regulations										
Explanation for each of the regulations and your perception of its impact on your product/service										

---

[15] 🌐 http://iab.worldbank.org. This can be a useful source of ranking markets.

8. Analysis of Financial and Market-entry Conditions

8.1. *Tax rates*

Rate the countries tax rates on a scale of 1–5, 1 being very high and 5 being fairly low. You may wish to add other tax rates. Your research may be used to explain the particular tax rates in each country and how they will impact the company.

Tax rates	Country 1					Country 2				
	1	2	3	4	5	1	2	3	4	5
Corporate Tax rates are favorable										
Personal Tax rates are favorable										
Any additional regulations										
Explanation for each of the Tax rates and your perception of its impact on your product/ service										

8.2. *Foreign exchange performance*

Check the country's foreign exchange performance and rate them on a scale of 1–5, 1 being poor performance and 5 being excellent performance.

You may wish to add other foreign exchange performance indicators. Your research may be used to explain the rates given and how the foreign exchange performance will impact the company. Include the current exchange rates from the host country's currency to the home country's currency.

Foreign exchange rate performance	Country 1					Country 2				
	1	2	3	4	5	1	2	3	4	5
The country's currency is convertible										
The country's current account is in good standing (Balance of Payments)										
The currency of the country has been stable										
Any additional regulations										
Explanation for each of the statements and your perception of its impact on your product/ service										

8.3. *Labor issues*

Score each of the criterion listed on a scale of 1–5 ; 1 being a major issue and 5 being a minor issue. You may wish to add other labor issues.

Labour issues	Country 1					Country 2				
	1	2	3	4	5	1	2	3	4	5
Child labor issues										
Labor wage rates										
Management–labor relations										
Strength of labor unions										
Any additional regulations										
Explanation for each of the issues and your perception of its impact on your product/service										

The LABORSTA[16] indicators are a useful database to consult in research country's labor market profiling. *Note*: For data from 2008 onwards, the ILOSTAT[17] databases will have to be used instead.

8.4. *Country infrastructures*

Rate the quality of each country's infrastructure; 1 being poor and 5 being excellent.

You may wish to add additional infrastructures. In the text-boxes, explain the rates given and how the condition of the infrastructure will impact the company.

Country infrastructure	Country 1					Country 2				
	1	2	3	4	5	1	2	3	4	5
Banking system										
Energy										
Internet connections										
Telecommunications system										
Transportation systems										
Any additional regulations										
Explanation for each of the infrastructure issues and your perception of its impact on your product/service										

8.5. *Market channel conditions*

A market channel is the path by which products/services flow from manufacturer or service provided to the final consumer or industrial user. Marketing channels can be short or long depending on how many intermediaries there are. Intermediaries include manufacturers, wholesalers, agents, distributors, and retailers. Usually, market channels of consumer goods are longer and indirect compared to industrial goods. Service providers typically use

---

[16]LABORSTA is available on: 🌐 http://laborsta.ilo.org/.
[17]This resource is available on: 🌐 http://www.ilo.org/ilostat.

direct channels. As the product moves down the line, there is a monetary transaction that occurs at each point. The price of the product increases as it moves from one intermediary to another until the product reaches the final buyer. When operating in host countries, companies need to assess the market channel conditions before they can set prices for the final consumer.

Rate each criterion on a scale of 1–5, 1 being less favorable and 5 being most favorable. You may wish to add other conditions. In the textboxes, explain the rates given and how the condition of the market channel will impact the company.

Market channel conditions	Country 1					Country 2				
	1	2	3	4	5	1	2	3	4	5
Distribution channels are regulated by the government										
Existing channels provide adequate national market coverage										
The company will be able to distribute its product/service using existing channels										
Any additional regulations										
Explanation for each of the market channel conditions and your perception of its impact on your product/service										

8.6. *Legal environment*

Rate the legal environment in each country on a scale of 1–5, 1 being least favorable and 5 being most favorable. Use the textboxes to explain the rates given and how the condition of the legal environment will impact the company.

Legal environment conditions	Country 1					Country 2				
	1	2	3	4	5	1	2	3	4	5
It is easy to establish presence or a business in the country										
The country has anti-trust legislation in place										
The country is a member of the WTO										
The country protects intellectual property										
The level of corruption in the country is low										
Any additional regulations										
Explanation for each of the market channel conditions and your perception of its impact on your product/service										

8.7. *Determining the best target market country*

All of the scores that you have been giving to the two countries under the five separate categories should now be calculated and included in a new matrix under "Average Rank".

VARIABLES	WEIGHT	AVERAGE RANK		WEIGHTED TOTAL	
		Country 1	Country 2	Country 1	Country 2
CONTACTS (average)					
MARKET & COMPANY SALES POTENTIAL					
COMPETITION					
COUNTRY ENTRY CONDITIONS					

VARIABLES	WEIGHT	AVERAGE RANK		WEIGHTED TOTAL	
		Country 1	Country 2	Country 1	Country 2
FINANCIAL & MARKET CONDITIONS					
	Total weight (100%)	Average rank sum		Weighted Total	
		Country 1	Country 2	Country 1	Country 2

In the table provided, assign weights to the five criteria listed. The most important criteria should be given a higher weight. Make sure the weights add up to 100%. Add the scores from your analysis.[18]

Once all the weights have been added up, one of the countries will have a higher score than the other. The country with the highest score is the country that the company will have a better chance to succeed in. You have now arrived at a market into which you will need to create an entry strategy.

The next chapter will be looking at the process of creating this entry strategy.

Endnotes

[a]Górecka, D., & Szałucka, M. (2013). *Country market selection in international expansion using multicriteria decision aiding methods.* International Workshop On Multiple Criteria Decision Making, 31–55. Academic Search Complete, EBSCOhost.

[b]Johanson J., & Vahlne J. E. (1977). The internationalization process of the firm — A model of knowledge development and increasing foreign market commitments. *Journal of Business Studies, 8*(1).

---

[18]The GMMSO4 software will perform a calculation, automatically, taking into consideration the weights and the scores given.

^cSilver, C., Jae-Hyup, L., & Jeeyoon, P. (2015). What firms want: Investigating globalization's influence on the market for lawyers in korea. Columbia Journal of Asian Law, *28*(1), 1–40. Academic Search Complete, EBSCOhost.

^dKoch A. J. (2001). Selecting overseas markets and entry modes: Two decision process or one? *Marketing Intelligence & Planning, 9*(1).

^eLascu D.-N. (2015). *International Marketing* 4/e. Texbook Media Press, pp. 218–225.

Additional Reading

Brewer, P. (2001). International market selection: Developing a model from Australian case studies. *International Business Review, 10*(2), 155–174.

Cavusgil, S. T. (2004). Complementary approaches to preliminary foreign market opportunity assessment: Country clustering and country ranking. *Industrial Marketing Management, 33*(7), 607–617.

Gaston-Breton, Ch., & Martín, M. O. (2011). International market selection and segmentation: A two-stage model. *International Marketing Review, 28*(3), 267–290.

Holtbrügge, D., & Baron, A. (2013). Market entry strategies in emerging markets: An institutional study in the BRIC countries. *Thunderbird International Business Review, 55,* 237–252.

Kumar, V. *et al.* (1994). An interactive multicriteria approach to identifying potential foreign markets. *Journal of International Marketing, 2*(1), 29–52.

Lasserre, P. (2012). *Global Strategic Management.* New York: Palgrave Macmillan.

Malhotra, S., & Papadopoulos, N. (2007). International market selection: An integrative review of empirical studies. *ASAC, 28*(8), 7–22.

Mullen, M. R. (2009). Foreign market analysis. *Irish Marketing Review, 20*(1), 47–56.

Ojala, A., & Tyr Väinen, P. (2008). Market entry decisions of US small and medium-sized software firms. *Management Decision, 46*(2), 187–200.

Ozturk, A., Joiner, E., & Cavusgil, S. T. (2015). Delineating foreign market potential: A tool for international market selection. *Thunderbird International Business Review, 57*(2), 119–141.

Reid, D., & Walsh, J. (2003). Market entry decisions in China. *Thunderbird International Business Review, 45,* 289–312.

Steenkamp, J.-B. E., & Ter Hofstede, F. (2002). International market segmentation: Issues and perspectives. *International Journal of Research in Marketing, 19*(3), 185–213.

Verster, K. (2014). *Evaluating market potential in emerging markets using marketing data (MBA mini dissertation).* University of Pretoria.

Online Resources in Determining Markets

1. **Analytical Trade Tables of The International Merchandise Trade Statistics Section (IMTSS)** — 🌐 goo.gl/FJ2EDx.

2. **ASEAN Macro Economic Indicators** — 🖐 tinyurl.com/hduz4an
3. **ASEAN TAX Guides** — 🖐 goo.gl/Mg6HGS.
4. **AsiaBizNews: Doing Business in Asia** — 🖐 goo.gl/f4iOxS.
5. **AT Kearney Ideas and Insights** — 🖐 goo.gl/WnKQI.
6. **Austrade Resources on Exporting** — 🖐 tinyurl.com/hrnmjlz.
7. **Bilateral Linkages Database** — 🖐 tinyurl.com/j8j478z.
8. **British Chambers of Commerce** — 🖐 tinyurl.com/hbp4wqx.
9. **Business.com** — 🖐 tinyurl.com/gletwel.
10. **CARIBLEX** — 🖐 goo.gl/PsZ7Q1.
11. **Center for Business Planning** — 🖐 tinyurl.com/jnq7pzt.
12. **Child Labour Statistics** — 🖐 goo.gl/9JbBlG.
13. **CISDOC Database** — 🖐 goo.gl/f4iOxS.
14. **comScore.com: International Solutions** — 🖐 www.comscore.com/International_Solutions.
15. **Corruption Perceptions Index** — 🖐 www.transparency.org/.
16. **Country Information, International Monetary Fund (IMF)** — 🖐 tinyurl.com/o6an8.
17. **Country Reports** — 🖐 www.countryreports.org/.
18. **Country Risk and Economic Research** — Available on 🖐 tinyurl.com/h4ha7tv.
19. **Country Risk and Economic Research** — 🖐 http://goo.gl/QV5VX.
20. **County Watch** — 🖐 www.countrywatch.com/.
21. **Data about Global Markets** — 🖐 www.oecd.org/.
22. **Database of Conditions of Work and Employment Laws** — 🖐 goo.gl/oshmNI.
23. **Deloitte International Tax Source: Country Guides and Highlights** — 🖐 tinyurl.com/jlbaw2k.
24. **Doing Business** — 🖐 www.doingbusiness.org/.
25. **Doing Business in Asian Countries** — 🖐 www.business—in—asia.com/.
26. **Economics & Country Risk** — 🖐 tinyurl.com/hm7pxcw.
27. **EconomyWatch** — 🖐 tinyurl.com/d5dx8n.
28. **eCrat.com: Bringing Together Resources for Addressing Today's Business, Social Enterprise and Intern** — 🖐 www.ecrat.com/home.html.
29. **EPLex — Employment Protection Legislation database** — 🖐 goo.gl/jYGgly.
30. **Euromonitor International** — 🖐 www.euromonitor.com/.
31. **Explore Export Markets** — 🖐 tinyurl.com/go6lcw4.
32. **Export.gov: Country Commercial Guides** — 🖐 export.gov/ccg/.
33. **Exporting from the EU** — 🖐 tinyurl.com/jkvhquu.
34. **Foreign Affairs and International Trade Canada** — 🖐 tinyurl.com/hk9stby.
35. **Gateway to the European Union** — 🖐 europa.eu/index_en.htm.
36. **Geography IQ** — 🖐 www.geographyiq.com/.
37. **Global Contact Inc.** — 🖐 globalcontact.com/.

38. **Global Trader Guides from the British Chambers of Commerce** — (⚓) tinyurl.com/h73dl2k.
39. **globalEDGE Country Insights** — (⚓) tinyurl.com/k4eotv2.
40. **Globstrategy Country Business Profiles** — (⚓) globstrategy.com/category/country—business—profiles/.
41. **GreenBook Directory** — (⚓) http://www.greenbook.org/.
42. **Human Development Report** — (⚓) tinyurl.com/krnf42.
43. **ILO Thesaurus** — (⚓) goo.gl/a24iPQ.
44. **ILOSTAT Database** — (⚓) www.ilo.org/ilos.tat.
45. **Inc.com** — (⚓) www.inc.com/entering—global—markets.
46. **International Business Center** — (⚓) tinyurl.com/j8hy8n7.
47. **International Customs Tariffs Bureau** — (⚓) www.bitd.org/.
48. **International Financial Statistics** — (⚓) tinyurl.com/8783h6g.
49. **International Monetary Fund (IMF): Staff Country Reports** — (⚓) tinyurl.com/jfjxngn.
50. **International Tax & Business Quides, Dilloitte** — (⚓) tinyurl.com/yg2p2f5.
51. **Internet Users** — (⚓) tinyurl.com/6ggchf.
52. **INTRACEN Online Databases** — (⚓) tinyurl.com/z6lyjyh.
53. **Key Indicators Database** — (⚓) tinyurl.com/jswpmh4.
54. **LABORSTA** — (⚓) laborsta.ilo.org/.
55. **Labour Force Surveys** — (⚓) goo.gl/yDp0M.
56. **Market Potential Index from Global Edge** — Avaliable on: (⚓) goo.gl/Gm3vp.
57. **Mellinger Co.** — (⚓) www.tradezone.com/trdzone.htm.
58. **Nation Master** — (⚓) www.nationmaster.com/.
59. **NetProspex** — (⚓) http://www.netprospex.com/.
60. **SICE — Foreign Trade Information System** — (⚓) http://www.sice.oas.org/.
61. **Tariff and Import Fees** — (⚓) http://tinyurl.com/yl6n4h.
62. **The British Exporters Association (BExA)** — (⚓) www.bexa.co.uk/exportinfo.html.
63. **The International Trade Centre** — (⚓) www.intracen.org/.
64. **The Nations Online Project — a portal of gateways to the countries, cultures and nations in the world** — (⚓) http://www.nationsonline.org/.
65. **The World Bank** — (⚓) www.worldbank.org/.
66. **Thomas Global** — (⚓) tinyurl.com/jdva4zk.
67. **Tourism Industry Highlights** — (⚓) tinyurl.com/cq2gc37.
68. **Tourism Indicators** — (⚓) tinyurl.com/2ofjdy.
69. **Tourism Market Trends** — (⚓) tinyurl.com/zuhkscm.
70. **U.S. Census Bureau** — (⚓) tinyurl.com/jhh7pl9.
71. **U.S. Department of Labor Occupational Safety & Health Administration** — (⚓) www.osha.gov/.

72. **U.S. Equal Employment Opportunity Commission** — Ⓕ tinyurl.com/ cw2qthk.
73. **U.K. Export Finance and Credit Insurance** — Ⓕ tinyurl.com/huwpvwc.
74. **U.K. National Statistics** — Ⓕ www.statistics.gov.uk/default.asp.
75. **U.K Trade & Investment (UKTI)** — Ⓕ tinyurl.com/glhbzlb.
76. **U.N. — Global Teaching and Learning Project** — Ⓕ www.cyberschoolbus. un.org/index.shtml.
77. **UNCTAD** — Ⓕ goo.gl/Z2DY7 .
78. **UNDATA** — Ⓕ data.un.org/.
79. **UNESCO Data Centre** — Ⓕ stats.uis.unesco.org/unesco/.
80. **UNIDO Statistical Country Briefs** — Ⓕ tinyurl.com/zwojyvm.
81. **United States Patent and Trademark Office** — Ⓕ www.uspto.gov/.
82. **U.S. Commercial Service Country Commercial Guides** — Ⓕ tinyurl.com/ llqvlcm.
83. **U.S. Customs and Border Protection** — Ⓕ www.cbp.gov/.
84. **U.S. Department of State** — Ⓕ www.state.gov/.
85. **U.S. Department of Treasury** — Ⓕ www.ustreas.gov/ofac.
86. **U.S. International Trade Commission** — Ⓕ www.dataweb.usitc.gov/.
87. **USA Trade Center** — Ⓕ usatc.doc.gov/.
88. **USDA Foreign Agriculture Service (FAS): Country Reports Selector:** — Ⓕ tinyurl.com/jzeh492.
89. **Values for Selected Variables about Global Markets** — Ⓕ tinyurl.com/ ycloe44.
90. **World Business Culture: Business Culture on the World Stage** — Ⓕ www. worldbusinessculture.com/index.html.
91. **World Integrated Trade Solution** — Avaliable on: Ⓕ http://goo.gl/pIoPO.
92. **World Trade Organization: Trade Policy Reviews** — Ⓕ tinyurl.com/6ex9ms.

Chapter 3

Creating an Entry Strategy into a Selected Market

Developing an entry strategy into the target market in the GMMS methodology involves the following structure:

1. Selecting an entry mode based on the firm's capabilities and objectives
2. Evaluating the business environment of the selected market
3. Creating a marketing plan with its firm specific goals and objectives
4. Developing a product strategy
5. Developing a pricing strategy
6. Creation of a promotional strategy
7. Developing of a distribution strategy
8. Creation of a financial strategy
9. Creating the organizational structure for the new market
10. Understanding possible exit strategies and scenarios

1. Selecting an Entry Mode into the Target Market

The entry mode strategy decision into the selected country with the highest market potential is one of the most important considerations on the part of the firm interested in internationalizing. An entry mode is defined as the institutional or organizational arrangement that is used in order to conduct an international business activity.[a] The choice of a suitable entry mode will determine the degree of

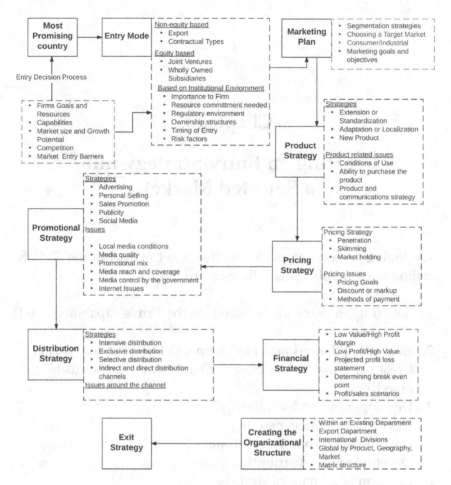

Figure 1:   Process-Driven Approach to Entry Strategy

resource commitment to the foreign market, the risks that the firm will have to manage in the target market and the level of control that the firm can exercise with its entry into the target market. It is key that the right entry mode is determined in the initial stages as a wrong entry mode can negatively impact the performance of the firm. It therefore follows that a brief review of the literature around entry modes should be addressed. Please note that the *mode of market entry* by itself is different from the *entry decision* process, which has been addressed in Chapter 2.

Classical literature identifies with entry modes being classified as *equity-based* and *non-equity-based* entry modes.[b] Non-equity based entry modes have been further divided into exports and contractual agreements by Pan and Tse (2000).[c] Figure 2 illustrates this. For those interested in reading further, a review of the theory on entry mode decisions can be read from Laufs and Schwens (2014).[d]

Another school of thought[1] looks at entry modes in terms of the institutional theory where entry modes are further differentiated:

- Based on the *level of activity* of the firm in the target market and the decision on how much of value activities can be transferred to this target market and the resource commitment required.
- The proposed *ownership structure*: The ownership aspect looks at whether firms should use wholly owned subsidiaries or share ownership with local partners to reduce pressures from local institutions as well as minimize investment risk.
- The *establishment mode* of operations in the target market: In terms of establishment, a decision can be made by the firm in making acquisitions of other forms of the target market or Greenfield investment.

The size of the firm is also a determinant of the choice of market entry modes. Small and medium-size enterprises (SMEs) will have limited financial and personnel resources as opposed to multinational enterprises (MNEs).[d] These resource constraints can force SMEs to choose low commitment for market entry modes.

Lasserre (2012) addresses both internal and external factors that impact on the type of the entry modes selected by the firm (Please see Figure 2).

---

[1]Holtbrügge, D., & Baron, A. (2013). Market entry strategies in emerging markets: An institutional study in the BRIC countries. *Thunderbird International Business Review, 55*(3), 237–252.

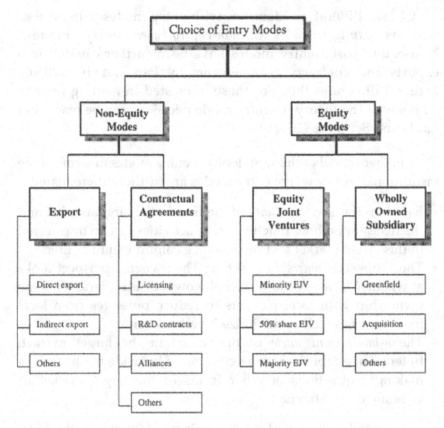

Figure 2:   A Hierarchical Approach to Entry Modes from Pan and Tse (2001)

A more recent contribution (De Villa, Rajwani & Lawton, 2015) to the literature on entry mode has been the emphasis on the role of the political environment of markets and the decision making around the choice of entry modes. Of particular interest to firms is a growing influence of TNCs or MNCs from developing countries like India, China, Russia, and Brazil in entering markets where the political environment is unpredictable. Figure 3 shows a snapshot of this article. Interested readers can find details about this article at the end of the chapter.

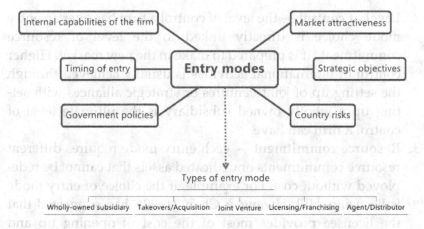

Figure 3: Factors Influencing Entry Modes based on Lasserre (2012)

1.1. *The GMMS process of selecting entry modes*

The GMMS philosophy is based on selecting entry modes from a process of ranking selection drivers on a scale of low to high based on the analyst perception of how this impacts on the firm's goals and objectives in the target market.

These selection drivers are:

1. **Goals and objectives of the firm in the target market** — Lasserre (2012)[e] distinguishes four types of strategic objectives:

   a) *Market development* objectives in which countries can offer a kind of market opportunity as a function of the population and income.

   b) *Resource access* objectives based on the presence of the key resource (mineral, agriculture or human) that can contribute to competitive advantage of the firm.

   c) *Learning objectives* — based on investment into markets through which a firm can gain knowledge and competencies by physical presence.

   d) *Coordination objectives* based on the need for a presence in a market to coordinate regional activities of other markets.

2. **Level of control** — the level of control a firm has over an entry
   mode choice is directly linked to the level of resource
   commitment,[f] if is prepared to make in the new market. Higher
   control of international activities is usually achieved through
   the setting up of joint ventures or strategic alliances with setting up a wholly owned subsidiary is the ultimate level of
   control a firm can have.

3. **Resource commitment** — each entry mode requires different
   resource commitments or dedicated assets that cannot be rede-
   ployed without cost. For example, if the choice of entry mode
   is licensing, Hill, Hwang & Chan, (1990)[g] had suggested that
   the licensee provides most of the cost of opening up and
   serving the foreign market and thus a low level of resource
   commitment is required.

4. **Experience in the use of selected entry mode** — having experience in operating in a global market can also have impact on
   the entry mode decision, where firms can reduce is uncertain,
   it is about entering a new market based on previous experience
   and prior knowledge of decision makers.

5. **The competitive aspect of the entry mode** — if the competitive
   market conditions in a country are intensive, small companies
   have difficulties to expand into these markets because of a lack
   of control. In markets and industries with high competition
   intensity, SMEs choose low investment modes (Ratten Dana,
   Han & Welpe, 2007).[h]

6. **Regulatory aspect of entry mode** — it is also imperative that
   firms understand the regulatory nature of the selected market.
   Governments have been known to implement policies that
   either favor or restrict the entry into the domestic markets. Some
   of the favorable measures can be tax incentives, financing for a
   specific industry sector and encouragement of the formation of
   industry clusters and networks in specific geographic regions.

7. **Market size** — the market potential regarding the size and
   growth of a country was found to be an important factor favor-
   ing high investment modes by Mayer Melitz & Ottaviano (2014).
   Further information on how competition across market

destinations affects both a firm's exported product range and product mix can be read from Mayer Melitz & Ottaviano. (2014).[i]

8. **Risk** — the ability of the firm to manage both macro-level country risk as well as business-specific risks is often dependent on its financial results, experience in international markets and the competitive environment (Koch, 2001).[j] Exporting as an entry mode for example will require engaging with a lower risk level.

9. **Flexibility of the entry mode** — in a dynamic environment, firms often have to change the entry mode strategy, perhaps in the extreme case withdraw from the market. In this event, a firm needs to identify changes in the market (strategic flexibility) and be able to react to changes in the market by allocating the right resources to managing these changes (Ulrich, Hollensen & Boyd, 2014).

10. Feedback of the entry mode to the international strategy of the firm.

The Analyst should carefully and critically evaluate the importance of each of these selection drivers and its effect on each type of entry mode. The entry mode that emerges with the highest score after ranking should be chosen to enter the market(s).

A **structured approach** that we suggest is as follows:

• Evaluate and select the best entry mode by ranking each one of the selection drivers listed below on a scale of 1–5. (Please see Figure 4 for an example of entry mode selection used for a project on the GMMSO4 software.

A = Goals/Objectives	F = Regulations
B = Control	G = Market size
C = Resources	H = Risk
D = Experience	I = Flexibility
E = Competition	J = Feedback

Note: A score of 1 = Low. A score of 3 = Medium.
A score of 5 = High.

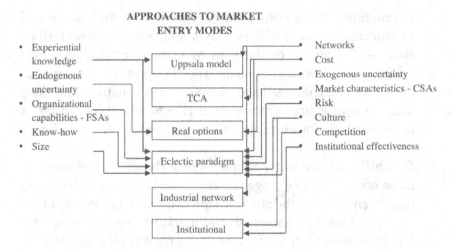

APPROACHES TO MARKET ENTRY MODES

- Experiential knowledge
- Endogenous uncertainty
- Organizational capabilities - FSAs
- Know-how
- Size

Uppsala model

TCA

Real options

Eclectic paradigm

Industrial network

Institutional

- Networks
- Cost
- Exogenous uncertainty
- Market characteristics - CSAs
- Risk
- Culture
- Competition
- Institutional effectiveness

Figure 4: Classification for Understanding and Developing Market Entry Modes Research from De Villa *et al.* (2015)

Corporate Owned Retail Stores

Goals/Objectives	Control	Resources	Experience	Competition
1	1	3	1	5

Regulations	Market Size	Risk	Flexibility	Feedback
3	3	1	4	4

Indirect Export

Goals/Objectives	Control	Resources	Experience	Competition
2	3	1	1	1

Regulations	Market Size	Risk	Flexibility	Feedback
1	3	4	2	3

Direct Export

Goals/Objectives	Control	Resources	Experience	Competition
5	3	4	4	4

Regulations	Market Size	Risk	Flexibility	Feedback
4	3	1	4	2

Figure 5: Ranking Entry Modes on the GMMSO4 System

You may wish to use the following Grid as a guide to the selection process

Entry mode	A	B	C	D	E	F	G	H	I	J	Total Score for entry mode
Corporate owned retail stores											
Indirect export											
Direct export											
Foreign-based sales branch											
Foreign-based marketing subsidiary											
Wholly owned manufacturing subsidiary											
Joint venture (manufacturing)											
Joint venture (marketing)											
Franchising											
Licensing											
Management contract											
E-commerce											

Having decided on the entry mode, explaining the reason for choosing the entry mode strategy is normally expected by management. Include the reasons for ranking the selection drivers and why the entry mode is better than the other entry possible entry modes.

2. The Business Environment of the Selected Market

The Local business environment of the selected target market should be the first point of reference for the analyst. The Doing business database provides individual country business environment

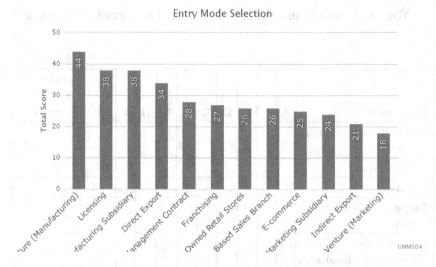

Figure 6:   Entry Mode Scoring on the GMMSO4 Software

profiling.[2] Regional Trade associations like the EU can also provide profiling of the local business environment. The EU has a dedicated online resource[3] that provides policy and market analysis of industry sectors. The OECD library[4] is also a useful resource to profile countries, markets, and industry sectors particularly those belonging to the OECD grouping.

The key aspect to be considered in the profiling of the selected market is as follows:

- You would have had a critical understanding of the target market from the process of in-depth market analysis carried out in chapter 2.
- At the stage of proposing an entry strategy into a new market, the analyst needs to identify any other issues or local market attributes which will influence your business or marketing plan, specific to the target market(s).

[2] 🌐 http://www.doingbusiness.org/reports/global-reports/doing-business-2016.
[3] 🌐 http://ec.europa.eu/growth/sectors/index_en.htm.
[4] 🌐 http://www.oecd-ilibrary.org/#.

- The political environment and market risk of the selected market: A useful article that addresses this including suggestions on how firms can manage political environment in a multipolar world is that of De Villa *et al.* (2015).[k]

Most national statistical agencies offer an analysis of the business environment as well as trade implications. An example of this analysis can be seen from the U.K. office of National statistics (ONS).[5]

3. Creating a Marketing Plan with Its Firm Specific Goals and Objectives

In order to develop a marketing plan, the first step is to identify and define the firm's target market(s) using segmentation strategies. Segmentation allows the firm to split its customers into specific groups with similar needs and wants. Thus, a firm can target and utilize its resources on a specific target segment.

The objectives of segmentation[l] are:

1) To reduce risk in deciding where, when, how, and to whom a product, service, or brand will be marketed.
2) To increase marketing efficiency by directing effort specifically toward the designated segment in a manner consistent with that segment's characteristics.

Market segmentation is a two-fold process that includes:

- Identifying and classifying people into homogeneous groupings, called segments.
- Determining which of these segments are viable target markets.

---

[5] http://www.ons.gov.uk/economy/nationalaccounts/balanceofpayments/bulletins/uktrade/2015-08-07.

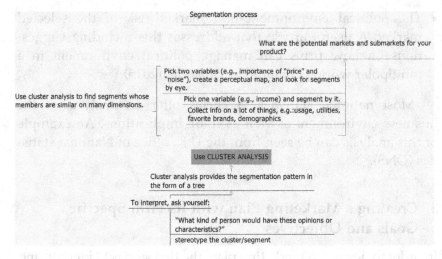

Figure 7:   Segmentation Process based on Prelec (2002)[m]

A course on how to write, conduct, and analyze a marketing research survey with emphasis on discovering market structure and segmentation is available on MIT OPEN.[6] In addition, Figure 7 describes a process of using cluster analysis to segment customers.

3.1. *Benefits of segmentation*

Some of the benefits of segmentation[n] are the following:

To the firm:

- Identification of valuable customers.
- More targeted promotions & marketing communication efficiency.
- Higher CLV sustainable profit growth.

   This ultimately leads to sustainable profit growth

To the customer:

- Customized products and services.

[6]Prelec, D. (2002). *15.822 Strategic Marketing Measurement*, Massachusetts Institute of Technology: MIT OpenCourseWare. ⑤ http://ocw.mit.edu. License: Creative Commons BY-NC-SA.

- Personalized experience.
- Increased customer satisfaction.

This ultimately leads to customer loyalty and retention.

3.2. *Choosing a target market from within a defined segment*[1]

While it is relatively easy to identify segments of consumers, most firms do not have the capabilities or the need to effectively market their product to all of the segments that can be identified. Rather, one or more target markets (segments) must be selected. A company selects its target market because it exhibits the strongest affinity to a particular product or brand. It is in essence the most likely to buy the product. While the market is initially reduced to its smallest homogeneous components (perhaps a single individual), business in practice requires the marketer to find common dimensions that will allow him to view these individuals as larger, profitable segments.

In order to better segment customers, the analyst would need to define whether the product or service is a consumer product/service or an industrial product or service. Within the GMMS methodology before segmentation, the following questions need to be asked to determine the selection of market variables for segmentation.

Answer the following questions:

- Is the product/service an industrial or consumer product/service?
- What needs does the product/service satisfy? How?
- Does the product/service need to be modified? Explain.

3.3. *Consumer product/service*

it is unrealistic to target the whole population or the entire industry in the chosen country. As a result, market segmentation is necessary. Use the tables provided to determine which variables will make up the target market profile.

If the product/service is a consumer product/service, use the "Consumer" table. If the product/service is an industrial product/ service, use the "Industrial" table.

It is possible that the product/service is both a consumer and industrial good, such as flour; in this case, think about how the product will be used. For example, if the flour will be sold in a supermarket, it is a consumer good. However, if the flour will be purchased by a factory in order to make bread, then it is an industrial good.

You may select variables in both tables if the company has primary and secondary markets and will be selling the product/ service to consumers and businesses. In this case, you will have to develop two profiles, one for the consumer market and one for the industrial market. You will also need to determine what the primary market is and what the secondary market is.

You may wish to add additional variables. In the "Define" column, explain how the chosen variable will be measured.

3.4. *Consumer product table*

The following list will guide in the selection of market variables for the purpose of segmenting the target market in the selected country.

Selected segmentation variables for consumer goods		Define each of the selected variables
Demographic	Age distribution	
	Birth rates	
	Death rates	
	Family size	

(Continued)

Table (*Continued*)

Selected segmentation variables for consumer goods		Define each of the selected variables
	Gender	
	Income	
	Population	
	Population density	
	Unemployment rate	
	Urban vs. rural	
	Climate	
Geographic	Topography	
	Vegetation and land use	
	Education	
Socio-Cultural	Language	
	Religion	
	Lifestyle	
Psychographic	Personality traits	
	Social class	

3.5. *Industrial product table*

Selected segmentation variables for industrial/institutional goods		Define each of the selected variables
	Industry	
	Location	
Organizational Characteristics	Management	
	Profitability	
	Size	
	Technology	
	Application	
Purchase/Use Situation	Distribution channels	
	Frequency of purchase	

(*Continued*)

Table (*Continued*)

	Importance of purchase	
	Purchasing procedure	
	Volume of purchase	
User's Needs/Preferences for Product Characteristics	Brand preferences	
	Desired features	
	Performance requirements	
	Quality	
	Service requirements	
	Supplier assistance	

3.6. *Target market*

As the final country screening for global market opportunity, the analyst must identify the target market(s) with the greatest potential for sales. Analysis of market conditions include demand analysis, competitive analysis, basic consumer purchase motivation and available channels of distribution.

In order to do that, the GMMS methodology looks at two aspects.

1. Estimating the total market potential (TMP) for a product or service in the target market and
2. Estimating the firm or company sales potential (CSP) in the target market.

The TMP = [Number of potential (eligible/qualified) consumers] × [Frequency of purchase on an annual basis] × [Selling price of the product].

While CSP = [Total Market Potential (TMP)] × [Desired Market Share (%)].

Goal	Objective	Time Frame
Expand to Africa	*To establish presence in 3 countries of Sub Saharan Africa.*	*To be completed in 3 years*

Figure 8: Setting Marketing Goals and Objectives

3.7. *Marketing goals and objectives*

It is important that the firm, in addition to having a clear vision, must define their marketing goals and objectives in terms of the firm resources/capabilities as well as local market conditions and competitive conditions. Figure 8 is an example of marketing goals and objective set in a real project created using the GMMSO4 software.

The GMMS methodology suggests:

- In the goal column, explain the goal that is to be achieved.
- In the objective column, explain the purpose of the goal.
- *Finally*, in the time column, explain the time frame for the goal.

Table 1: Setting Marketing Objectives

Goal	Objective	Time frame
Expand to Africa	To establish presence in three countries of Sub-Saharan Africa.	To be completed in 3 years

4. Developing a Product Strategy

Based on the assumption that the analyst has already defined the product or service to be taken to the new market as well as identified its characteristics (see Chapter 1 for more on this), we suggest the following questions to be answered:

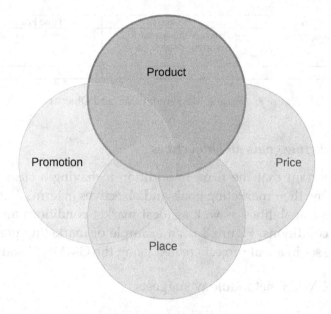

Figure 9:   Marketing Mix Strategies

1. What kind of product development or modification is required in the new market?

2. Is there an *unmet* need that has been identified through segmentation?

3. Are there product or service-specific issues that need to be resolved between the home market and the target market?

4. What are the conditions of use for the selected product or service?

5. What are the attributes behind the ability (buying power) to purchase the product in the selected market?

6. Is there a regulatory environment for the sales and marketing of the product?

7. What kind of product/service communication strategy needs to be identified for the market?

8. What kind of product strategies are going to be used in the market? An extension of existing products, standardization, adaptation, or localization?

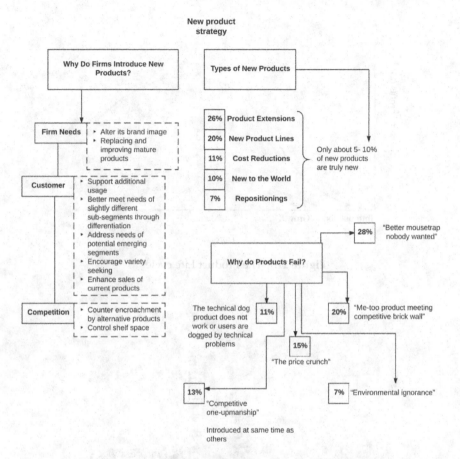

Figure 10: Understanding New Product Strategy[n]

9. Are you looking at the development of new products? The analyst should note that a vast majority of product introduction into new markets fail. (Please see Figure 11 for an explanation.)

5. Developing a Pricing Strategy

5.1. *Pricing strategy*

In order to address a pricing strategy, the following questions regarding the pricing issues must be addressed:

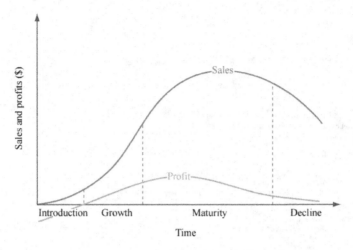

Figure 11: The Product Life cycle[n]

Figure 12: Social Media Options[7]

1. Is the rate of inflation under control in the country? Explain how the rate of inflation has shifted and changed over the past few years. Predict future changes in the inflation rate and how they may impact the company.
2. Is the exchange rate of the country's currency stable? Explain the changes in the exchange rate for the past few years. Predict future changes of the exchange rate and how they will impact the company.
3. Is the "country of origin" factor an important element affecting the price/quality perception of the product/service? Do the local consumers favor domestic or international brands? Explain the trends in local consumer behavior.
4. Are there any price controls imposed by the government of the country that may have an impact on the price of the product/service? List specific price controls. Explain how the price controls will impact the final price of the product.

The table below can be used to determine a pricing strategy.

Pricing Issue	Yes	No	Explain your reasoning
Is the rate of inflation under control in the country?			
Is the exchange rate of the country's currency stable?			
Is the "country of origin" factor an important element affecting the price/quality perception of the product/service?			
Are there any price controls imposed by the government of the country that may have an impact on the price of the product/service?			

Every stage of the product life cycle should have particular pricing goals. Keep these in mind when setting pricing goals.

---

[7]Image is courtesy of PIXABAY.

The PLC includes the following:

1. Introduction: Low penetration pricing to build market share quickly OR high skim price to cover development costs.
2. Growth: Maintain set prices. Demand for the product/service will be increasing and there will be little competition.
3. Maturity: Adjust the price depending on how the company needs to react to increasing competition.
4. Decline: Reduce the price and offer the product to a loyal niche segment.

PLC stage	Country/Market
Introduction	
Growth	
Maturity	
Decline	

5.2. Pricing goals

1. The best pricing strategy for the company's product/service in the target market: Is it Market Skimming or Penetration Pricing or Market Holding Pricing.
2. The selling price of the company's product/service in the target market.

   Will the price be same in both the home country and the target country?

   Different in the target country than in the home country?

   If different, the price in the target country, will the price be higher or lower?

5.3. Pricing method to be used in the target country

Use the glossary to define the pricing methods given. You may want to choose between Cost-plus, Marginal-cost pricing, Return on export investment (target pricing), Negotiated price or Arm's length. Please explain your reasoning.

5.4. *Determining the manufacturing price*

If the firm will manufacture a product in the target country, determine the costs associated with manufacturing the product in both the home country and the target country. If the firm will not be manufacturing in the target country, determine the manufacturing price for the home country only.

	Home country	Target market
Manufacturer's cost		
Manufacturer's selling price		
Selling price paid by the final consumer or industrial user		

5.5. *Determining export price*

If the firm will be exporting to the target country instead of manufacturing the product in the target country, complete the export price calculations.

	Target market
Selling price	
Total shipping costs	
Insurance costs	
Foreign freight forwarder's fees	
Total C.I.F price or landed cost (£)	
Import duties (Tariffs)	
Value-added tax	
Other taxes if any	
Total cost (£)	

5.6. *Determining the discount or the mark up (%) the company will offer to channel members*

As the product/service passes through the various intermediaries on its way to the final consumer or industrial user, the firm may offer a discount or mark-up on the product based on the Manufacturer's Suggested Selling Price (MSRP). The discount or markup (%) given to channel members by the manufacturer may vary from country to country due to the following factors:

- Local market/competitive conditions.
- Contractual agreements.
- Import duties, etc.

If there are other channel members involved in the process, please use the same process for these channels.

6. Creation of a Promotional Strategy

Use the chart below to create a promotional mix. Decide what the company will need to use to market its product/service in the target country. Keep in mind the goals and objectives you came up with from creating the marketing objectives and goals, the availability and cost of the media, and the promotional strategies of the key competitors.

Determine the cost per unit and the number of units needed.

Add up the total cost for each variable chosen and the total budget for the promotional mix.

Promotional mix		Cost/Unit	Units required	Total cost
Advertising	Movies			
	Newspaper			
	Outdoor advertising			
	Radio			
	TV			
Personal selling				
Sales promotion				
Publicity				
Trade shows				
Government sponsored trade missions				
Direct mail				
Internet				
Total Promotional Budget				

The use of an integrated marketing communications (IMC) if appropriate may be explored if the customer needs to be presented with a seamless 'Brand' experience.

The primary role of IMC° is to systematically evaluate the communication needs and wants of the buyer and, based on that information, design a communication strategy that will:

(1) Provide answers to primary questions of the target audience.
(2) Facilitate the custom ability to make correct decisions, and
(3) Increase the probability that the choice they make most often will be the brand of the information provider, i.e., the sponsor or marketer.

You may wish to read about the case of using an innovative promotional strategy to de-market Tobacco use.[8]

6.1. *Evaluation of local media issues*

The ability to use any of these promotional strategies in the market.

- Advertising
- Personal selling
- Sales promotion
- Publicity
- Social media[9]

Address any of media issues like

- Local media conditions
- Media quality
- Promotional mix
- Media reach and coverage
- Media control by the government
- Internet issues
- Any other market specific media issues

7. Developing of a Distribution Strategy

7.1. *Distribution strategy in the target country*

Determine the best strategy for the company's product/service in the target country and explain why the chosen strategy is the best for the company to pursue.

- Intensive distribution

---

[8] http://socialmarketing.blogs.com/r_craiig_lefebvres_social/2009/09/the-4ps-of-demarketing-tobacco-use.html

[9] A free course on Branding, content, and social media by OHIO University is available on ITUNEs. https://itunes.apple.com/us/course/branding-content-social-media/id824354707?ign-mpt=uo%3D8

- Exclusive distribution
- Selective distribution

7.2. *Distribution channels*

Determine the distribution channels in the target market.

- Are you going to create a new distribution channel?
- Or will you be using a local company's distribution channel?
- Can you use existing distribution channel?

7.3. *Channel issues*

You may wish to critically examine the local channel issues.

Does the government require a license to establish presence in the country?

Is it difficult to dismiss a channel member such as a Distributor/Agent with whom you have an agreement?

7.4. *Select the best channel method*

Determine the best channel in the local market. The matrix below from the GMMSO software can be used here.

Channel alternatives		Reasoning behind the choice
Direct: Selling directly to consumer	Company-Owned Retail Stores	
	Marketing Subsidiaries	
	Sales Branches	
Indirect: selling through intermediaries	Agents	
	Import Distributor	
	Industrial Supply Houses	
	Manufacturing Representatives	
	Retailers	
	Wholesalers	
E-commerce	Internet	

8. Creation of a Financial Strategy

8.1. *Projected P/L statement*

In the case of a manufacturer or service provider, determine the number of units that will be sold in the first, second, and third years the company is operating in the target country.

To determine the selling price and the price per unit, keep in mind the TMP, CSP, and the pricing goals from previous chapters.

Step 1: *Determine cost of goods sold (CGS) and operating expenditure (OP)*

To determine the CGS, look back at the manufacturing price and the export price. Another place to look for the CGS and Operating Expenses (OP) is the Income Statement of the firm.

You may want to use the same CGS and OP % or adjust it to account for local manufacturing costs and market conditions.

Use the glossary at the end of this book to define unfamiliar terms in the table. Make sure the CGS and the OE is in terms of all units and not per unit. For example, if the CGS is £4.00/unit, and the company plans to sell 1,000 units in its first year, the CGS will be £4,000.

The following matrix may help:

	Year 1	Year 2	Year 3
Unit			
Unit Price			
Calculate net sales in the target Market			
(No of Units × unit price)			
Cost of goods sold			
Calculate Gross profit (loss)			
Opex			
Net Profit (loss) after Tax			

In the case of a retail Establishment, determine and enter the total retail sales for each year in the "Unit" box and the number of stores in the "Unit Price" box.

You should project annual sales for one unit (one retail store for the first year). For years 2 and 3, consider increasing the number of stores (enter the number of new stores in the "Unit Price" box) by opening additional stores in the target country. Also consider increasing the sales ("Unit") by a certain % for the next 2 years along with the OE.

Calculate the net sales in the target country, gross profit/loss, and net profit/loss.

Step 2: *Break-Even point*

Included in the analysis of the profitability of a Target Market is the computation of the break-even point (BEP). The BEP should be used simultaneously with the development of product strategies and action plans to ensure that the marketing program meets the required level of sales successfully.

Percentage Gross Profit = Total Gross Profit/Total Net Sales.

BEP sales = Total OE/Percentage Gross Profit.

	Year 1	Year 2	Year 3
Gross profit			
BEP sales			

Using the P/L statement and the break-even analysis, figure out the best and worst case scenarios for the first 3 years of operation in the target country. Be consistent with the CSP.

Include the percentage of the target market the company will capture. Then determine the best and worst case scenarios for the first, second, and third years of operation.

Some examples of scenarios that can impact your financial projections are:[10]

- Can you relocate production from affected areas with minimum risk and loss of revenues?
- What is your response to terrorism and what about disaster management plans?
- The impact of natural disaster/risks on your supply chain — Automobile supply chain disruption in Japan?
- Labor disputes/Plant shutdowns
- Impacts of currency fluctuations on profitability
- Insurance risks and the Acts of God clause
- Pandemics and Global Climate change effects on long-term strategies

Use your research of the local market to briefly describe and explain each scenario.

Year	Profit		Sales	
1	Best case		Best case	
	Worst case		Worst case	
2	Best case		Best case	
	Worst case		Worst case	
3	Best case		Best case	
	Worst case		Worst case	

After determining the various scenarios, you may wish to explain the reasoning behind each scenario.

9. Creating the Organizational Structure for the New Market

The nature of the organizational structure in the new market is clearly a function of the objectives of the firm, its resources and the proposed

---

[10]Suresh George's Lecture at Coventry University.

commitment to the market. You might want to start by describing how the country-level operational structure might look like.

Following from this, a description of the value creating as well as valid transferring activity that is expected to be performed in the market may be addressed. Some questions that may be asked at this juncture can be

1. Is the new organizational structure going to be responsible for its local market or will it have organizational responsibility for the regional market as well?
2. How does the proposed organizational structure fit into the overall structure of the firm?
3. Will it be part of its global business unit, will it need to be a country-level unit or will it have to be a product-level organizational structure?

A useful discussion on *"The Pros & Cons of 7 Popular Organizational Structures"*[11] can be a guide to understanding different organizational structures. Some of the common types of organizational structures are:

9.1. *Functional structure*

Organizations can also be created as a functional structure based on activities that determine how the firm performs and operates in a particular market.

9.2. *Divisional structure*

Another structure is the divisional structure which can be used to manage the activities of the firm in a new market.

---

[11] http://blog.hubspot.com/marketing/team-structure-diagrams#sm.0001m8zxl m7lad24u4712u60xgc21.

9.3. *Matrix Structure*

Many organizations are changing their international structure into a matrix or at the least, one with matrix elements. Burton, Obel & Håkonsson (2015)[p] have identified three factors that are critical to matrix success:

(1) having strong reasons for choosing a matrix structure.
(2) aligning key contingencies with the matrix and its purpose, and
(3) carefully managing the junctions at which dimensions of the matrix come together.

The basic matrix configuration is a cross-functional organization with product/service/customer and functional dimensions. See Figure 13 below for an example.

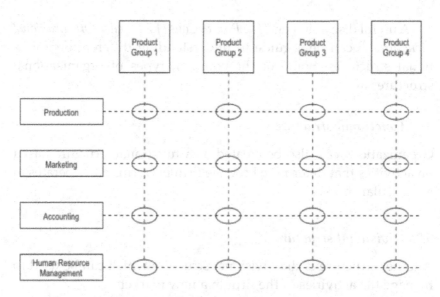

Figure 13:   The Matrix Configuration (*Source*: Burton, *et al.*, 2015)

A case study in building a global procurement organization can be a valuable insight to understanding the limitations of the global structure. Read it on the Bain consultancy[12] website.

10. Understanding Exit Strategy and Scenarios

Most business analysts would like to be positive and think that a well-designed market entry strategy will become profitable. However, it is our recommendation that during the process of designing the entry strategy, an understanding of exit options must be included in your planning. An exit strategy is the mode through which the firm intends to exit the market.

The literature on exit strategies has primarily addressed three issues (DeTienne & Chirico, 2013[q]):

1. The importance of construct definition due to exit's multi-level nature (i.e., exit of firms from the market and exit of founders from the firm)
2. The critical distinction between exit and failure
3. The various routes of entrepreneurial exit

The following exit strategies from Stever Robbins[13] can be a way forward to address this final aspect of entering a new market.

1. Bleed the business dry
2. Liquidate the business
3. Sell the business to either a competitor or an employee
4. Sell it to a competitor who wants to acquire your business
5. Take your company public

---

[12]🖲 http://www.bain.com/publications/articles/building-a-world-class-global-procurement-organization.aspx.
[13]🖲 https://www.entrepreneur.com/article/78512.

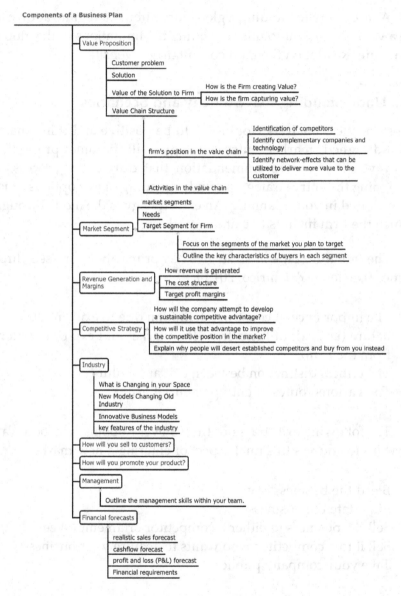

Figure 14:   Components of a Business Plan[14,r]

[14]Based on Data from Joseph Hadzima's Lecture Notes at MIT and information from the Gov.uk website.

11. Summary

At this point, the firm will have determined the best possible entry strategy into the selected market, the potential offered by the market, local market environment, and the financial costs associated with the entry.

All you now need is to present this in a business plan to the stakeholders of the company and proceed with the entry process. Figure 14 is an example of the key components of a business plan that you may want to use. In addition, the GOV.UK site[15] offers resources that can help with writing business plans: https://www.gov.uk/write-business-plan.

Endnotes

[a]Holtbrügge, D., & Baron, A. (2013). Market entry strategies in emerging markets: An institutional study in the BRIC countries. *Thunderbird International Business Review*, 55(3), 237–252.

[b]Kumar, V., & Subramaniam, V. (1997). A contingency framework for the mode of entry decision. *Journal of World Business*, 32(1), 53–72.

[c]Pan, Y., & Tse, D. K. (2000). The hierarchical model of market entry modes. *Journal of International Business Studies*, 31(4), 535–554.

[d]Laufs, K., & Schwens, C. (2014). Foreign market entry mode choice of small and medium-sized enterprises: A systematic review and future research agenda. *International Business Review*, 23(6), 1109–1126.

[e]Lasserre, P. (2012). *Global Strategic Management*. Palgrave Macmillan.

[f]Ulrich, A. M. D., Hollensen, S., & Boyd, B. (2014). Entry mode strategies into the Brazil, Russia, India and China (BRIC) Markets. *Global Business Review*, 15(3), 423–445.

[g]Hill, C., Hwang, P., & Chan, K. (1990). An eclectic theory of the choice of international entry mode'. *Strategic Management Journal*, 11(2), 117–128.

[h]Ratten, V., Dana, L. P., Han, M., & Welpe, I. (2007). Internationalisation of SMEs: European comparative studies. *International Journal of Entrepreneurship and Small Business*, 4(3), 361–379.

[i]Mayer, T., Melitz, M. J., & Ottaviano, G. I. (2014). Market size, competition, and the product mix of exporters. *The American Economic Review*, 104(2), 495–536.

---

[15] https://www.gov.uk/write-business-plan.

[j] Koch, A. J. (2001). Factors influencing market and entry mode selection: Developing the MENS model. *Marketing Intelligence & Planning, 19*(5), 351–361.

[k] De Villa, M. A., Rajwani, T., & Lawton, T. (2015). Market entry modes in a multipolar world: Untangling the moderating effect of the political environment. *International Business Review, 24*(3), 419–429.

[l] *Source*: Boundless (2016, 20 May). "The Importance of Market Segmentation." *Boundless Marketing.* (§) https://www.boundless.com/marketing/textbooks/boundless-marketing-textbook/consumer-marketing-4/market-segmentation-36/the-importance-of-market-segmentation-187-4063/.

[m] Prelec, D. *15.822 Strategic Marketing Measurement,* Massachusetts Institute of Technology: MIT OpenCourseWare. (§) http://ocw.mit.edu. License: Creative Commons BY-NC-SA.

[n] Mizik, N. *15.810 Marketing Management,* Massachusetts Institute of Technology: MIT OpenCourseWare. (§) http://ocw.mit.edu. License: Creative Commons BY-NC-SA.

[o] Burnett, J. (2008). Core concepts of marketing. Published by the Global Text project. (§) https://archive.org/details/ost-business-core-concepts-of-marketing.

[p] Burton, R. M., Obel, B., & Håkonsson, D. D., (2015). How to get the matrix organization to Work. *Journal of Organization Design, 4*(3), 37–45.

[q] DeTienne, D. R. & Chirico, F. (2013). Exit strategies in family firms: How socioemotional wealth drives the threshold of performance. *Entrepreneurship Theory and Practice, 37*(6), 1297–1318.

[r] Hadzima, J. *15.S21 Nuts and Bolts of Business Plans, January IAP 2014.* Massachusetts Institute of Technology: MIT OpenCourseWare. (§) http://ocw.mit.edu. License: Creative Common BY-NC-SA.

Additional Reading

1. A blog that shows how SUBARU created its new market entry. (§) https://teamsubaru.wikispaces.com/Marketing+Strategy.

2. A course on creating Business plans is by Hadzima, J. *15. S21 Nuts and Bolts of Business Plans, January IAP 2014,* (Massachusetts Institute of Technology: MIT OpenCourseWare). (§) http://ocw.mit.edu License: Creative Commons BY-NC-SA.

3. A free online course on the working knowledge of the analytical tools that bear most directly on the economic decisions firms must regularly make is available on: (§) http://ocw.mit.edu/courses/sloan-school-of-management/15-010-economic-analysis-for-business-decisions-fall-2004/#.

4. A reading on entry mode decision-making can be seen in Laufs, K. & Schwens, C. (2014). Foreign market entry mode choice of small and

medium-sized enterprises: A systematic review and future research agenda. *International Business Review, 23*(6), 1109–1126.

5. An excellent article (though dated) on entry modes is Hill, C., Hwang, P., & Chan, K. (1990). An Eclectic theory of the choice of international entry mode. *Strategic Management Journal, 11*(2), 117–128.

6. An excellent article on how the personal characteristics of a business owner can influence the entry mode is by Parker, S. C. & Van Praag, C. M., (2012). The entrepreneur's mode of entry: Business takeover or new venture start? *Journal of Business Venturing, 27*(1), 31–46.

7. Business Plans Templates. 🖐 https://www.princes-trust.org.uk/help-for-young-people/tools-resources/business-tools/business-plans.

8. Exit Strategies for Your Business. 🖐 https://www.entrepreneur.com/article/78512.

9. How To Identify Your Market And Size Up Competitors. Available on *Forbes* 🖐 http://www.forbes.com/sites/rebeccabagley/2013/10/02/how-to-identify-your-market-size-up-competitors/#3aa4c1062463.

10. The selection of entry mode when penetrating a foreign market by Annica Gunnarsson. 🖐 http://www.diva-portal.org/smash/get/diva2:421070/FULLTEXT01.pdf.

11. This article is useful to understand how to get a matrix to work by Burton, R. M., Obel, B. & Håkonsson, D.D. (2015). How to get the matrix organization to work. *Journal of Organization Design, 4*(3), 37–45.

12. This paper finds that different motives and theories influence the choice of foreign market entry by SMEs Nisar, S., Boateng, A., Wu, J., & Leung, M. (2012). Understanding the motives for SMEs entry choice of international entry mode. *Market Intelligence & Planning, 30*(7), 717–739.

Online Resources

1. **Business Corruption Country Profiles** — 🖐 tinyurl.com/jgpwrtv.
2. **Choose Your Business Structure** — 🖐 tinyurl.com/jjznax4.
3. **Commisceo Country Guides** — 🖐 www.commisceo-global.com/country-guides.
4. **Doing Business in Asian Countries** — 🖐 www.business-in-asia.com/.
5. **Economist Intelligence Unit** — 🖐 www.eiu.com/.
6. **eCrat.com: Bringing Together Resources for Addressing Today's Business, Social Enterprise and Intern** — 🖐 www.ecrat.com/home.html.
7. **Export.Gov: Helping US Companies Export** — 🖐 www.export.gov/.
8. **Five Smart Exit Strategies** — 🖐 www.businessinsider.com/startup-exits-should-be-positive-and-planned-early-2011-1.
9. **Foreign Affairs and International Trade Canada** — 🖐 tinyurl.com/hk9stby.
10. **Gateway to the European Union** — 🖐 europa.eu/index_en.htm.

11. **Global Edge: Resource Desk** — globaledge.msu.edu/ibrd/ibrd.asp.
12. **Global Information Network for SMEs** — 🌐 www.gin.sme.ne.jp/.
13. **How to Choose an Exit Strategy** — 🌐 tinyurl.com/8wz5aqa.
14. **Index of Economic Freedom** — 🌐 tinyurl.com/e8nu.
15. **Industry Canada** — 🌐 tinyurl.com/zlbo82v.
16. **International Shipping Worldwide** — 🌐 www.shipping-worldwide.com/.
17. **Lonely Planet** — 🌐 www.lonelyplanet.com/worldguide/.
18. **Mellinger Co.** — 🌐 www.tradezone.com/trdzone.htm.
19. **Nation Master** — www.nationmaster.com/.
20. **Portals of the World From the Library of Congress** — 🌐 www.loc.gov/rr/international/portals.html.
21. **The Economist Intelligence Unit's Country Profiles and Country Reports** — 🌐 tinyurl.com/jfktpfo.
22. **The Economist Intelligence Unit's Country Profiles and Country Reports** — 🌐 www.eiu.com/home.aspx.
23. **The EU Doing Business portal** — 🌐 europa.eu/youreurope/business/.
24. **The EU Doing Business portal** — 🌐 europa.eu/youreurope/business/.
25. **The Marketing Mix 4P's and 7P's Explained** — 🌐 marketingmix.co.uk/.
26. **The UK's Monthly Statistics on Trade in Goods** — 🌐 tinyurl.com/zgvl9z2.
27. **The UK's Monthly Statistics on Trade in Goods** — 🌐 tinyurl.com/zgvl9z2.
28. **The World Bank** — 🌐 www.worldbank.org/.
29. **Thomas Global** — 🌐 http://goo.gl/UFgis5.
30. **US International Trade Commission** — 🌐 www.dataweb.usitc.gov.
31. **What Makes a Business** — 🌐 tinyurl.com/z4g7doy.
32. **Write Your Business Plan** — 🌐 tinyurl.com/hayzwkh.

Part B

The GMMSO4 Software System

GMMSO

The Global Marketing Management System Online (GMMSO) software (GMSMO4©) http://www.book.gmmso4.com is an online management planning tool designed to aid research of global markets and develop international marketing plans and strategies. It is based on the GMMS methodology described in Part A of this book.

Not only is the GMMSO4 designed to be user friendly, but it is also more comprehensive, practical and interactive than the previous version. The GMMSO4 has been greatly enhanced by using a new state-of-the-art platform, a database, a report generator, and dynamically generated results.

New and exciting features include:

- An up-to-date list of targeted websites
- Detailed instructions
- Spell checking
- Chat functionality
- New sample case studies
- Power Point presentation examples
- Most importantly, an Instructor's Manual and User Guide

1. What Is GMMSO?

The GMMSO is a research and strategic planning management tool designed to help your company enter or expand its presence into foreign markets.

The GMMSO, consisting of three dynamic modules, will enable you to systematically:

1. Conduct a company situation analysis in a global context.
2. Identify the country with highest market potential for your company and select the most effective entry mode strategy.
3. Develop the business or marketing plan.

2. Bridge the Gap

- The GMMSO software addresses one of the most important challenges faced by international business faculty: how to bring the real world into the classroom or training environment by providing the platform needed to support students in their roles as managers and decision makers in a global setting.
- Students are provided with an interactive, engaging, and innovative web-based software which helps bridge the gap between theory and the rigorous decision-making process of solving real, complex business problems.
- Results based on surveys conducted by instructors confirm that the software enhanced their students' international business understanding, and improved their team work and critical thinking skills.

3. Benefits

Learn to:

- Apply classroom and textbook context
- Integrate knowledge from experience
- Perform a situation analysis of a company in a global context
- Practice how to research global markets
- Identify and evaluate high potential country markets for company's products/services
- Conduct competitive analysis
- Determine best entry mode strategies
- Develop customized marketing plans and strategies

- Use internet resources and information effectively
- Make informed business decisions in a global context

4. Background to the Development of the Online Version of the GMMS Method

The introduction and integration of various emerging technologies into the teaching and learning classroom experience seems to be a growing and irreversible trend. This more experiential hands-on approach that aims to bring reality into the classroom enables students to apply, and to a certain extent, test the theoretical knowledge being acquired.

The GMMSO web-based software addresses one of the most important challenges faced by international business faculty, that is, how to bring the real world into the classroom or training environment by providing the needed platform and systematic step-by-step process to support students in their roles as managers and decision makers in a global setting.

Students are provided with an interactive, engaging, and innovative research and planning tool which helps them to bridge the gap between theory and the rigorous decision-making process of solving real, complex business problems.

The GMMSO, http:book.gmmso4.com is essentially a project-based learning (PBL) tool designed to be used for international business projects as part a of course or on its own.

5. Learning Outcomes

As a result of using the GMMSO software as a key teaching and learning tool students should learn how to:

- Research, analyze, interpret, and use data to make business decisions in a global setting

- Apply what they learn in the classroom or training environment
- Integrate knowledge from all functional business areas and be able to make decisions in a global context
- Perform a situation analysis of a company in a global context
- Practice how to research global markets
- Identify and evaluate high potential country markets for company's products/services
- Conduct competitive analysis
- Determine best entry mode strategies
- Develop customized marketing plans and strategies
- Use internet resources and information effectively

The twin engines of global economic development, information technology and globalization have accelerated the growth of web-based pedagogical resources and revolutionized the teaching and learning methodologies through the use of the internet.

Research evidence seems to indicate that one of the immediate consequences of increasing adoption of technology into the classroom is the shift from lecturer and lecture discussion to student center learning (Marcus, 2006). It is important to mention that this is a key aspect of the GMMSO system analyzed in this paper. Recent research by Samarawickrema and Stacey corroborate previous studies showing that innovation and technology adoption in teaching and learning provide "effective, efficient, relevant, interesting, learner-centered, web-based learning experiences" (Samarawickrema & Stacey, 2007, p. 317).

Several surveys have proven (Janavaras, 2007; Janavaras, Gomes, Ceema & George, 2008; Gomes, Janavaras & Cheema, 2008) that the software had enhanced the skills of the students, such as critical thinking, web-based research, team working, and decision-making. However, further research is needed in the area of PBL and interactive learning to determine the benefits and pitfalls associated with web-based software and other simulations.

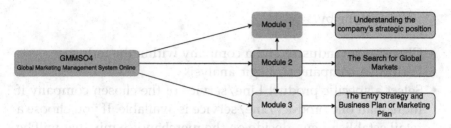

The GMMSO4 system layout

Each module defines a set of objectives and provides

1) Steps
2) Instructions
3) Resource links to accomplish these objectives

- Apply classroom and textbook context
- Integrate knowledge from experience
- Perform a situation analysis of a company in a global context
- Practice how to research global markets
- Identify and evaluate high potential country markets for company's products/services
- Conduct competitive analysis
- Determine best entry mode strategies
- Develop customized marketing plans and strategies
- Use internet resources and information effectively
- Make informed business decisions in a global context

5.1. *Outline of each module*

5.1.1. *Module 1 — Understanding the company's strategic position*

The objective of Module 1 is for project teams and/or management to conduct a company situation analysis. Not only does this assist project teams in conducting more effective and targeted studies, but it also helps management redefine their business within the framework of a global marketing imperative.

This is done by:

- Choosing an industry and a company within the industry
- Perform a company strategic analysis
- Select a specific product Line/service of the chosen company if more than one product Line/service is available. If you choose a retail establishment, decide on the merchandise mix that will be included in the overseas operation, along with the number of stores that will be opened during the first, second and third years of international operation
- Determine the target market profile
- Determine the international involvement, if any, of the company
- Conduct an internal analysis of the company
- Conduct an external analysis of the Industry
- Determine the company's global business readiness in the international arena

5.1.2. *Module 2 — The search for global markets*

The objective of Module 2 to is to identify the country with the highest market potential for your company, using a country attractiveness screening process consisting of three stages, and determine the most effective entry mode strategy for the targeted country as shown below:

1. Macro-level criteria
2. Micro-level criteria
3. Accessibility criteria
4. Market entry strategy criteria

The criteria selected should assist the company to identify the country that offers the most business opportunity for your company based on:

1. Need/desire for the product
2. Market size and growth

3. Ability to purchase the product
4. Ability to enter the market

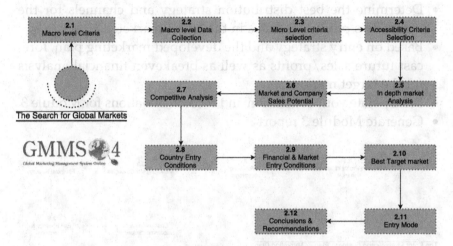

Figure 2: Structure of Module 2 of the GMMSO4 Software

5.1.3. *Module 3 — The entry strategy and business plan or marketing plan*

The objective of Module 3 is to determine the most effective entry strategy and marketing plan based on company's goals, resources, strengths relative to the competition and market conditions by using the following procedure:

• Develop marketing strategies and action plans that will most successfully penetrate the target market country.
• Identify the target market in the country using key segmentation variables.
• Develop market penetration and coverage objectives that fully exploit market opportunity.
• Determine whether the company should create, extend, and/or adapt its current product/service.
• Determine the best pricing strategy and method for the company's product after investigating terms of sale and value-added costs in the target market.

- Develop an effective promotional strategy by carefully matching company resources with perceived product/service benefits and buyer behavior in the target market.
- Determine the best distribution strategy and channels for the company's product/service in the target market.
- Based on entry strategy and the developed marketing plan, forecast future sales/profits as well as breakeven financial analysis for the target market.
- Briefly state your conclusion and recommendations for Module 3
- Generate Module 3 report

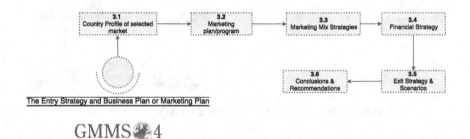

Figure 3:   Structure of Module 3 of the GMMSO4 Software

5.2. *Teaching with the GMMSO4 software*

5.2.1. *Instructor benefits*

- Minimum preparation time
- Instructor's manual and PP presentations
- Ability to monitor student progress and review completed projects online
- Real-time business tools
- User friendly (need basic computer skills only; detailed instructions are provided to guide you in completing the process)
- Interactive and integrative (students can work independently or as a members of a team from anywhere in the world)
- Cognitive and experiential (hands-on)

- Resourceful and innovative (up-to-date websites and targeted resources are included for each phase)
- Multidimensional (can be used for global, regional and, individual country markets)
- It can be used from anywhere in the world with Internet connections!
- Generate reports, provide feedback, and keep scores

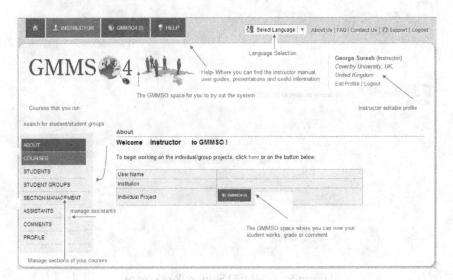

Figure 4:   GMMSO Instructor Workspace

5.3. *Teaching suggestions*

- Review the GMMSO prior to assigning it to your students for the class project
- Assign it early, that is, the first or second week of classes.
- Assign it as a group project (up to five (5) students per group). Individual assignments should also be considered on a case-by-case basis, depending on circumstances.
- Recommend an industry and publicly held companies or provide a list of companies to choose from.
- Require a project proposal consisting of Module 1.1a–1.2.e.

- Allow students to work on the project during class time (If you teach an online course, specify a time students can contact you with project-related questions).
- Visit with the groups while working on the project in class.

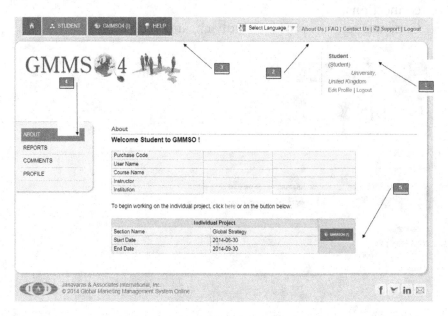

Figure 5:   GMMSO Student Workspace

5.4. *Allowing the use of group assignments*

- The GMMSO4 enables the instructor to create groups of students.
- When a group is created, an automated e-mail with group information will be sent to all group members.
- Each member of the group will use his or her own username and password to log in
- Two group members should not be working on one screen simultaneously.
- Communicate with your group members frequently to keep track of each others progress.

- If it should occur that two members are working on one screen, when one of those persons clicks "Save", the other person will lose all of his or her entered data.

5.5. *Correlation between GMMSO and international business topics:*

Topic	Module I	Module II	Module III
Globalization imperative	X		
Global economic environment	X		
Global financial environment	X	X	
Global cultural environment and buyer behavior	X	X	
Political and legal environment	X	X	
Global marketing research		X	X
Global segmentation and positioning		X	
Global marketing strategies		X	X
Global market entry strategies		X	X
Global sourcing strategy: R&D, manufacturing, and marketing interfaces		X	X
Global Product policy decisions:Developing new products for global markets		X	X
Global product policy decisions: Marketing products and services		X	X
International pricing		X	
Communicating with the world customer		X	X
Sales management		X	X
Global logistics and distribution		X	X
Export and import management		X	X
Global marketing and the internet			X

5.6. *Using the software*

Please login to www.gmmso4.com and select the "register" tab as shown in the below. Choose the type of registration.

User Registration

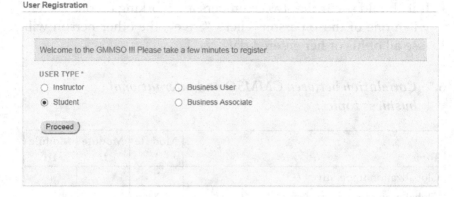

Once you have finished your registration, you will be sent your login details to the registered email id. Please use this to login to the GMMSO4 system. After logging in, you will be able to see your welcome screen that indicates your subscription details. If you are a student, you will be able to click on the individual project as well as your group project if the instructor has allocated you to a group.

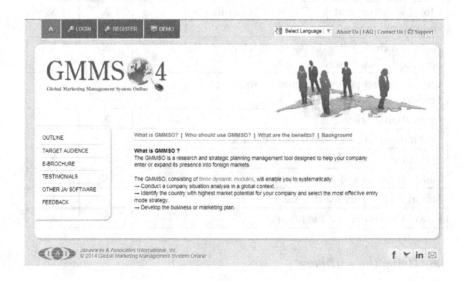

5.7. *Starting on the GMMSO4*

Welcome Student to GMMSO !

Purchase Code		
User Name		
Course Name		
Instructor		
Institution		

To begin working on the individual project, click here or on the button below:

Individual Project		
Section Name	Global Strategy	GMMSO4 (I)
Start Date	2014-06-30	
End Date	2014-09-30	

To begin working on the group project, click here or on the button below:

Group Project		
Section Name	Global Strategy	GMMSO4 (G)
Start Date	2014-06-30	
End Date	2014-09-30	

Figure 6: The Welcome Screen on the GMMSO4 Software

5.8. *The GMMSO4 workspace*

1) Personal profile — edit your details as well as see details of your course.
2) Choose a language to use the system, a support tab that allows you to contact us in the event of a technical issue, a list of frequently asked questions (FAQs) on the GMMSO4 and contact forms to send us a message.
3) Home page , view your individual and group report areas as well as a help section that provides you with user guides, case studies, and examples of reports that have been created using the system.

4) View any scores or comments made by an instructor, create reports, and manage your profile.
5) GMMSO4 individual or group areas.

5.9. *Navigating the GMMSO4*

The top left-hand section of the GMMSO4 is key to navigating to your projects. You can toggle from the Individual (GMMSO4 (I)) as well as a group project (GMMSO4(G)) if your instructor has allowed it.

Clicking on the resources tab will open a window with glossary, suggested websites and useful articles that are relevant to the section you are working on as shown below

Click on the "ADD Bibliography" Tab to add references to your project as you enter data. Your personal list of references will be listed as shown below:

5.10. *Student layout and workspace*

The layout of the student view of the GMMSO4 software is quite simple and all the tools are displayed neatly as shown in Figure 7 below:

Some of the useful icons/tabs are as follows:

1. Personal Profile: This area is your personal profile here. You can edit your details as well as see details of your course.
2. This area allows you to choose a language to use the system, a support tab that allows you to contact us in the event of

a technical issue, a list of FAQs on the GMMSO4 and contact forms to send us a message.

3. This section allows you to return to your home page at any time, view your individual and group report areas as well as a help section that provides you with user guides, case studies, and examples of reports that have been created using the system.

4. This section will allow you to view any scores or comments made by an instructor, create reports, and manage your profile.

5. This section will allow you to access the GMMSO4 either through the individual or group areas.

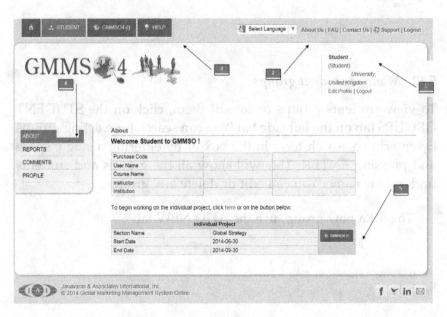

Figure 7: The GMMSO4 Workspace

5.11. *Manage students*

To view students or to edit them. Click on the STUDENTS tab on the left side bar. You can search for existing students by entering a search term in the box or by entering a single space and pressing ENTER. This will show all the students under your name. You can edit or delete any course.

To add a new student, use the ADD NEW tab

5.12. *Manage student groups*

To view students groups or to edit them, click on the STUDENT GROUPS tab on the left side bar. You can search for existing groups by entering a search term in the box or by entering a single space and pressing ENTER. This will show all the groups and students under your name. You can edit or delete any group.

To add a new group, use the ADD NEW tab

Manage Student Groups

Add New   New Search

Search Student Groups *

Search

5.13. *Suggested semester schedule for course delivery*

Week 1	Introduction to the GMMSO using the PP presentation along with the user guide and instructor's manual.
Week 2	Formation of teams, teams research, and decide on the industry, company, and its product(s)/service(s).
Week 3	Module 1: Understanding the company's strategic position. Make company contacts and begin to collect data pertaining to the company and its product(s)/service(s).
Week 4	Complete the research and collection of data for Module 1.
Week 5	Progress report on Module 1.
Week 6	Module 2: The search for global markets. Determine the criteria necessary for success in a foreign market.
Week 7	Screening and selections of possible markets.
Week 8	In-depth market analysis and competitive analysis of two countries and selection of best country market.
Week 9	Progress report on module 2
Week 10	Module 3: Business/marketing plan development
Week 11	Market segmentation, target market, goals, and objectives
Week 12	The marketing mix, P/L statement, and scenario development
Week 13	Executive summary and bibliography
Week 14	Final report and PP presentation

5.14. *Suggested quarter schedule for course delivery*

Week 1	Introduction to the GMMSO using the PP presentation along with the user guide and instructor's manual. formation of teams, teams research, and decide on the industry, company and its product(s)/service(s).
Week 2	Module 1: Understanding the company's strategic position. Make company contacts and begin to collect data pertaining to the company and its product(s)/service(s).
Week 3	Complete the research and collection of data for Module 1.
Week 4	Progress report on Module 1.
Week 5	Module 2: Global market search. Selecting Country Markets. Determine the criteria necessary for success in a foreign market and screen for best markets.

Week 6	In-depth market and competitive analysis of two countries and selection of best country market.Screening and selection of possible markets.
Week 7	Progress Report on Module 2.
Week 8	Module 3: Business/marketing plan development, market segmentation, target market, goals and objectives.
Week 9	The marketing mix, P/L statement, and scenario development. Executive Summary and Bibliography.
Week 10	Presentation of final reports.

Part C: Case Study

**Lafkiotis Winery Entry
into United States: A Report Created by
Using the GMMSO4 System**

Case Study

Executive Summary

This report was created by the Global marketing management system online software, (GMMSO4) and analyzes the entry of a firm into a new market.

The firm is analyzed using a structured approach in three modules.

Module 1   looks at understanding the company's Strategic Position
Module 2   is the search for global markets
Module 3   is the entry strategy and business plan or marketing plan

1. Lafkiotis Winery's Strategic Analysis

In 1963, Konstantinos Lafkiotis and his two brothers (Dimitris and Petros) founded the Lafkiotis Winery located in Ancient Kleones, Nemea, region of Peloponnese. Today, the Lafkiois Winery (owned and managed by the five children of the founders), supported by the experience of many years of producing premium wines, continues the tradition by selecting high quality vineyards and producing premium wine in modern state-of-the-art facilities using the latest wine-making methods and techniques. Some of the wines are stored in stainless steel tanks, but most of the Lafkiotis wines are aged in oak French and American barrels in environmentally-controlled cellars. The high quality of limited production of Lafkiotis wines express the distinct flavors of native grapes and the unique micro-climates and terroir where they are grown such as that of St. George (Agiorgitiko) in the area of Nemea. More than 85% of the Lafkiotis wines are exported to selected European countries, North America and Australia (www.lafkiotis.gr).

Purpose

The purpose of this study is to develop an international marketing plan and strategy for the Lafkiotis Winery and its channels that could be used in its global expansion and marketing efforts.
More specifically, the study will:

1. Analyze the Lafkiotis, winery in terms of its current resources, capabilities, strategies, and readiness to expand to new country markets.
2. Identify, analyze, and evaluate the country with the highest market potential, perform a detailed competitive analysis, and determine the most viable entry mode strategy for the selected market.
3. Develop the marketing and plan, strategy and tactics to be implemented at the local level by the importer and the distributor in the selected market.

Research Methodology

The research for this project was mainly based on secondary data, which were found online. Also, primary data were collected and used through a visit to the winery and personal interviews with Mrs. Yianna Lafkiotis, one of the winery owners and Communications Director and with Mr. Basil and Mrs. Linda Janavaras (Janavaras Enterprises LLC Â– JE) wine importers based in Minnesota, USA. Primary data were also collected by the author in cooperation with

Vinocopia, the wine Distributor of JE in Minnesota, in the form of wine tastings for selected clients and participation in direct sales calls and trade shows.

Key Findings — Module 1

Module 1 includes a company analysis and evaluation of the Lafkiotis Winery. Their sustainable growth is primarily based on a belief and strategy of producing high quality wines using mainly indigenous grapes, product differentiation, consistency, and transparency with both the supply chain and their distribution channels.

Lafkiotis exports, directly for the most part, 85% of its wines in 17 different countries. Their sales have increased by an average of 22% the last 3 years. The three main competitors of the winery are 'Domaine Skouras', 'Papaioannou Wines' and 'Semeli Wines' all located in the region of Nemea. Compared to their domestic and international competitors, the Lafkiotis Winery has fewer resources and productive capacity. In light of the Lafkiotis resources, experience and knowledge base, the most appropriate method of international expansion is to continue with the direct exporting strategy.

Key Findings — Module 2

In this module, the countries with the highest market potential were identified, analyzed, and evaluated. GMMSO4 proposed countries according to selected Macro, Micro, and Accessibility criteria related to market size and growth potential. Some of the key criteria used were population, the political environment, the market size, as well as the existing and potential consumers of wines. Based on the results, the top two countries were USA and Australia. Next step was the comparison between USA and Australia as potential markets for the Lafkiotis wines. USA was selected as the best country for exports for the company's products.

Key Findings — Module 3

In this module, the marketing plan and strategy were developed in an effort to assist the Lafkiotis Winery and the USA, based importer/distributor to successfully enter and penetrate the market in Minnesota and other states. In light of the prevailing market and competitive conditions, there is a need for a differentiation strategy with communications and selective distribution. The entire marketing mix was carefully analyzed and evaluated as well as the possible revenues and profits for the company were estimated. In addition, expansion into other U.S. states, may require a different approach and marketing plan.

Conclusion

This study resulted in an international marketing plan and strategy for the Lafkiotis Winery and its channels that could be used in its global expansion and marketing efforts. The countries which were considered as potential target markets for future exports and distribution of Lafkiotis wines were USA, Australia, China, and Canada. In the final analysis, the USA market was selected for entry and expansion. More specifically, Lafkiotis wines will be exported to a USA importer based in the state of Minnesota where the wines will be first distributed by the importer's distributor and later in other states in the midwest. The entire marketing mix was carefully analyzed and evaluated as well as the possible revenues and profits for the company were estimated. All things considered, the proposed Marketing Plan, if carefully implemented, should achieve the specific goals and objectives of the parties involved including the sales and profit targets.

Recommendations to the company

The Lafkiotis winery while continuing to serve existing customers domestically and internationally should also consider expanding to new markets. In order to do so successfully and in light of market and competitive pressures, it should consider creating an export department and/or devote more time and resources to this effort. This action has to be seriously considered by the company's management, as the recession in the domestic market has a direct impact on the wine market for Greek consumers. According to the results of this study, it will be beneficial for the company to try to increase its export to the USA and its presence in other states in cooperation with its Minnesota, based distributor or others for that matter. In order for Lafkiotis and its USA based distributor to have an increase in sales in the target market and be able to expand in other states, it may be necessary for both to be more actively and directly involved in increasing awareness and promoting the Lafkiotis wines at all levels.

1.1	1.2	1.3	1.4	1.5	1.6	1.7	1.8	1.9
Company Strategic Analysis	Product Analysis	Target Market Profile	International Involvement	Analysis of Internal Environment	Analysis of External Environment	S.W.O.T Matrix	Global Readiness	Conclusion & Recommendations

Start Module-1 Analysis

The objective of Module 1 is for project teams and/or management to conduct a company situation analysis. Not only does this assist project teams in conducting more effective and targeted studies, but it also helps management redefine their business within the framework of a global marketing imperative.

This is done by:
- Choosing an industry and a company within the industry.
- Perform a company strategic analysis.
- Select a specific?Product?Line/service of the chosen company if more than one?Product?Line/service is available. If you choose a retail establishment, decide on the merchandise mix that will be included in the overseas operation, along with the number of stores that will be opened during the first, second and third year of international operation.
- Determine the Target market profile.
- Determine the international involvement, if any, of the company.
- Conduct an internal analysis of the company.
- Conduct an External Analysis of the Industry.
- Determine the company's global business readiness in the international arena.

1.1. *Company strategic analysis*

(a) Background information

1.1.1 (a) - Background Information

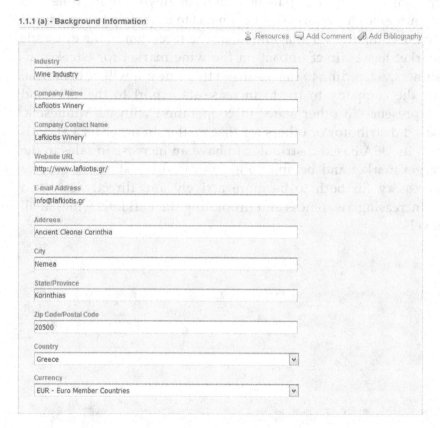

(b) Company background

In 1963, Konstantinos Lafkiotis and his two brothers (Dimitris and Petros) founded the Lafkiotis Winery located in Ancient Kleones, Nemea, region of Peloponnese. Today, the Lafkiotis Winery (owned and managed by the five children of the founders), supported by the experience of many years of producing premium wines, continues the tradition by selecting high quality vineyards and producing premium wine in modern state-of-the art facilities using the latest wine-making methods and techniques. Some of the wines are stored in stainless steel tanks, but most of the Lafkiotis wines are aged in oak French and American barrels in environmentally-controlled cellars.

The high quality of limited production of Lafkiotis wines express the distinct flavors of native grapes and the unique micro-climates and terroir where they are grown such as that of St. George (Agiorgitiko) in the area of Nemea. More than 85% of the Lafkiotis wines are exported to selected European countries, North America, and Australia.

(c) Sales and net profit (profit after taxes) for the last three years

1.1.1 (c) - Sales and net profit (profit after taxes) for the last three years

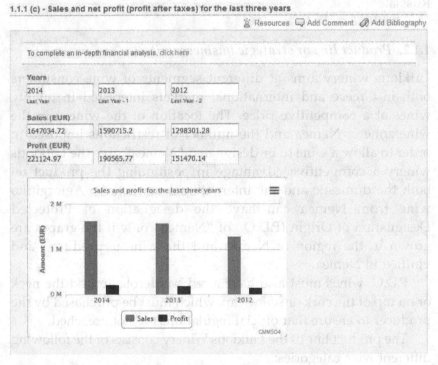

Is the company part of a group or an individual company? — Individual

1.1.1. *Corporate-level strategies*

The strategy of the Lafkiotis Winery is producing high-quality wines in limited quantities using indigenous grapes, product differentiation, completive prices (Value for the money), and product consistency and transparency with both the supply chains and their distribution channels. By focusing on exporting directly the majority of their wines to selected countries Lafkiotis has experienced a sustained growth in both sales and profits during the last few the years. They plan to continue their international market development strategies targeting countries with high future growth market potential, such as USA, Canada, and Russia.

1.1.2. *Product line or strategic business unit*

Lafkiotis winery aims at different segments of wine consumers both in Greece and international markets interested in quality wines at a competitive price. The location of the winery in the wine zone of Nemea and the number of restrictions imposed in order to allow a wine to be designated "Nemea" give the Lafkiotis winery a competitive advantage in positioning the product on both the domestic and the international market. An Agiorgitiko wine from Nemea can have the designation of Protected Designation of Origin (P.D.O.) of "Nemea" only if the grapes are grown in the region of Nemea and the wine is produced and vinified in Nemea.

P.D.O. wines must also have a red banderole around the neck or on top of the cork or screw cap, which must be purchased by the producer to ensure that official regulations are not breached.

The product line of the Lafkiotis Winery consists of the following different wine categories:

1. Upscale/Premium wines: Syrah and Agiorgitiko (blend) and Lafkioti and Agionimo

2. Mid-priced wines: Agiorgitiko Lafkioti, Nemea, Ninemos Wine, Moschofilero, Lafkiotis Rose, and Rodamo, and Mavrodaphne de Patras
3. Everyday Wines: Kleoni Red, Kleoni Rose, Kleoni White, and Retsina

1.1.3. *Business-level strategies*

The Lafkiotis Winery is committed to producing and selling high quality wines using competitive pricing and product differentiation strategies worldwide. They export directly to selected importers, wholesalers, and retail establishments, particularly in countries with high number of people of Greek origin.

The domestic strategy of Lafkiotis is based on direct and indirect sales to selected restaurants and wine cellars. In addition, they promote their wines using wine tastings, sponsoring and holding special events and tours at the attractive facilities, participating in trade shows, and collaborating with other wineries in an effort to promote the region of Nemea and its premium Agiorgitiko wine.

1.2. *Product strategy and analysis*

This section determines the product(s) or service(s) that the selected company markets and to seek information on whether the selected product is ready for internationalization

(a) Product Details

(a) Is the product a consumer or industrial good?	Consumer
(c) Selling price of the product	5–20 euros retail price (EUR)
(e) Comparison to competition in terms of Quality	High
(e) Comparison to competition in terms of price	Medium
(f) Technology level of the product	Medium

(b) Strengths and Weaknesses of the product

Strengths	Weaknesses
— Good quality wine made from a well-known variety — Competitive price — Success in foreign markets by Direct Exports	— Low production capacity than the compertitiors

(c) Company product life cycle

Company Domestic PLC — Maturity (Strength)

Company International PLC — International Introduction (Strength)

(d) Industry product life cycle

Industry Domestic PLC — Maturity (Strength)

Industry International PLC — Maturity (Strength)

1.3. *Target market profile*

This section determines the segment of customers that the company serves with the selected product or product line. It also explains the user characteristics as well as any product usage characteristics in the domestic market as well as in any international markets if the company is present.

(a) End user description

Consumers of Lafkiotis Wines are usually between 35 and 65 years old, have higher education, middle and upper income. They look for premium wines in the medium-price category and usually, they purchase their wines on a monthly basis.

(b) Compare and contrast the end users in the foreign and domestic markets.

Globalization seems to minimize the differences in consumption patterns worldwide including that of the wine industry. Consumers seem to be more sensitive on the effects of wine consumption due to a large extent on health reasons. Thus, most of them prefer lower alcohol wines. However, the positive findings of studies on the effects of wine on health have helped in the increase of wine consumption worldwide. Moreover, the increasing disposable incomes of households in many countries and the fact that more consumers in comparison to the previous decades are caring about health issues have led consumers to demand more quality alcoholic beverages, especially wine.

1.4. *International involvement*

The level of internationalization of a company is primarily determined by the method(s) the company has chosen to enter foreign markets and distribute its products/services. The rank assigned to each method of international involvement used by a company should represent the level of resource(s) (such as financial, human, technological, etc.) commitment a company has made to internationalization along with the desired level of control, profitability, and risk the company is willing and able to assume. Below is the analysis carried out in this section.

(a) Company's international involvement

Is the company involved internationally?. **Yes**

(b) Domestic/International Competitors

1) Domaine Skouras
2) Papaioannou Wines
3) Semeli Wines

(c) Methods of international involvement
Rated on a Scale of 1–3, 1 being Very Low and 3 being Very High

	Lafkiotis Winery	Domaine Skouras	Papaiaonnou Wines	Semeli Wines
Direct Exporting	3	4	2	3
Total	3 (25 %)	4 (33.33 %)	2 (16.67 %)	3 (25 %)

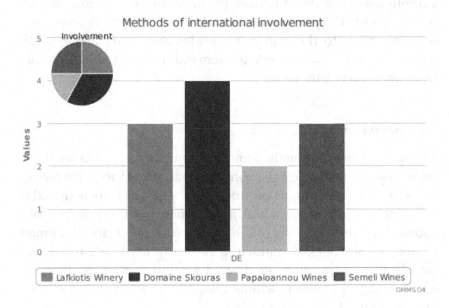

(d) Organization of international function

	Lafkiotis Winery	Domaine Skouras	Papaioannou Wines	Semeli Wines
Within sales/marketing team	Y	Y	Y	Y

(e) International experience

	Lafkiotis Winery	Domaine Skouras	Papaioannou Wines	Semeli Wines
5 or more years of international experience	Y	Y	Y	Y

1.5. *Analysis of the internal environment*

In this section, the process of analyzing the internal environment is carried out in two steps:

First, a Resource Audit is performed.

Secondly, an SW analysis of the strengths and weakness of the company is carried out. For business strategies to be effective, the company must exploit and expand on its strengths, as well as reduce or eliminate its weaknesses creating or improving its competitive advantage in order to achieve profitability.

(a) Resource Audit

Strengths	Weaknesses
Financial Resources — Increase in Sales and Profits **Physical Resources** — New technology, Adequate equipment **Intangible Resources** — Family business (personal interest) Export orientation by owners and managers Direct Export as the main entry strategy	**Human Resources** — The main personnel is responsible for more than one activities (ex. Marketing, Sales, Exports)

(b) List the company's Strengths & Weaknesses (Internal Factors)

Strengths	Weaknesses
— Knowledgeable personnel — Up-to-date facilities — Quality products and competitive price	— Limited knowledge about companies product by the consumers — Small presence in foreign countries — Lack of Business and Marketing Plan

1.6. *Analysis of the external environment*

The external environment of a company is often complex but dynamic as it constantly changes and increasingly is becoming global. A company's external environment has two major parts: its macro-environment and the industry context in which it operates.

This section determines the key trends and drivers in the industry as well as the competitive position of the company within the industry.

(a) Industry analysis

Which industry group does the organization belong to — Food, Beverages and Tobacco

(b) Industry sales and growth rates for the past 2 years

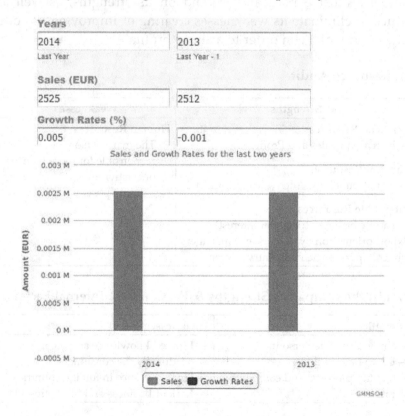

Years	
2014	2013
Last Year	Last Year - 1

Sales (EUR)	
2525	2512

Growth Rates (%)	
0.005	-0.001

GMMS04

(c) Key Trends and Drivers in the Industry

The fine wine category, where Silicon Valley Bank expects the strongest growth, is defined as US $ 20 and above per bottle.

The demand for lower-priced wines (US $ 15 and below) has been lagging, leading to excess supply. At the moment about 33 million gallons of wine are available in the bulk market.

(d) Competitive Analysis of the Industry

Threat of new entrants:

The entry of new players in the wine market can be done through the creation of a new wine-making business, through diversification of industries in which an existing company acts or through exports.

The legislation on alcoholic beverages in many countries of the world is rigid and it certainly reduces the threat of the entry of new competitors. Imported wine is subjected to tariffs, taxes, and VAT, which vary by country. There are also legislative restrictions in relation to the advertising of products containing alcohol as well as alcohol consumption by minors.

Market penetration can be achieved through selling designation of origin wines, which are sold at higher prices, so that the winery has high profit margin and invest in equipment, vineyards, etc. However, large companies often sell both high quality, as well as ordinary table wines through supermarkets, which makes it more difficult for new wineries to enter the market. As a result, the distribution of the wine can be difficult, less appealing and profitable.

Threat of substitutes:

The main substitutes for wine are other alcoholic beverages such as beer, whiskey, liqueurs, ouzo, tequila, vodka, rum, etc. The shift costs from the wine to the substitutes are very high, and this increases their preferability for other drinks. Also, the price per liter of wine is less than the price of alcoholic beverages such as whiskey, but higher than the price per liter of beer. Beverages with high alcohol content have been increased in foreign markets and the economic crisis during the last years means less expenditures for luxury goods like beverages and it is more interesting for wines that have lower quality and price. In conclusion, the power of substitute products is particularly strong.

Determinants of supplier power:

The suppliers of the Lafkiotis winery are independent suppliers for grapes, barrels, bottles, and equipment. Furthermore, Lafkiotis winery has not owned vineyards, but it purchases grapes or grapes must from come grape producers in the region of Peloponnese.

However, the number of grape producers is quite large and as a result, the grape producers do not have great power. Nevertheless, when wineries sign long-term contracts with grape producers, they do not easily consider other suppliers in order to maintain the quality of the final product. This increases the strength of the grape producers.

The barrels that Lafkiotis winery buys come mostly from France and the United States of America. The number of companies from which the winery can buy the barrels, like every winery, is quite large, and even larger is number of the suppliers for bottles. Thus, suppliers for barrels and bottles have little power, which is not the case with suppliers for equipment, where the costs of switching to another company are high.

More generally, the power of suppliers is assessed as moderate.

Determinants of buyer power:

Final wine consumers are more price sensitive in the case of table wines and as a result, their pricing should be competitive.

The customer loyalty is very low in most countries. That is probably the reason the imported wines are successful in foreign markets, as consumers prefer variety. This and the fact that there are several substitutes can enhance the power of consumers.

Consequently, the power of buyers (intermediate and mainly of the supermarkets) is considered as very high.

Determinants of competitive rivalry:

Both the Greek and the world wine market are fragmented, as there is a very large number of competitors, and a small number of major "players". There are thousands of wine brands in the market that can attract consumers precisely because the last ones are confused. Wine producers can reduce the level of competition that exists in the wine market by diversifying their products, offering different varieties like producing wines that have a specific origin or different type of wines like champagnes and sparkling wines and also offering wines of different style. The product differentiation and the right marketing planning, which can help the brand and the products to be recognizable to the general public, reduce the power of consumers, something that can have reduced switching costs as the consumers can choose from a large variety of wines. This enhances the competition between the wineries.

(e) List the company's Threats & Opportunities (External Factors)

Threats	Opportunities
— There is good number of Greek wineries with more resources and with higher level of commitment to further export expansion — Consumers in foreign markets may not have a good perception about Greece and its products due to the financial crisis — Wine consumers in foreign countries have limited awareness and knowledge about Greek Wines	— Agiorgitiko from Nemea is known as a great variety and Lafkiotis main products are based on this variety — The role of (wine) tourism can be supportive for Lafkiotis winery — Higher number of people of Greek origin in some foreign markets may contribute to an increase in the demand and the consumption of Greek Wines — Since Lafkiotis winery has successfully exported its wines, it can grow its business by more systematically pursuing entry to new foreign markets

1.7. *Strengths, weaknesses, opportunities, threats*

This section uses the SWOT matrix to analyze the company.

1.7.1. *SWOT matrix*

Strengths	Weaknesses
(1) Good quality wine made from a well-known variety (2) Competitive price (3) Company Domestic PLC — Maturity (4) Company International PLC — International Introduction (5) Industry Domestic PLC — Maturity (6) Industry International PLC — Maturity (7) Increase in sales and Profits (8) New technology, adequate equipment (9) Family business (personal interest) Export orientation by owners and managers Direct Export as the main entry strategy (10) Knowledgeable personnel (11) Up-to-date Facilities (12) Quality products and competitive price (13) Success in foreign markets by Direct Exports	(1) Lower production capacity then the competitors (2) The main personnel is responsible for more than one activities (ex. Marketing, sales, Exports) (3) Limited knowledge about companies products by the consumers (4) Small presence in foreign countries (5) Lack of Business and Marketing Plan
Opportunities	Threats
(1) Agiorgitiko from Nemea is known as a great variety and Lafkiotis main products are based on this variety (2) The role of (wine) tourism can be supportive for Lafkiotis winery (3) Higher number of people of Greek origin in some foreign markets may contribute to an increase in the demand and the consumption of Greek Wines (4) Since Lafkiotis winery has successfully exported its wines, it can grow its business by more systematically pursuing entry to new foreign markets	(1) There is good number of Greek wineries with more resources and with higher level of commitment to further export expansion (2) Consumers in foreign markets may not have a good perception about Greece and its products due to the financial crisis (3) Wine consumers in foreign countries have limited awareness and knowledge about Greek Wines

1.7.2. *SWOT analysis*

(a) WT Strategy:

The low awareness for Lafkiotis wines and the very high competition from thousands of wine brands in foreign markets can be a serious threat for the company in the near future. Moreover, the lack of a comprehensive Business and Marketing Plan can adversely affect the future growth and profits of the business.

(b) WO Strategy:

Lafkiotis can promote the region of Nemea and the Agiorgitiko variety in order to gain the awareness of the consumers for the company and its products and increase gradually its presence in the foreign markets. The wine tourism can be very supportive for this action.

(c) ST Strategy:

The company can decrease the low awareness about it and promote the Lafkiotis brand and its wines through wine tourism by inviting tourists in the up-to-date facilities.

(d) SO Strategy:

The quality of Lafkiotis wines and the great price that these wines are offered at can create a competitive advantage and make Lafkiotis wines to be considered as value for money wines in some foreign markets. The export experience can be used by the company to enter and distribute its wines to new markets. Working with selected channels can help the winery to increase its market penetration in existing and new markets.

(e) The future dimension:

Lafkiotis winery has to face hard competition in the foreign markets, in which it is mainly active. The consistency in the quality of the wines that the company produces is of paramount importance. Lafkiotis winery also has to take careful and gradual steps in order to have the same or increasing presence in the markets that it is already in or in new markets. The creation and the implementation of a strategic marketing plan that can support this requires investments for knowledgeable personnel about exports and foreign markets or even the creation of an export department.

1.8. *Assessment of global readiness based on the ranking of specific questions*

(a) Assessment of Global Readiness

Questions	Rank on a scale from 1–5
Is the foreign market similar to the domestic market? *(The more similar the market the more favorable)*	3
Is the End User of the product in the foreign market the same as in the domestic market? *(The more similar the End User the more favorable)*	3
Is the product successful in the domestic market? *(The more unique the product the more favorable)*	2
Is the product unique? *(The more successful the more favorable)*	3
Does the product perform the same function in the foreign market as it does in the domestic market? *(If yes, the more favorable)*	4
Are the product use conditions the same in the foreign market as they are in the domestic market? (If yes, the more favorable)	3
Does the product need modifications to meet the needs of the customers in the foreign market? *(High level of modification will make is less favorable)*	2
What is the stage of the product's life cycle in the home market? *(Early stage is more favorable)*	3
What is the stage of the product's life cycle in the international market? *(Early stage is more favorable)*	4
Does the product require after-sales service? *(if yes, the less favorable)*	5

(Continued)

(Continued)

Questions	Rank on a scale from 1–5
Is the company in a position to provide after sales-service to its customers in the foreign market? *(if yes, the more favorable)*	2
Would export orders hurt domestic sales? (if yes, the less favorable)	2
Does the company have the financial resources necessary for export? *(if yes, the more favorable)*	3
Does the company have in-house personnel with export related knowledge/experience? *(if yes, the more favorable)*	3
Is international/global participation part of the Mission Statement of your company? *(if yes, the more favorable)*	4
Is international expansion a part of the strategic business plan of the company? *(if yes, the more favorable)*	4
Would the company be willing to investigate export market opportunities? *(if yes, the more favorable)*	3
Would the company be willing to attend and/or participate in Trade Shows abroad? *(if yes, the more favorable)*	3
Is the company be willing to translate company literature into one or more foreign languages? *(if yes, the more favorable)*	4
Are the company's top competitors involved internationally? *(If yes, less favorable but this could also serve as one of the key reasons to internationalize)*	1
Is the industry highly regulated? *(if yes, the less favorable)*	2
Is the company certified- ISO 9000 or other certification? *(if yes, the more favorable)*	5
Total	**68**

(b) Results

Based upon the company's score of 62%, it is suggested that the company proceeds with the following options:

Score: 62% (68 out of 110)

Direct Exporting:

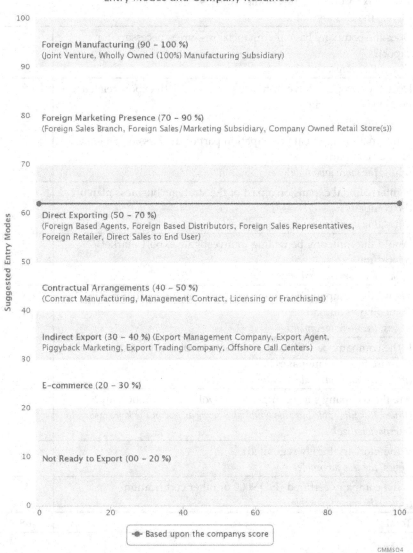

Entry Modes and Company Readiness

100

Foreign Manufacturing (90 – 100 %)
(Joint Venture, Wholly Owned (100%) Manufacturing Subsidiary)

90

80 Foreign Marketing Presence (70 – 90 %)
(Foreign Sales Branch, Foreign Sales/Marketing Subsidiary, Company Owned Retail Store(s))

70

60 Direct Exporting (50 – 70 %)
(Foreign Based Agents, Foreign Based Distributors, Foreign Sales Representatives,
Foreign Retailer, Direct Sales to End User)

50

Contractual Arrangements (40 – 50 %)
(Contract Manufacturing, Management Contract, Licensing or Franchising)

40

Indirect Export (30 – 40 %) (Export Management Company, Export Agent,
Piggyback Marketing, Export Trading Company, Offshore Call Centers)

30

E-commerce (20 – 30 %)

20

10 Not Ready to Export (00 – 20 %)

0

Suggested Entry Modes

0   20   40   60   80   100

-●- Based upon the companys score

GMMS04

— Foreign based agents
— Foreign based distributors
— Foreign sales representatives
— Foreign retailer
— Direct sales to end user

This is graphically represented in the graph below:

1.9. *Conclusion and recommendations*

Conclusions and recommendations based on analysis of the company strategic position are given below:

(a) Conclusion

This module includes the Company Strategic Analysis for Lafkiotis Winery. Furthermore, the main competitors of the company were identified.

Lafkiotis winery offers a wide range of wines at competitive prices mainly based on the variety Agiorgitiko. The winery has experienced increase in sales and profits and appears to grow in exports.

(b) Recommendations

Globalization and the major changes which are taking place in the wine industry and the increasing number of countries that produce excellent wines have increased the competition among wineries. To successfully compete in the marketplace, the companies are required to develop a strategic business plan with emphasis on exports and devote enough financial and human resources in order to strengthen the existing relationship with their customer base and expand in new markets.

In order for Lafkiotis Winery to continue having growth in sales and profits, it should pursue direct exports by selecting and entering new markets.

This can be helped through the following steps:

(1) Proper study, evaluation and selection of target markets, segmentation and targeting different labels in different consumer segments, and create appropriate marketing strategy:

(2) Export potential of business: Production capacity, staff training, and rational allocation of financial and human resources.

(3) Competitive Price.

(4) Knowledge of distribution channels, finding selected local distributors, cooperation and exchange of information: The greater the exchange of information, the better the company reacts to the foreign market. A long, well-grounded relationship with distributors, based on personal contact is required as well as the support of distributors with promotional material, proper training and on time delivery for the wines.

(5) The use of the Internet and social media.

(6) Participation in international competitions and fairs to acquire knowledge and create awareness of the wines.

2. The Search for Global Market

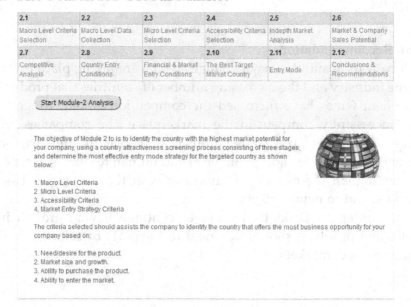

2.1	2.2	2.3	2.4	2.5	2.6
Macro Level Criteria Selection	Macro Level Data Collection	Micro Level Criteria Selection	Accessibility Criteria Selection	Indepth Market Analysis	Market & Company Sales Potential
2.7	2.8	2.9	2.10	2.11	2.12
Competitive Analysis	Country Entry Conditions	Financial & Market Entry Conditions	The Best Target Market Country	Entry Mode	Conclusions & Recommendations

Start Module-2 Analysis

The objective of Module 2 to is to identify the country with the highest market potential for your company, using a country attractiveness screening process consisting of three stages, and determine the most effective entry mode strategy for the targeted country as shown below:

1. Macro Level Criteria
2. Micro Level Criteria
3. Accessibility Criteria
4. Market Entry Strategy Criteria

The criteria selected should assists the company to identify the country that offers the most business opportunity for your company based on:

1. Need/desire for the product.
2. Market size and growth.
3. Ability to purchase the product.
4. Ability to enter the market.

2.1. *Macro level criteria selection*

(a) Select macro-level criterion (criteria) used to identify global market opportunity

The purpose of selecting criteria is to identify the country with the highest market potential for the company's product/service. The criteria listed below are quantifiable and can be measured objectively.

GMMSO will automatically assign a score to each selected criterion. Negative relationships will be assigned lower scores, while positive relationships will be assigned higher scores.

ECONOMIC CRITERIA	DEMOGRAPHIC CRITERIA	GEOGRAPHIC CRITERIA	SOCIO-CULTURAL CRITERIA
• Level of economic development (IC, NIC, LDC, BEM) • Gross national product • Income per capita • Interest rates • Exchange rate performance • Availability of hard currency • National health spending • Disposable income • Distribution of wealth • Housing starts • Banking system • Economic affiliations (EEC, EFTA, ANCOM) • Major industries • Energy consumption	• Population • Average age of population • Age distribution • Life stage • Population growth • Population density • Urban vs. rural • Male vs. female • Labour distribution by industry or profession • Labor unions	• Land area • Topography • Vegetation and land use • Climate	• Major religions • Level of education • Social indicators • Spoken and written languages • Holidays and celebrations • Business practices: Code of ethics, Pricing, Promotions, Negotiations, Distribution, Payment methods, Employee relations • Role of business in society

The following list is designed to guide the selection of macro level product/market criteria that is essential in determining the success of marketing the product in foreign markets. Some of the variables may not need analysis, others may need further analysis.

Criteria Selection:
To include criteria in the analysis, assign a weight (>0 and <100) to the criteria. However, while selecting criteria, keep in mind the relationship each criterion has with its' value. If the criterion has a negative relationship with the value selected, check the box directly next to that criterion. If the criterion has a positive relationship with the value selected, leave the box next to the criterion blank. For example, a country with high import duties (tariffs) is unfavorable; therefore, the relationship between that criterion and the value given to that criterion is negative.

Adding Criteria:
Use the textbox (Add New Criteria) at the end of the list to enter a criterion that does not appear in the list.

(b) Selected macro-level criteria weight distribution

Capital & financial account

Foreign direct investment, net inflows
Units: % of GDP — (-ve) — Weight (%)

Foreign direct investment, net outflows
Units: % of GDP — (-ve) — Weight (%)

Current Account

Current account balance
Units: % of GDP — (-ve) — Weight (%)

Net trade in goods and services
Units: BoP, current US$ (Million) — (-ve) — Weight (%)

Demography

Population — 15
Units: Million — (-ve) — Weight (%)

Birth rate, crude
Units: per 1,000 people — (-ve) — Weight (%)

Death rate, crude
Units: per 1,000 people — (-ve) — Weight (%)

Life expectancy at birth, total
Units: years — (-ve) — Weight (%)

Population ages 0-14
Units: % of total — (-ve) — Weight (%)

Population ages 15-64
Units: % of total — (-ve) — Weight (%)

Population ages 65 and above
Units: % of total — (-ve) — Weight (%)

Doing Business

Ease of doing business
Units: 1=easiest — (-ve) — Weight (%)

Cost to get electricity
Units: % of income per capita — (-ve) — Weight (%)

Cost to register property
Units: % of property value — (-ve) — Weight (%)

Cost to start a business
Units: % of income per capita — (-ve) — Weight (%)

Procedures required to start a business — ☑ — 5

Profit tax Units: %	☑ (-ve)	10 Weight (%)
Resolving Insolvency: cost Units: % of estate	☐ (-ve)	 Weight (%)
Time required to start a business Units: days	☐ (-ve)	 Weight (%)
Total tax rate Units: % of profit	☑ (-ve)	10 Weight (%)
Trade: Cost to export Units: US$ per container	☐ (-ve)	 Weight (%)
Trade: Cost to import Units: US$ per container	☐ (-ve)	 Weight (%)
Trade: Time to export Units: days	☐ (-ve)	 Weight (%)
Trade: Time to import Units: days	☐ (-ve)	 Weight (%)

Economic Criteria

Gross Domestic Product (GDP) Units: $s billion	☐ (-ve)	10 Weight (%)
Gross National Product PPP Units: $s billion	☐ (-ve)	 Weight (%)
Income per Capita Units: $	☐ (-ve)	 Weight (%)
Disposable Income Units: $	☐ (-ve)	20 Weight (%)
Personal Income Tax Units: %	☐ (-ve)	 Weight (%)
Business Tax (average) Units: %	☐ (-ve)	 Weight (%)

Financial Sector

Automated teller machines (ATMs) Units: per 100,000 adults	☐ (-ve)	 Weight (%)
Borrowers from commercial banks Units: per 1,000 adults	☐ (-ve)	 Weight (%)
Commercial bank branches Units: per 100,000 adults	☐ (-ve)	 Weight (%)

Macro Criteria	(+ve/-ve)	Measuring Units	Weight (%)
Disposable Income	+ ve	$	20
GDP per capita growth	+ ve	annual %	15
Population	+ ve	Million	15
Gross Domestic Product (GDP)	+ ve	$s billion	10
Trade	+ ve	% of GDP	10
Profit tax	- ve	%	10
Total tax rate	- ve	% of profit	10
Procedures required to start a business	- ve	number	5
Internet users	+ ve	per 100 people	5
		Total Weight:	100 (%)

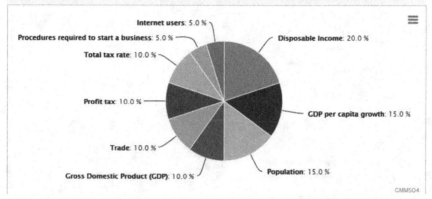

(c) List of top countries based on macro-level criteria selected

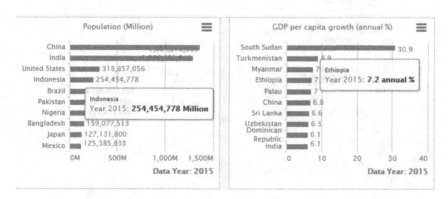

Trade (% of GDP)

Singapore	351
Maldives	196
United Arab ...	186
Seychelles	184
Vietnam	170
Estonia	167
Belgium	165
Lithuania	163
Czech Republic	160
Equatorial Guinea	158

0   100   200   300   400

Data Year: 2015

Profit tax (%)

Zambia	1.3
Sri Lanka	1.6
Saudi Arabia	2.1
Singapore	2.2
Canada	3.9
Luxembourg	4.2
Latvia	4.9
Bulgaria	5
Lebanon	6.1
Lithuania	6.1

0   2   4   6   8

Data Year: 2015

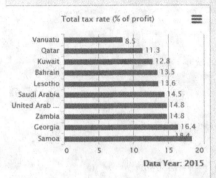

Total tax rate (% of profit)

Vanuatu	8.5
Qatar	11.3
Kuwait	12.8
Bahrain	13.5
Lesotho	13.6
Saudi Arabia	14.5
United Arab ...	14.8
Zambia	14.8
Georgia	16.4
Samoa	18.4

0   5   10   15   20

Data Year: 2015

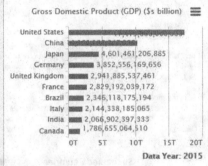

Gross Domestic Product (GDP) ($s billion)

United States	
China	
Japan	4,601,461,206,885
Germany	3,852,556,169,656
United Kingdom	2,941,885,537,461
France	2,829,192,039,172
Brazil	2,346,118,175,194
Italy	2,144,338,185,065
India	2,066,902,397,333
Canada	1,786,655,064,510

0T   5T   10T   15T   20T

Data Year: 2015

Procedures required to start a business (number)

Canada	1
New Zealand	1
Armenia	2
Georgia	2
Jamaica	2
Slovenia	2
Afghanistan	3
Australia	3
Azerbaijan	3
Belgium	3

0   1   2   3   4

Data Year: 2015

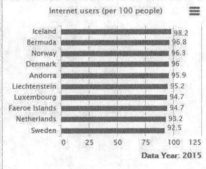

Internet users (per 100 people)

Iceland	98.2
Bermuda	96.8
Norway	96.3
Denmark	96
Andorra	95.9
Liechtenstein	95.2
Luxembourg	94.7
Faeroe Islands	94.7
Netherlands	93.2
Sweden	92.5

0   25   50   75   100   125

Data Year: 2015

2.2. *Macro-level data collection*

(a) GMMSO system suggested list of candidate markets

The GMMSO4 system has generated a list of possible markets based on the selected macro-variables given below:

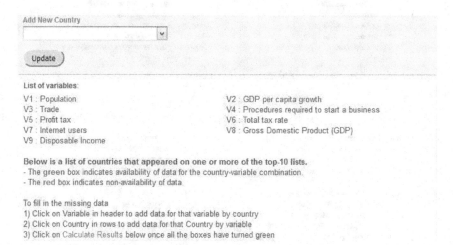

Add New Country

Update

List of variables:

V1 : Population	V2 : GDP per capita growth
V3 : Trade	V4 : Procedures required to start a business
V5 : Profit tax	V6 : Total tax rate
V7 : Internet users	V8 : Gross Domestic Product (GDP)
V9 : Disposable Income	

Below is a list of countries that appeared on one or more of the top-10 lists.
- The green box indicates availability of data for the country-variable combination.
- The red box indicates non-availability of data.

To fill in the missing data
1) Click on Variable in header to add data for that variable by country
2) Click on Country in rows to add data for that Country by variable
3) Click on Calculate Results below once all the boxes have turned green

Suggested Countries	V1	V2	V3	V4	V5	V6	V7	V8	V9
☑ Australia									
☑ Canada									
☑ China									
☑ United States									
☐ Afghanistan									
☐ Andorra									
☐ Armenia									
☐ Azerbaijan									
☐ Bahrain									
☐ Bangladesh									
☐ Belgium									
☐ Bermuda									
☐ Brazil									
☐ Bulgaria									
☐ Czech Republic									

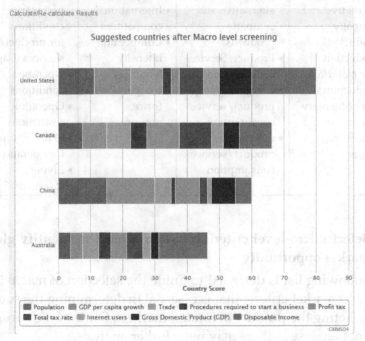

☐ ≡≡ Denmark
☐ ≡≡ Dominican Republic
☐ ≡ Equatorial Guinea
☐ ═ Estonia
☐ ≡ Ethiopia
☐ ✚ Faeroe Islands
☐ ▮▮ France
☐ ✣ Georgia
☐ ═ Germany
☐ ≡ Iceland
☐ ═ India
☐ ═ Indonesia
☐ ▮▮ Italy
☐ ✕ Jamaica
☐ ● Japan

(b) Suggested country list after macro-level screening

Calculate/Re-calculate Results

Suggested countries after Macro level screening

United States

Canada

China

Australia

0   10   20   30   40   50   60   70   80   90
Country Score

■ Population ■ GDP per capita growth ■ Trade ■ Procedures required to start a business ■ Profit tax
■ Total tax rate ■ Internet users ■ Gross Domestic Product (GDP) ■ Disposable Income

CMMS04

2.3. *Micro-level indicators of market accessibility*

Although all chosen criteria sholud be product/market specific, micro level variables are specific to the attributes and benefits of the company's principle product (eg. Number of food processing plants, computer sales, number of machine tools manufactures, agricultural production and products).

Because the developed micro-level variables will be entirely unique to each company, the following list of croteria are only a suggestion. Note that both direct and proxy variables can be used as micro-level indicators. It may also be helpful for the analyst to create a research letter and/or questionnaire. This letter/questionnaire can be sent to those organizations previously.

PRODUCTION CRITERIA	CONSUMPTION CRITERIA	COMPETITON CRITERIA	OPERATION/ USAGE CRITERIA
• Exports (complimentary, alternative and company product(s)) • Production of raw materials • Production of complimentary product(s) • Processing Plants	• Imports (complimentary, alternative and company product(s)) • Product/Service consumption • Complimentary product/service consumption • Alternative product/service consumption	• Local competitors • International competitors • Competition intensity • Nature of competition (price, non-price)	• Ideal, expected, and/or necessary conditions for product/ services usage • Operation conditions • Operation restrictions • Skills required for operation • Living standards

(a) Select micro-level criterion (criteria) used to identify global market opportunity

The following list is designed to guide the selection of macro level product/market criteria that is essential in determining the success of marketing the product in foreign markets. Some of the variables may not analysis, others may need futher analysis.

Criteria Selection:

To include criteria in the analysis, assign a weight (>0 and <100) to the criteria. However, while selecting criteria, keep in mind relationship each criterion has with its value. If the criterion has a negative relationship with the value selected, check the box directly next to that criterion. If the criterion has a positive with the value selected, leave the box next to the criterion balnk. For example, a country with high import duties (tariffs) is unfavrable; therefore the relationship between that criterion and the value given to that criterion is negative.

Adding Criteria:

Use the textbox (Add New Criteria) at the end of the list to enter a criterion that does not appear in the list.

Competition

| Local competitors | ☑ | 15 |
| Units: | (-ve) | Weight (%) |

| International competitors | ☑ | 15 |
| Units: | (-ve) | Weight (%) |

| Competition Intensity | ☑ | 20 |
| Units: | (-ve) | Weight (%) |

| Nature of competition (price, non-price) | ☐ | |
| Units: | (-ve) | Weight (%) |

Consumption

| Imports (complimentary, alternative and company product(s | ☑ | 10 |
| Units: | (-ve) | Weight (%) |

| Product/Service consumption | ☐ | 10 |
| Units: | (-ve) | Weight (%) |

| Complimentary product/service consumption | ☐ | |
| Units: | (-ve) | Weight (%) |

| Alternative product/service consumption | ☑ | 15 |
| Units: | (-ve) | Weight (%) |

Product usage / Operation

| Ideal, expected, and/or necessary conditions for product/se | ☐ | |
| Units: | (-ve) | Weight (%) |

| Operation conditions | ☐ | |
| Units: | (-ve) | Weight (%) |

| Operation restrictions | ☐ | |
| Units: | (-ve) | Weight (%) |

| Skills required for operation | ☐ | |
| Units: | (-ve) | Weight (%) |

| Living Standards | ☐ | 15 |
| Units: | (-ve) | Weight (%) |

(-ve): If the criterion has a negative relationship with the value selected, check the box directly next to that criterion.

Weight (%): Enter Weight for criteria to be used for screening Countries.

Unselect Variable: Remove Weight to unselect an already selected variable.

Production

Exports (complimentary, alternative and company product(s	☐ (-ve)	Weight (%)
Units:		
Production of raw materials	☐ (-ve)	Weight (%)
Units:		
Production of complimentary product(s)	☐ (-ve)	Weight (%)
Units:		
Production of alternative product(s)	☐ (-ve)	Weight (%)
Units:		
Processing Plants	☐ (-ve)	Weight (%)
Units:		
Add New Criteria		
	☐ (-ve)	Weight (%)
Measuring Units		

(b) Selected micro-level criteria weight distribution

Micro Criteria	(+ve/-ve)	Measuring Units	Weight (%)
Competition Intensity	- ve		20
Local competitors	- ve		15
International competitors	- ve		15
Alternative product/service consumption	- ve		15
Living Standards	+ ve		15
Imports (complimentary, alternative and company product(s))	- ve		10
Product/Service consumption	+ ve		10
		Total Weight:	100 (%)

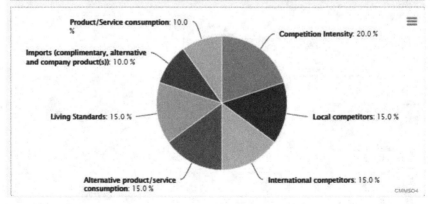

Product/Service consumption: 10.0 %
Imports (complimentary, alternative and company product(s)): 10.0 %
Living Standards: 15.0 %
Alternative product/service consumption: 15.0 %
Competition Intensity: 20.0 %
Local competitors: 15.0 %
International competitors: 15.0 %

CMMSO4

- Below is a list of top 4 countries after the Macro Level Screening.
- The green box indicates availability of data for the country-variable combination.
- The red box indicates non-availability of data.
- To fill in the missing data or exclude a country from the below list CLICK HERE

List of variables:

V1 : Imports (complimentary, alternative and company
product(s))
V3 : Alternative product/service consumption
V5 : International competitors
V7 : Living Standards

V2 : Product/Service consumption
V4 : Local competitors
V6 : Competition Intensity

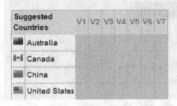

(c) Country filtering micro-variables

- The green box indicates availability of data for the country-variable combination.
- The red box indicates non-availability of data.

To fill in the missing data
1) Click on Variable in header to add data for that variable by country
2) Click on Country in rows to add data for that Country by variable
3) Click on Calculate Results below once all the boxes have turned green

List of variables:

V1 : Imports (complimentary, alternative and
company product(s))
V3 : Alternative product/service consumption
V5 : International competitors
V7 : Living Standards

V2 : Product/Service consumption
V4 : Local competitors
V6 : Competition Intensity

Scroll to the right if you have more than 17 variables

Update

* Please be patient. This Update might take longer than normal to process due to high volume of data.

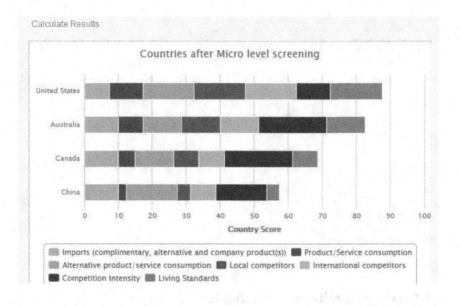

2.4. *Indicators of market accessibility*

Access to a make is just as important as market potential. Even though they are quick to change, accessibililty criteria play an integral part in determining the success of entering foreign markets. Again, the following list in not exhaustive, and is only meant as a guide for the analyst in developing product/market specific criteria.

GMMSO will automatically assign a score to each selected criterion. Negative relationships will be assigned lower scores, while positive relationships will be assigned higher scores.

EXPORT CONTROLS	HOST COUNTRY IMPORT CONTROLS	POLITICAL/ LEGAL ASSESMENT	PHYSICAL ENVIRONMENT & INFRASTRUCTURE
• Licensing (general, validated) • National Security	• Licensing • Tariffs/duties • Quotas • Documentation • Packaging • Labeling	• Type of Government • Government Stability • Government Procurement Policies	• Location (distance) • Major ports of entry • Airports • Transportation system (road, air, water, rail) • Communication systems

Table (*Continued*)

EXPORT CONTROLS	HOST COUNTRY IMPORT CONTROLS	POLITICAL/ LEGAL ASSESMENT	PHYSICAL ENVIRONMENT & INFRASTRUCTURE
		• Attitudes towards: Imports, Foreign Direct Investment, Technology transfer • Code or common law • Product liability (Health & safety) • Contractual requirements • Patents/ trademarks/copy • Legislative process	• Free-trade zones

The following list is designed to guide the selection of micro level product/market criteria that is essetial in determining the success of marketing the product in foreign markets. Some of the variables may not need analysis, others may need futher analysis.

Criteria Selection:

To include criteria in the analysis, assign a weight (>0 and <100) to the criteria. However, while selecting criteria, keep in mind relationship each criterion has with its value. If the criterion has a negative relationship with the value selected, check the box directly next to that criterion. If the criterion has a positive with the value selected, leave the box next to the criterion balnk. For example, a country with high import duties (tariffs) is unfavrable; therefore the relationship between that criterion and the value given to that criterion is negative.

Adding Criteria:

Use the textbox (Add New Criteria) at the end of the list to enter a criterion that does not appear in the list.

Export Controls		
Licensing (general, validated)	☐	
Units:	(-ve)	Weight (%)
National security	☐	
Units:	(-ve)	Weight (%)
Host Country Import Controls		
Licensing	☑	10
Units:	(-ve)	Weight (%)
Tariffs / duties	☑	10
Units:	(-ve)	Weight (%)
Quotas	☐	
Units:	(-ve)	Weight (%)
Documentation	☑	5
Units:	(-ve)	Weight (%)
Packaging	☐	
Units:	(-ve)	Weight (%)
Labeling	☑	10
Units:	(-ve)	Weight (%)
Infrastructure requirements		
Location (distance)	☑	5
Units:	(-ve)	Weight (%)
Major ports of entry	☐	10
Units:	(-ve)	Weight (%)
Airports	☐	
Units:	(-ve)	Weight (%)
Transportation system (road, air, water, rail)	☐	10
Units:	(-ve)	Weight (%)
Communication Systems	☐	10
Units:	(-ve)	Weight (%)
Free trade zones	☐	
Units:	(-ve)	Weight (%)

Political / Legal Assessment

Type of Government	☐	5
Units:	(-ve)	Weight (%)
Government stability	☐	15
Units:	(-ve)	Weight (%)
Government procurement policies	☐	
Units:	(-ve)	Weight (%)
Attitude toward: Imports; Foreign direct investment; T	☐	
Units:	(-ve)	Weight (%)
Code or common law	☐	

Units:	(-ve)	Weight (%)
Contractual requirements	☐	
Units:	(-ve)	Weight (%)
Patents / Trademarks / Copyrights	☐	10
Units:	(-ve)	Weight (%)
Legislative process	☐	
Units:	(-ve)	Weight (%)
Add New Criteria		
	☐	
Measuring Units	(-ve)	Weight (%)

Save

(a) Selected accessibility criteria weight distribution

Accessibility Criteria	(+ve/-ve)	Measuring Units	Weight (%)
Government stability	+ ve		15
Licensing	- ve		10
Tariffs / duties	- ve		10
Labeling	- ve		10
Major ports of entry	+ ve		10
Transportation system (road, air, water, rail)	+ ve		10
Communication Systems	+ ve		10
Patents / Trademarks / Copyrights	+ ve		10
Documentation	- ve		5
Location (distance)	- ve		5
Type of Government	+ ve		5
		Total Weight:	**100 (%)**

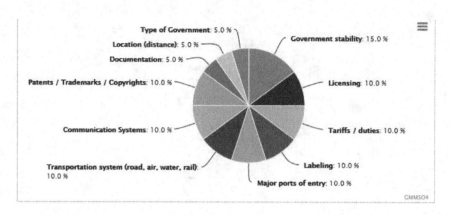

(b) Country filtering after micro level screening

- Below is a list of top 10 countries after the Micro Level Filtering.
- The green box indicates availability of data for the country-variable combination.
- The red box indicates non-availability of data.
- To fill in the missing data or exclude a country from the below list click here

List of variables:

V1 : Licensing	V2 : Tariffs / duties
V3 : Documentation	V4 : Labeling
V5 : Type of Government	V6 : Government stability
V7 : Patents / Trademarks / Copyrights	V8 : Location (distance)
V9 : Major ports of entry	V10 : Transportation system (road, air, water, rail)
V11 : Communication Systems	

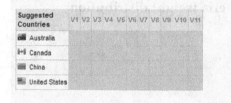

(c) Country filtering accessibility variables

- The green box indicates availability of data for the country-variable combination.
- The red box indicates non-availability of data.

To fill in the missing data
1) Click on Variable in header to add data for that variable by country
2) Click on Country in rows to add data for that Country by variable
3) Click on Calculate Results below once all the boxes have turned green

List of variables:

V1 : Licensing   V2 : Tariffs / duties
V3 : Documentation   V4 : Labeling
V5 : Type of Government   V6 : Government stability
V7 : Patents / Trademarks / Copyrights V8 : Location (distance)
V9 : Major ports of entry   V10 : Transportation system (road, air, water, rail)
V11 : Communication Systems

Scroll to the right if you have more than 17 variables

Suggested Countries	V1	V2	V3	V4	V5	V6	V7	V8	V9	V10	V11
☑ Australia											
☑ Canada											
☑ China											
☑ United States											

(d) Country selection

Your Top two markets are listed below. The top two markets will be used in the following sections for an indepth analysis.

Top Ranked Country

United States (167.5)

Second Ranked Country

Australia (82.50)

If you decide not to conduct business in the highest ranking country listed above, explain your reasoning

2.5. *In-depth market analysis*

In-depth market analysis and estimates of sales potential in any one country market would be difficult, to say the least, without making contact with those who are more familiar with the Target Market(s).

(a) Contacts in target markets

Potential agents and/or distributors, U.S. and foreign governments, associations and organizations all can be helpful in this specialized networking endeavor. Research and sales letters of inquiry can provide in-depth market research and establish relationships that may facilitate bringing the company's product or service to the marketplace.

Contacts are key to most new markets as they help in understanding the size and potential from their local knowledge.

* Note: Add at least 1 contact for each country.

1) Australia

Miloway Wines	Miloway Wines
Name of Contact	Organization

miloway@bigpond.com
Address

(02) 9559 5673	miloway@bigpond.com
Phone	E-mail

Australia	Strength 0 1 ●2 3 4 5
Country	

2) Australia

Ioanna Gouvatsou	Australian Embassy
Name of Contact	Organization

Corner Kifisias & Alexandras Ave, Ambelokipi
Address

210 870 4000	ioanna.gouvatsou@austrade.gov.au
Phone	E-mail

Australia	Strength 0 1 ●2 3 4 5
Country	

3) United States

Dionysos Imports Inc	Liquor Imports
Name of Contact	Organization

11581 Robertson Drive Manassas, VA 20109
Address

703-392-7073	info@dionysosimports.com
Phone	E-mail

United States
Country   Strength   0   1   2   **3**   4   5

4) United States

Janavaras Enterprises LLC	Wine Imports
Name of Contact	Organization

27 Capri Drive, Mankato, Minnesota 56001 USA
Address

507-345-5824	wine@janavaras.com
Phone	E-mail

United States
Country   Strength   0   1   2   3   4   **5**

(b) Average score of contacts in each market

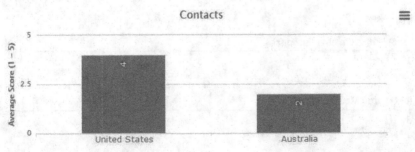

GMMSO4

2.6. *Market & company sales potential*

As the final country screening for global market opportunity, the analyst must identify the target market(s) with the greatest potential for sales. Analysis of market conditions include demand analysis, competitive analysis, basic consumer purchase motivation, and available channels of distribution.

Estimate **Total Market Potential (TMP)** for the product in the chosen countries: TMP = [Number of potential (eligible/qualified) consumers] × [Frequency of purchase on an annual basis] × [Selling price of the product]

Estimate **Company Sales Potential (CSP)** for the product:

$$CSP = [TMP] \times [Desired\ Market\ Share\ (\%)]$$

(a) Estimate the TMP and CSP for your target markets

(a) Number of potential (eligible/qualified) consumers

594000	546000
United States	Australia

(b) Frequency of purchase on an annual basis

48	48
United States	Australia

(c) Selling price of the product

13	13
United States	Australia

(d) Desired Market Share (%)

3	2
United States	Australia

Calculate

(b) TMP and CSP

Total Market Potential (TMP):

| 370656000 | 340704000 |
| United States | Australia |

Company Sales Potential (CSP)

| 11119680 | 6814080 |
| United States | Australia |

(c) Average score of TMP and CSP in each market

Market & Company Sales Potential

2.7. *Competitive analysis*

Competitor profiles in each target market enable the selection of the best primary target market country for the company and its product, as well as the development of an effective marketing program. While proprietary information may be inaccessible, industry/annual reports, competitors' clients, channel members and company literature can, in many cases, provide a wealth of competitor information.

(a) Profiling of two key competitors in the target markets

	United States		Australia	
	Domaine Skouras	Semeli Wines	Domaine Skouras	Semeli Wines
Product/Service Name:	Wines	Wines	Wines	Wines
Total Sales (countrywide):	200,000	150,000	200,000	150,000
Total Sales (worldwide):	800,000	700,000	800,000	700,000
Number of Employees:	55	50	55	50
Years in Business:	20	37	20	37

(b) Evaluation and analysis of top two competitors

	United States		Australia	
	Domaine Skouras	Semeli Wines	Domaine Skouras	Semeli Wines
Distribution e-Commerce	Direct export to US based importer/ distributor with presence in a good number of states	Direct export to US based importer/ distributor with limited presence	No E-commerce	No E-commerce
	Rating: 4/5	Rating: 3/5	Rating: 1/5	Rating: 1/5
Pricing Strategy:	Price holding	Price holding	Overall very competitive prices	Overall, very competitive pricing
	Rating: 4/5	Rating: 4/5	Rating: 4/5	Rating: 4/5
Product Attributes and Benefits	Very good wines and well received by customers	Very good wines		
	Rating: 4/5	Rating: 3/5	Rating: 4/5	Rating: 3/5

(*Continued*)

(Continued)

	United States		Australia	
	Domaine Skouras	**Semeli Wines**	**Domaine Skouras**	**Semeli Wines**
Promotion Strategy:	Aggressive promotional efforts. Participation in trade shows and journals	Limited promotional efforts		
	Rating: 4/5	Rating: 3/5	Rating: 3/5	Rating: 2/5
Quality:	Very good good quality	Very good quality	Very good quality	Very good quality
	Rating: 5/5	Rating: 5/5	Rating: 5/5	Rating: 5/5
Service	Very good service	Good service	Good service	Fair service
	Rating: 4/5	Rating: 3/5	Rating: 3/5	Rating: 2/5
Target Market Profile:	Middle class consumers	Middle class consumers	Middle to upper middle class consumers	Middle and upper middle class consumers
	Rating: 4/5	Rating: 4/5	Rating: 3/5	Rating: 3/5
Other:	Rating:1/5	Rating: 1/5	Rating: /5	Rating: /5

(c) Average score of the strength of competition

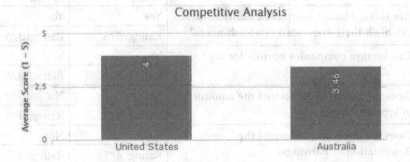

2.8. *Country entry conditions*

In addition to the preliminary screening for market accessibility, in-depth analysis of the conditions of market entry further ascertains the feasibility and cost-effectiveness of entering any one target market country alternative. It also prepares the company for development of the marketing program. It is important to note, however, that countries with the best market entry conditions may not always be the ones with the greatest potential for sales.

(a) Import regulations

	United States	Australia
Administrative Barriers	A few	A good number
	Rating: 3/5	Rating: 2/5
Import Licensing requirements	Import license is required and it is expensive	Import license is required
Quotas	Rating: 3/5	Rating: 4/5
	None	None
Tariffs	Reasonable	Reasonable
	Rating: 3/5	Rating: 3/5
Other	Rating: /5	Rating: /5

(b) Foreign Direct Investment (FDI) regulations

	United States	Australia
Are foreign based companies allowed 100% Equity Ownership of domestic firms?	Yes	Yes
	Rating: 4/5	Rating: 3/5
Are foreign based companies allowed to establish their own retail establishments?	Yes	Yes
	Rating: 5/5	Rating: 3/5
Can foreign companies borrow locally?	Yes	Yes
	Rating: 5/5	Rating: 3/5
Does the government restrict the amount or type of investment?	No	No
	Rating: 4/5	Rating: 4/5
Does the government restrict the Repatriation of Earnings?	No	No
	Rating: 4/5	Rating: 3/5
Other:	Rating: /5	Rating: /5

(c) Average score of entry conditions in each market

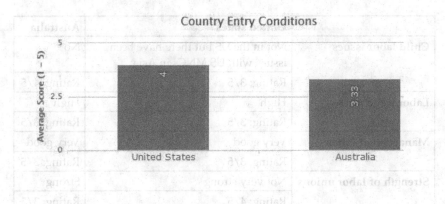

2.9. *Financial and market entry conditions*

(a) Tax rates

	United States	Australia
Corporate Tax rates are favorable	Reasonable	High
	Rating: 4/5	Rating: 3/5
Personal Tax rates are favorable	Yes	Somewhat
	Rating: 3/5	Rating: 2/5
Other	Rating: /5	Rating: /5

(b) Foreign exchange rate performance

	United States	Australia
The country's currency is convertible	Yes	Yes
	Rating: 5/5	Rating: 3/5
The country's current account is in good standing (Balance of Payments)	Trade balance deficits particularly with China	Good standing
	Rating: 3/5	Rating: 4/5
The currency of the country has been stable	Yes	Somewhat
	Rating: 4/5	Rating: 3/5
other	Rating: /5	Rating: /5

(c) Labor issues

	United states	Australia
Child labor issues	Not in the US but there have been issues with US MNCs in Asia.	No
	Rating: 3/5	Rating: 4/5
Labor wage rates	High	High
	Rating: 3/5	Rating: 3/5
Management-labor	Very good	Very good
	Rating: 3/5	Rating: 3/5
Strength of labor unions	Not very strong	Strong
	Rating: 4/5	Rating: 3/5
Other	Rating: /5	Rating: /5

(d) Country infrastructure

	United states	Australia
Banking system	Sound system	Sound system
	Rating: 4/5	Rating: 4/5
Energy	Available and reasonably priced	Available and reasonably priced
	Rating: 4/5	Rating: 4/5
Internet connections	Excellent	Very good
	Rating: 5/5	Rating: 3/5
Telecommunications system	Excellent	Very good
	Rating: 4/5	Rating: 3/5
Transportation systems	Excellent	Very good
	Rating: 4/5	Rating: 3/5
other	Rating: /5	Rating: /5

(e) Market channel conditions

	United States	Australia
Distribution channels are regulated by the government	To some extend yes	To some extend yes
	Rating: 2/5	Rating: 2/5
Existing channels provide adequate national market coverage	A few do. These channels dominate the market	yes
	Rating: 3/5	Rating: 4/5
The company will be able to distribute its product/service using existing channels	Yes	
	Rating: 4/5	Rating: 4/5
Other	Rating: /5	Rating: /5

(f) Legal environment

	United states	Australia
It is easy to establish presence or a business in the country	Yes	Yes
	Rating: 4/5	Rating: 3/5
The country has anti-trust legislation in place	Yes	Yes
	Rating: 4/5	Rating: 3/5
The country is a member of the WTO	Yes	Yes
	Rating: 4/5	Rating: 5/5
The country protects intellectual property	Yes	
	Rating: 4/5	Rating: 3/5
The level of corruption in the country is low	Low but it is present	Low but it is present
	Rating: 3/5	Rating: 3/5
Other:	Rating: /5	Rating: /5

(g) Average score of financial and market entry conditions in each market

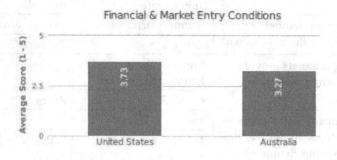

2.10. *The best target market country*

(a) Variable weight

CONTACTS

4	2	25
Average Score (United States)	Average Score (Australia)	Weight (%)

MARKET & COMPANY SALES POTENTIAL

5	4	35
Average Score (United States)	Average Score (Australia)	Weight (%)

COMPETITION

4	3.46	15
Average Score (United States)	Average Score (Australia)	Weight (%)

COUNTRY ENTRY CONDITIONS

4	3.22	10
Average Score (United States)	Average Score (Australia)	Weight (%)

FINANCIAL & MARKET CONDITIONS

3.73	3.27	15
Average Score (United States)	Average Score (Australia)	Weight (%)

TOTAL

20.73	15.95	100
Avg Score Sum (United States)	Avg Score Sum (Australia)	Weight Sum (%)

Calculate

(b) The best target market

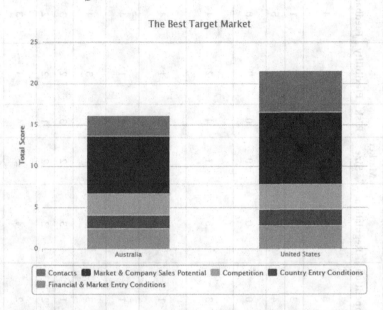

(c) Country selection

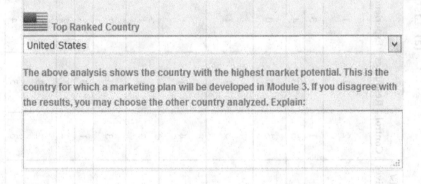

2.11. *Entry mode*

This section evaluates the best entry mode by ranking each one of the selection drivers on a scale of 1–5. A score of 1 = Low. A score of 3 = Medium. A score of 5 = High. The Entry Mode with the highest score will be the one which should be chosen in entering the foreign market.

(a) List of Entry Modes

	Goals/objectives	Control	Resources	Experience	Competition	Regulations	Market Size	Risk	Flexibility	Feedback
Corporate Owned Retail Stores	1	2	1	1	3	1	3	3	2	4
Indirect export	3	1	5	3	3	1	1	3	5	1
Direct export	5	5	3	4	4	4	4	3	5	5
Foreign based sales branch	1	3	0	0	0	0	0	0	0	0
Foreign Based Marketing Subsidiary	1	3	1	1	3	3	1	4	2	4
Wholly Owned Manufacturing Subsidiary	1	4	1	1	1	1	2	1	1	4
Joint Venture (Manufacturing)	1	3	1	1	1	1	2	1	1	4
Joint Venture (Marketing)	3	3	3	2	3	3	3	4	3	4
Franchising	2	1	3	1	1	3	2	3	2	3
Licensing	2	2	3	2	2	3	2	1	2	2
Management Contract	3	2	3	3	2	4	3	4	4	3
E-Commerce	4	3	5	4	2	4	5	4	4	5

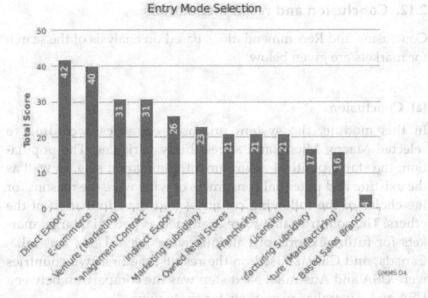

(b) **Entry mode strategy and reason**

Entry mode strategy selected: **Direct Export**

Reason for choosing the entry mode strategy: The main reason for the choice of the direct export as the method for the entry in the new market is that this option is the only realistic scenario for companies with limited resources and experience in doing business in countries other than their own. In addition, the winery is able to sell wines to a qualified and experienced importer and distribution channels, maintain control over the production and product quality while reducing the financial and market associated risks. Also, the ecommerce cannot easily work because of the nature of the product and of the relevant legislation (no postage of wines to China and Canada is allowed and it is allowed only under strict conditions in some states of the USA).

2.12. Conclusion and recommendations

Conclusion and Recommendations based on analysis of the search for markets are given below:

(a) Conclusion

In this module, the system proposes countries according to selected Macro, Micro, and Accessibility variables. The population, the stable political environment, the market size, as well as the existing and potential consumers of wine were the reasons for the choice of the following countries and the elimination of the others. The countries that were examined as potential target markets for future exports of Lafkiotis wines were USA, Australia, Canada, and China. Based on the results, the first two countries were USA and Australia. Next step was the comparison between USA and Australia, as markets for these wines.

Contacts, through which the company will be able to export its wines, the potential profits from this export activity, the regulations applicable in each country, and the relevant competition were examined. The best country for export of the company's products was the United States.

(b) Recommendations

According to the results, it will be beneficial for the company to try to export its wines in the USA. The next module will include the development of the Marketing Plan and the strategy designed to assist the Lafkiotis Winery and its USA-based distributor to successfully market the wines in the state of Minnesota and beyond.

3. Entry Strategy into the U.S. Market

3.1	3.2	3.3	3.4	3.5	3.6
Country Profile Of Selected Market	Marketing Plan/Program	Marketing Mix Strategies (4P's)	Financial Strategy	Exit Strategy and Scenarios	Conclusions & Recommendations

(Start Module-3 Analysis)

The objective of Module 3 is to determine the most effective entry strategy and marketing plan based on company's goals, resources, strengths relative to the competition and market conditions by using the following procedure:

- Develop marketing strategies and action plans that will most successfully penetrate the Target Market country.

　　1) Identify the Target Market in the country using key segmentation variables.

　　2) Develop Market Penetration and coverage objectives that fully exploit market opportunity.

　　3) Determine whether the company should create, extend, and/or adapt its current product/service.

　　4) Determine the best pricing strategy and method for the company's product after investigating terms of sale and value added costs in the Target Market.

　　5) Develop an effective promotional strategy by carefully matching company resources with perceived product/service benefits and buyer behaviour in the Target Market.

　　6) Determine the best distribution strategy and channels for the company's product/service in the Target Market.

- Based on entry strategy and the developed marketing plan, forecast future sales/profits as well as breakeven financial analysis for the Target Market.

- Briefly state your conclusion and recommendations for Module 3

- Generate Module 3 Report

3.1. *Country profile of selected market*

(a) "Doing business" conditions in the selected market

Lafkiotis winery already exports its wines in the state of California, in the state of Florida, and in the state of Minnesota. The marketing plan will focus on the state of Minnesota, one of the midwestern states, with the prospect of future expansion in other states in the region. Some of the reasons for selecting Minnesota and the midwest are: the working relationship between the Lafkiotis Winery and the importer in Minnesota in terms of common goals and objectives, the high household income and the limited number of other competing wines from Greece in the region.

3.2. *Marketing plan/program*

(a) Products (consumer/industrial) or services
The product is a Consumer product.

(b–g) Segmentation variables for a consumer product and its definitions

Segmentation variables for a consumer product:

Income:
Middle or Higher

Education:
Higher education

Personality Traits:
Willingness to try new and different wines

Social Class:
Middle or Higher

Target market
Definition of the target market based on the selected variables:

As stated previously, the Marketing Plan for this study will focus on the state of Minnesota with the prospect of expanding to other states in the region. The state of Minnesota is the 19th highest in value of imports of wines in USA. The annual expenditure of a household for wine (US $150.84 in 2014) is higher than the average of the same expenditure for the whole country. The target market for Lafkiotis wines consists of individuals who are age & 35–70 years old, have higher education, middle and upper income. These consumers look for premium and competitively priced wines (value for the money), are open to tasting new wines and usually they purchase their wines on a weekly or monthly basis. A good number of the wine buyers and consumers in

Minnesota are women who buy wines for themselves, family consumption, special events or as gifts.

(i) Marketing goals and objectives

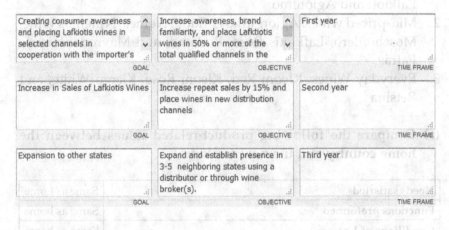

GOAL	OBJECTIVE	TIME FRAME
Creating consumer awareness and placing Lafkiotis wines in selected channels in cooperation with the importer's	Increase awareness, brand familiarity, and place Lafkiotis wines in 50% or more of the total qualified channels in the	First year
Increase in Sales of Lafkiotis Wines	Increase repeat sales by 15% and place wines in new distribution channels	Second year
Expansion to other states	Expand and establish presence in 3-5 neighboring states using a distributor or through wine broker(s).	Third year

3.3. *Marketing mix strategies*

3.3.1. *Product Strategy*

(From Section 1.1.2.)

Lafkiotis winery aims at different segments of wine consumers both in Greece and international markets interested in quality wines at a competitive price. The location of the winery in the wine zone of Nemea and the number of restrictions imposed in order to allow a wine to be designated "Nemea" give the Lafkiotis winery a competitive advantage in positioning the product on both the domestic and international markets. An Agiorgitiko wine from Nemea can have the designation of P.D.O. of "Nemea" only if the grapes are grown in the region of Nemea and the wine is produced and vinified in Nemea.

P.D.O. wines must also have a red banderole around the neck or on top of the cork or screw cap, which must be purchased by the producer to ensure that official regulations are not breached.

The product line of the Lafkiotis Winery consists of the following different wine categories:

1. Upscale/Premium wines: Syrah and Agiorgitiko (blend) Lafkioti and Agionimo.
2. Mid-priced wines: Agiorgitiko Lafkioti, Nemea, Ninemos Wine, Moschofilero, Lafkiotis Rose, Rodamo, and Mavrodaphne de Patras.
3. Everyday Wines: Kleoni Red, Kleoni Rose, Kleoni White, and Retsina

(a) Compare the following product-related issues between the home country and the new market

Needs satisfied	Same as home
Functions preformed	Same as home
Conditions of Use	Same as home
Ability (buying power) to purchase the product in the new market	Yes
Need government permission to enter market	Yes
Import license and license from Food and Drug Administration are required	

(b) Product/communications strategy

Based on the comparisons above, the most appropriate product and communications strategy for the chosen market is product standardization/communications adaptation (same product/different message)

Reason: The wine consumers in most countries have usually similar wine preferences and consumption patterns. So the product will be the same as it is in the home market, but the front and back labels will be in English and will meet regulatory requirements. However, there is a need for a different communications strategy, as the target group, channels, the sale points, and the media in Minnesota are different compared with the ones in Greece.

3.3.2. *Pricing Strategy*

(a) Pricing issues

Is the rate of inflation under control in the country? Explain.

| The rate of inflation is low and under control in the USA. However, it is expected to increase in the future. | ◉ Yes | ○ No |

Is the exchange rate of the country's currency stable? Explain.

| The US $dollar is one of the most stable currencies during the last decade. | ◉ Yes | ○ No |

Is the 'country of origin' factor an important element affecting the price/quality perception of the product/service? Explain.

| The recent financial crisis along with the new tax laws in Greece could result in price increase of the wines and have a negative | ◉ Yes | ○ No |

Are there any price controls imposed by the government of the country that may have an impact on the price of the product/service? Explain.

| No, there are no price controls on wines but Liquor taxes can affect the final price of the product. | ◉ Yes | ○ No |

(b) For the target country, set pricing goals for all stages of the product life cycle

PLC Stage: Introduction

Cost-plus pricing strategy and a little higher price than the competition will be used in order the comsumers to perceive the price as an indicator of quality.

PLC Stage: Growth

Same as in previous stage

PLC Stage: Maturity

Same as in previous stage

PLC Stage: Decline

Price will be reduced as the company wants to sell the remaining quantity and exit the market

(c) Based on the marketing goals and objectives determine

The best pricing strategy for the company's product/service in the target market: **Market Holding Pricing**

The selling price of the company's product/service will be: **Same in United States.**

(d) Final selling price to the end customer in the Target market vs. the Home market

Home Country:
5–15 €

The United States:
10–30 €

(e) Pricing method to be used in the target country

The best pricing strategy for the company's product/service in the target market: **Cost-plus** — The pricing policy takes into account all costs and includes profit margins of all channel members involved in the process both on the production and marketing side.

(f) Calculate export price (if the product is exported to the new country)

Selling Price

3.42

Total shipping costs

0.80

Insurance costs

0.03

Foreign Freight Forwarder's Fees

0.02

TOTAL C.I.F PRICE OR LANDED COST

4.27

Import duties (Tariffs)

0.13

Value-added tax

0.13

Other

0.46

TOTAL COST

4.99

Calculate

(g) Discount or markup (%) that will be offered to channel members

Importer's Markup = 30%
Distributor's Markup = 35%
Liquor Store's Markup = 40%
Restaurant's Markup = 250%

(h) Method of Payment

Drafts: Time Draft

Facilitating trade to broaden partnerships that will lead to increased sales. Existence of trust between transacting parties. However, there are disadvantages in case there is lack of immediate liquidity or non-payment during the defined timeframe.

3.3.3. *Promotional strategy*

(a) Evaluate local media issues

Media availability:

Several media are available for the promotion of wines. The cost along with the effectiveness of each is different of course. The more direct and targeted each medium is the more expensive but also more effective usually is. Personal selling is considered to be the most effective medium for wines.

Media quality:
The majority of the media that are going to be used are considered as high quality media.

Media reach and coverage:
The existing media have adequate coverage in the state of Minnesota.

Media control by the government:
The media control by the government is minimal. However, in the State of Minnesota, there are restrictions on using print media, such as newspapers, for advertising alcoholic products, including wine.

Media affordability: The media costs are high, but if all parties involved (Winery, importer and distributor) contribute to it, the cost can be affordable.

Any other issues:
The most effective way to market wine is giving the customer the opportunity to taste and purchase the wine. This has an effective multiplier and leads to word-of-mouth advertising.

(b) Promotional mix

	Cost/Unit	Units	Total Cost
Magazine	1,100	1	1,100
TV	2,100	1	2,100
Personal Selling	40,000	1	40,000
Trade shows	2,700	2	5,400
Internet	2,000	1	2,000
Winetastings	1,000	2	2,000
Print of flyers of import and distribution company	1,000	1	1,000
Total Budget			**53,600**

(c) Goals and objectives that are to be achieved using the selected promotional strategy

The company would like to increase the awareness of and sales to the consumers of Greek wines in general and Lafkiotis wines in particular. That's the reason for the selection of different promotion strategies, which targets various segments of wine consumers.

3.3.4. *Distribution strategy (the place)*

(a) Channel issues

Does the government require a license to establish presence in the country? — **Yes**

Is it difficult to dismiss a channel member such as a distributor/agent with whom you have an agreement? — **Yes**

Other Issues:

In every state the distributor needs a distribution license, along with the retailer (liquor store, restaurants). The license's fee varies from state to state. This license is annual.

Explanation:

An import license and a distribution license are required. An existing channel cannot be easily dismissed as the company may not have the required product knowledge and personnel for the adequate coverage of this specific market.

(b) Best distribution strategy in the target country

Selective distribution — A distribution company, which can provide adequate market coverage and presence and selected retail stores, like liquor stores and restaurants, is of paramount importance.

(c) Distribution channels

Select all Indirect and Direct Channels that apply (United States)

Indirect Channels
- ○ Broker/Agent
- ◉ Importer/Wholesaler
- ○ Retailer

Direct Channels
- ◉ Use an existing channel
- ○ Acquire an existing channel
- ○ Create a new channel

E-Commerce
- ○ B2B
- ◉ B2C

Explain reasons for your selection

> The low budget of the company makes the use of an existing channel as the only
> viable solution. The E-commerce can not be used at this point, as a different
> license is needed and wine consumers in Minnesota rarery buy wine online.

3.3.5. *Select the international targeting strategy*

Based on the analysis of the marketing mix, the best targeting strategy is *differentiated.*

Reason for above selection:

An adaptation needs to be done as the labels of each bottle need to be translated to English. Taking into account the differences between the home market's and the new market's target groups and the market structure, a differentiated approach needs to be considered regarding the distribution and the promotional strategies. The emphasis should be on the quality and uniqueness of the indigenous Greek grapes, region of Nemea, and the Agiorgitiko along with all other wines of Lafkiotis. The pricing strategy is generally based on the coverage of the additional costs in comparison to the strategy for the home market.

3.4. *Financial strategy*

(a) Projected P/L statement

Number of Units to be Sold *

8400	10080	12096
Year-1	Year-2	Year-3

Unit Price *

16.5	16.5	16.5
Year-1	Year-2	Year-3

Net sales in the Target Market

138600	166320	199584
Year-1	Year-2	Year-3

CGS *

40488	48586	58303
Year-1	Year-2	Year-3

Gross Profit (loss)

98112	117734	141281
Year-1	Year-2	Year-3

Operational Expenditure

65000	75000	85000
Year-1	Year-2	Year-3

Net profit (loss) after taxes

33112	42734	56281
Year-1	Year-2	Year-3

[Calculate]

(b) Break-even point

Included in the analysis of the profitability of a Target Market is the computation of the break-even point (BEP). The BEP should be used simultaneously with the development of product strategies and action plans to ensure that the marketing program meets the required level of sales successfully.

Percentage Gross Profit = [Total Gross Profit] / [Total net sales]
BEP sales = [Total operating expenses] / [Percentage Gross Profit]

% Gross Profit

70.787878787879	70.787638287638	70.787738496072
Year-1	Year-2	Year-3

BEP Sales

468	604	795
Year-1	Year-2	Year-3

(c) Profit/sales scenarios

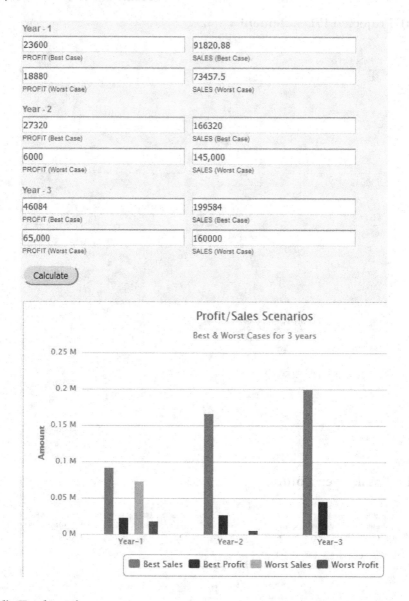

Year - 1

23600		91820.88
PROFIT (Best Case)		SALES (Best Case)

18880		73457.5
PROFIT (Worst Case)		SALES (Worst Case)

Year - 2

27320		166320
PROFIT (Best Case)		SALES (Best Case)

6000		145,000
PROFIT (Worst Case)		SALES (Worst Case)

Year - 3

46084		199584
PROFIT (Best Case)		SALES (Best Case)

65,000		160000
PROFIT (Worst Case)		SALES (Worst Case)

Calculate

Profit/Sales Scenarios
Best & Worst Cases for 3 years

Legend: Best Sales, Best Profit, Worst Sales, Worst Profit

(d) Explanation

The assessment of bottles of wine to be sold in 2017 (Year-1) is based on the export of a 20 ft. Shipping Container and a rise in sales by 20% and 30% for 2018 and 2019, respectively. The predicted increase in sales for 2019 is based on the plans of the company for the distribution of wines to additional states. The cost of sales is based on the CIF method with the state of Minnesota as destination and the related costs added for the implementation of the Marketing Plan. Regarding the different profit scenarios for the company, the sales are based on the projected sales and the possible costs.

3.5. Exit strategy and scenarios

In the event of having to exit from the local market, the possible scenarios are listed below.

Exit strategy and scenarios
In the event of having to exit from the local market, please discuss the possible scenarios. You may want to consider liquidation, selling to a JV partner or stay the course:

Different options could be considered in the event there is a reason such as:

Sell the business as a going concern, sell part of the business to a third party, liquidate the inventory and shot down and lastly, go bankrupt and reorganize. In all instances, one should take into account the tax ramifications, existing financial obligations, if any, and future consequences.

What are the legal issues on terminating a business at the local level?

There are no legal issues on terminating a business at the local level.

3.6. *Conclusion and recommendations*

Conclusion and Recommendations based on the entry strategy have given below:

(a) Conclusion
In this module, a strategic marketing plan was developed in an effort to assist the Lafkiotis Winery and especially its Minnesota-based distributor, to each achieve their own and their mutually

agreed upon goals and objectives. More specially, Lafkiotis wines will be exported to a USA importer based in the state of Minnesota where the wines will be first distributed by the importer's distributor in Minnesota and later in other states in the midwest. The entire marketing mix was carefully analyzed and evaluated as well as of the possible revenues and profits for the company were estimated. All things considered, the proposed Marketing Plan, if carefully implemented, should achieve the specific goals and objectives of the parties involved including the sales and profit targets.

(b) Recommendations

The wine consumers in most countries usually have similar wine preferences and consumption patterns. However, there is a need for a different communications strategy, as the target group, the sale points and the media that will be used for the promotion of the product, are different in comparison to those in the home markets. For a business plan of this nature to succeed, all parties involved would need to communicate frequently, cooperate, use due diligence, and best business practices.

Appendix A
Glossary

Glossary of Common Terms Used in International Business

A

Accession — Becoming a member of the WTO, signing on to its agreements. New members have to negotiate terms: bilaterally with individual WTO members multilaterally, (1) to convert the results of the bilateral negotiations so that they apply to all WTO members, and (2) on required legislation and institutional reforms that are need to meet WTO obligations.

ACP — African, Caribbean and Pacific countries. Group of countries with preferential trading relations with the EU under the former Lomé Treaty now called the Cotonou1 Agreement.

Ad valorem equivalent (AVE)[a] — A tariff that is not a percentage (e.g., dollars per ton) can be estimated as a percentage of the price — the ad valorem equivalent.

Ad valorem tariff[a] — A tariff rate charged as percentage of the price

Administrative Barriers — The ongoing administrative, discriminatory, and ad hoc safeguard actions and practices to protect home industries. Typical NTBs include exclusion orders, standards, exclusionary distribution, and administrative delays.

Advertising — A paid form of non-personal communication about an organization and/or its products that is transmitted to a target audience through a mass medium.

Agenda 2000[a] — EC's financial reform plans for 2000-06 aimed at strengthening the union with a view to receiving new members.

Agenda 21[a] — The Agenda for the 21st Century — a declaration from the 1992 Earth Summit (UN Conference on the Environment and Development) held in Rio de Janeiro.

Agent — A representative in a foreign market who attempts to sell your good or service through his or her network. Agents may be exclusive or represent many companies. They usually do not take responsibility for delivery or servicing of your product and are paid on a commission basis.

Air Bill (Air Waybill) — A shipping document used by the airlines for air freight. It is a contract for carriage that includes carrier conditions of carriage including such items as limits of liability and claims procedures. The air waybill also contains shipping instructions to airlines, a description of the commodity and applicable transportation charges. Air waybills are used by many truckers as through documents for coordinated air/truck service.

Amber Box[a] — Domestic support for agriculture that is considered to distort trade and therefore subject to reduction commitments. Technically calculated as "Aggregate Measurement of Support" (AMS).

Andean Community[a] — Bolivia, Colombia, Ecuador, Peru and Venezuela.

Anti-dumping duties[a] — GATT's Article 6 allows anti-dumping duties to be imposed on goods that are deemed to be dumped and causing injury to producers of competing products in the importing country. These duties are equal to the difference between the goods' export price and their normal value, if dumping causes injury.

APEC[a] — Asia Pacific Economic Cooperation forum.

Appellate Body[a] — An independent seven-person body that considers appeals in WTO disputes. When one or more parties to the dispute appeals, the Appellate Body reviews the findings in panel reports.

Applied tariff / Applied rates[a] — Duties that are actually charged on imports. These can be below the bound rates.

Arm's Length Price — The price at which two unrelated and non-desperate parties would agree to a transaction.

Article XX[a] (i.e. 20) — A GATT article listing allowed "exceptions" to the trade rules.

ASEAN[a] — Association of Southeast Asian Nations. Eight ASEAN members are members of the WTO — Brunei, Cambodia, Indonesia, Malaysia, Myanmar, the Philippines, Singapore and Thailand. The other ASEAN members — Laos and Vietnam — are negotiating WTO membership.

ASEAN Free Trade Area — "The Association of Southeast Asian Nations (ASEAN) agreed in January 1992 to create a free trade area (ASEAN Free Trade Area, or AFTA) with use of a common effective preferential tariff. Under the agreement ASEAN members will cut tariff rates within 15 years.

Automatic import licensing[a] — when applications for import licenses are approved in all cases.

Automaticity[a] — In disputes, the "automatic" chronological progression for settling trade disputes in regard to panel establishment, terms of reference, composition and adoption procedures.

B

Backward vertical integration — A strategy that involves a buyer entering the industry that it purchases goods or services from.

Balance of payments basis[a] — Trade data conforming with national income accounting methods (the value of trade in goods and services changing hands between residents and non-residents sometimes without crossing borders); the figures for goods trade are derived and adjusted from customs data (the value of goods trade crossing borders).

Barriers to Entry — The obstacles a new firm may face when trying to enter into an industry or new market.

Basel Convention[a] — A multilateral environmental agreement dealing with hazardous waste.

Berne Convention[a] — Berne Convention A treaty, administered by WIPO, for the protection of the rights of authors in their literary and artistic works.

Big Emerging Markets (BEMs) — A group of fast growing economies that the Department of Commerce has identified as major U.S. export.

Big Mac Index — The index, published by the Economist is based on the theory of purchasing-power parity, which says that exchange rates should eventually adjust to make the price of a basket of goods the same in each country. The Big Mac index works by calculating the exchange rate that would leave a Big Mac costing the same in each country.

Bill of Lading — A document issued by a carrier to a shipper, signed by the captain, agent, or owner of a vessel, furnishing written evidence regarding receipt of the goods (cargo), the conditions on which transportation is made (contract of carriage), and the engagement to deliver goods at the prescribed port of destination to the lawful holder of the bill of lading. A bill of lading is, therefore, both a receipt for merchandise and a contract to deliver it as freight. There are number of bills of lading: straight bill of lading, shipper's order bill of lading, air waybill, clean bill of lading and closed bill of lading.

BIT[a] — Bilateral investment treaties.

Blue Box[a] — Amber Box types of support, but with constraints on production or other conditions designed to reduce the distortion. Currently not limited.

Border protection[a] — Any measure which acts to restrain imports at point of entry.

Bottom up[a] — drawing on members' positions.

Box[a] — In agriculture, a category of domestic support.

Green box: supports considered not to distort trade and therefore permitted with no limits.

Blue box: permitted supports linked to production, but subject to production limits, and therefore minimally trade-distorting.

Amber box: supports considered to distort trade and therefore subject to reduction commitments.

Bracketed[a] — In official drafts, square brackets indicate text that has not been agreed and is still under discussion.

Break – Even Analysis — A break-even analysis is an analysis to determine the point at which revenue received equals the costs associated with receiving the revenue. Break-even analysis calculates what is known as a margin of safety, the amount that revenues exceed the break-even point. This is the amount that revenues can fall while still staying above the break-even point.

BTA[a] — Border tax adjustment.

Bunker Adjustment Factor (BAF) — An adjustment in shipping charges to offset price fluctuations in the cost of bunker fuel.

Business-level strategies — Plans or methods companies use to conduct various functions in their business operations. Companies often use business-level strategies to provide guidelines for owners, managers and employees to follow when working in the business.

Buyers — Purchasers of the goods or services that the competitors in an industry create.

C

C.I.F. (Cost Insurance and Freight) — An international trade term of sale in which, for the quoted price, the seller/exporter/manufacturer clears the goods for export and is responsible for delivering the goods to the named port of destination. However, once the goods pass the ship's rail at the port of shipment, the buyer assumes responsibility for risk of loss or damage as well as any additional transport costs. The seller is also responsible for procuring and paying for marine insurance in the buyer's name for the shipment. The Cost and Freight term is used only for ocean or inland waterway transport.

Cabotage[a] — In maritime transport, sea shipping between ports of the same country, usually along coasts.

Cairns Group[a] — Group of agricultural exporting nations lobbying for agricultural trade liberalization. It was formed in 1986 in Cairns, Australia just before the beginning of the Uruguay Round.

CAP[a] — Common Agricultural Policy — The EU's comprehensive system of production targets and marketing mechanisms designed to manage agricultural trade within the EU and with the rest of the world.

Caricom[a] — The Caribbean Community and Common Market, comprising 15 countries.

Carrier — An individual or legal entity that is in the business of transporting passengers or goods for hire. Shipping lines, airlines, trucking companies, and railroad companies are all carriers.

Carry forward[a] — When an exporting country uses part of the following year's quota during the current year.

Carry over[a] — When an exporting country utilizes the previous year's unutilized quota.

Cash-in-Advance — Payment method in which an order is not processed until full payment is received in advance. Also called cash with order.

Certificate of Origin — A document attesting to the country of origin of goods. A certificate of origin is often required by the customs authorities of a country as part of the entry process. Such certificates are usually obtained through an official or quasi-official organization in the country of origin such as a consular office or local chamber of commerce. A certificate of origin may be required even though the commercial invoice contains the information.

Channel Strategy — The broad principles by which the firm expects to achieve its distribution objectives for its target market(s).

Circumvention[a] — Getting around commitments in the WTO such as commitments to limit agricultural export subsidies. Includes: avoiding quotas and other restrictions by altering the country of origin of a product; measures taken by exporters to evade anti-dumping or countervailing duties.

CITES[a] — Convention on International Trade in Endangered Species. A multilateral environmental agreement.

Codex Alimentarius[a] — FAO/WHO commission that deals with international standards on food safety.

Commercial Invoice — A document identifying the seller and buyer of goods or services, identifying numbers such as invoice number, date, shipping date, mode of transport, delivery and payment terms, and a complete listing and description of the goods and services being sold including prices, discounts and quantities.

Commercial Presence — Having an office, branch, or subsidiary in a foreign country. In services, "mode 3" (see "modes of delivery").

Common Law — Law that forms the foundation of the legal system in Anglo American countries; based on cumulative findings of judges in individual cases.

Competitive Advantage — A total offer, Vis à Vis relevant competition, that is more attractive to customers. It exists when the competencies of a firm permit the firm to outperform its competitors.

Competitive Strategy — A plan that attempts to define a position for the business that utilizes the competitive advantages that the business has over its competitors.

Competitors — The set of firms that produce goods or services within an industry.

Complementary Products — The products that are manufactured together, sold together, bought together, or used together. One aids or enhances the other.

Compulsory licensing[a] — For patents: when the authorities license companies or individuals other than the patent owner to use the rights of the patent — to make, use, sell or import a product under patent (i.e. a patented product or a product made by a patented process) — without the permission of the patent owner. Allowed under the WTO's TRIPS (intellectual property) Agreement provided certain procedures and conditions are fulfilled.

Confirming Houses — An agent who assists the overseas buyer by confirming, as a principal, orders already placed.

Consignment sales — Trading arrangement in which a seller sends goods to a buyer or reseller who pays the seller only as and when the goods are sold.

Consular Invoice — An invoice covering a shipment of goods certified (usually in triplicate) by the consul of the country for which the merchandise is destined. This invoice is used by customs officials of the country of entry to verify the value, quantity, and nature of the merchandise imported.

Consumer Goods — Goods and services bought for personal use.

Consumer price index (CPI)[c] — A measure of a country's general level of prices based on the cost of a typical basket of consumer goods and services.

Container Freight Charge — Charge made for the packing or unpacking of cargo into or from ocean freight containers.

Contract Manufacturing — Process of outsourcing manufacturing to other firms to reduce the amount of a firm's financial and human resources devoted to the physical production of its products.

Contract Manufacturing — The production of goods by one firm, under the label or brand of another firm.

Contractual Requirements — Agreements between the company and its foreign based agents/distributors, licensees/franchisees or joint venture partners.

Convertibility[b] — The ability to freely use a currency for international transactions by the residents of any country.

Convertible — Currency that can be quickly and easily bought and sold for other currencies.

Corporate fit — The degree to which the company's existing practices, resources, and capabilities fit the new market.

Corporate level strategy — Strategy that involves all the strategic decisions that are made by a company that affects the whole organization or company. Most organizations will only use this one strategic plan in all their operations.

Corporate Strategy — The overall scope and direction of a corporation and the way in which its various business operations work together to achieve particular goals.

Corporate Tax — A tax that must be paid by a corporation based on the amount of profit generated. The amount of tax, and how it is calculated, varies depending upon the region where the company is located.

Cost - Plus Pricing — A pricing method whereby the purchaser agrees to pay the vendor an amount determined by the costs Incurred by the vendor to produce the goods or services purchased, plus a fixed percentage of that cost for profit.

Counterfeit[a] — Unauthorized representation of a registered trademark carried on goods identical or similar to goods for which the trademark is registered, with a view to deceiving the purchaser into believing that he/she is buying the original goods.

Countertrade — An exchange of goods or services which are paid for, in whole or part, with other goods or services, rather than with money.

Countervailing measures[a] — Action taken by the importing country, usually in the form of increased duties to offset subsidies given to producers or exporters in the exporting country.

Credit Risk Insurance — Insurance designed to cover risks of non-payment for delivered goods.

CRTA[a] — Committee on Regional Trade Agreements.

CTD[a] — The WTO Committee on Trade and Development.

CTE[a] — The WTO Committee on Trade and Environment.

CTG[a] — Council for Trade in Goods — oversees WTO agreements on goods.

Current membership are : Argentina, Australia, Bolivia, Brazil, Canada, Chile, Colombia, Costa Rica, Guatemala, Indonesia, Malaysia, New Zealand, Pakistan, Paraguay, Peru, Philippines, South Africa, Thailand, Uruguay.

Customs union[a] — Members apply a common external tariff (e.g. the European Union).

D

Date draft — Bill of exchange that becomes payable (matures) on a fixed date, irrespective of the date it was accepted by the payer.

DDA[a] — Doha Development Agenda, sometimes Doha Round. Unofficial name of the Doha Work Programme on negotiations and implementation.

De minimis[a] — Minimal amounts of domestic support that are allowed even though they distort trade — up to 5% of the value of production for developed countries, 10% for developing.

Deficiency payment[a] — A type of agricultural domestic support, paid by governments to producers of certain commodities and based on the difference between a target price and the domestic market price or loan rate, whichever is the less.

Demographic Environment — The human population characteristics that surround a firm or nation and that greatly affect markets. The demographic environment includes such factors as age distributions, births, deaths, immigration, marital status, sex, education, religious affiliations, and geographic dispersion — characteristics that are often used for segmentation purposes.

Differentiation strategy — A generic positioning that attempts to convince customers to pay a premium price for its good or services by providing unique and desirable features A firm following a differentiation strategy attempts to convince customers to pay a premium price for its good or services by providing unique and desirable feature.

Direct Exporting — Selling directly to an importer or buyer located in a foreign market area.

Dispatch — An amount paid by a vessel's operator to a charter if loading or unloading is completed in less time than stipulated in the charter agreement.

Disposable Income — Personal income minus income taxes and other taxes paid by an individual, the balance being available for consumption or savings.

Distortion[a] — When prices and production are higher or lower than levels that would usually exist in a competitive market.

Distributor (Foreign Based) — The foreign distributor purchases the product and is always responsible for payment of the export item. They assume financial risk and generally provide support and service for the product. Distributors often buy to fill their own inventories and typically carry a range of non-competitive, but complementary products.

Dock Receipt — A receipt issued by a warehouse supervisor or port officer certifying that goods have been received by the shipping company. The dock receipt is used to transfer accountability when an export item is moved by the domestic carrier to the port of embarkation and left with the international carrier for movement to its final destination.

Domestic support[a] — (Sometimes "internal support".) In agriculture, any domestic subsidy or other measure which acts to maintain producer prices at levels above those prevailing in international trade; direct payments to producers, including deficiency payments, and input and marketing cost reduction measures available only for agricultural production.

Dumping[a] — Occurs when goods are exported at a price less than their normal value, generally meaning they are exported for less than they are sold in the domestic market or third-country markets, or at less than production cost.

E

Electronic commerce[a] — The production, advertising, sale and distribution of products via telecommunications networks.

Embargo — A government prohibition against the shipment of certain products to a particular country for economic or political reasons.

Emerging Markets[b] — The capital markets of developing countries that have liberalized their financial systems to promote capital flows with nonresidents and are broadly accessible to foreign investors.

End User — The ultimate user for which something is intended.

Entry Mode — Method selected by a firm to enter into a foreign market to conduct business.

Equity Ownership — Ownership interest in a corporation in the form of common stock or preferred stock.

European Union (EU) — A regional economic and political organization with a combined GDP of more than U.S. $7 trillion and a population of 370 million. Its 15 members are Austria, Belgium, Denmark, Finland, France, Germany, Greece, Ireland, Italy, Luxembourg, The Netherlands, Portugal, Spain, Sweden, and the United Kingdom.

Ex Works — An international trade term of sale in which, for the quoted price, the seller/exporter/manufacturer merely makes the goods available to the buyer at the seller's "named place" of business. This trade term places the greatest responsibility on the buyer and minimum obligations on the seller. The seller does not clear the goods for export and does not load the goods onto a truck or other transport vehicle at the named place of departure. The parties to the transaction, however, may stipulate that the seller be responsible for the costs and risks of loading the goods onto a transport vehicle. Such a stipulation must be made within the contract of sale. If the buyer cannot handle export formalities the Ex Works term should not be used. In such a case Free Carrier (FCA) is recommended.

Exclusive Distribution — A very highly selective pattern of distribution is used at each level of the marketing channel.

Exit Barriers — Factors that make it difficult for a firm to stop competing in an industry.

Exit Strategy — Timing and means with which an investor cashes the investment in a startup venture or a buyout arrangement.

Export Agent — An intermediary who acts on behalf of a company to open up or develop a market in a foreign country. Export agents are often paid a commission on all sales and may have exclusive rights in a particular geographic area.

Export Controls — To exercise control over exports for statistical and strategic purposes, Customs enforces export control laws for the U.S. Department of Commerce and other Federal agencies.

Export License — A document prepared by a government authority, granting the right to export a specified quantity of a commodity to a specified country. This document may be required in some countries for most of the exports and in other countries only under special circumstances.

Export Management Company (EMC) — An EMC is a private firm that serves as the export department for several manufacturers, soliciting and transacting export business on behalf of its clients in return for a commission, salary, or retainer plus commission. An EMC maintains close contact with its clients and is supply driven. An EMC may take title to the goods it sells, making a profit on the markup, or it may charge a commission, depending on the type of products being handled, the overseas market, and the manufacturer client's needs.

Export Merchant — A company that engages in export and buys and sells on its own account.

Export Price List — Shows the list price (retail) for the merchandise to give the importer an idea of what the items sell for to the consumer so the importer can plan the markup.

Export Trading Companies — A corporation or other business unit organized and operated principally for the purpose of exporting goods and services, or of providing export related services to other companies. An ETC can be owned by foreigners and can import, barter, and arrange sales between third countries, as well as export.

F

FDI[a] — Foreign direct investment.

Focused cost leadership — A generic business strategy that requires competing based on price to target a narrow market. A focused cost leadership strategy requires competing based on price to target a narrow market A firm that follows this strategy does not necessarily charge the lowest prices in the industry. Instead, it charges low prices relative to other firms that compete within the target market.

Focused differentiation — A generic business strategy that requires offering unique features that fulfill the demands of a narrow market. A focused differentiation strategy requires offering unique features that fulfill the demands of a narrow market.

Foreign Based Agents — A representative in a foreign market who attempts to sell your good or service through his or her network. Agents may be exclusive or represent many companies. They usually do not take responsibility for delivery or servicing of your product and are paid on a commission basis.

Foreign Based Distributors — The foreign distributor purchases the product and is always responsible for payment of the export item. They assume financial risk and generally provide support and service for the product. Distributors often buy to fill their own inventories and typically carry a range of non-competitive, but complementary products.

Foreign Branch — A foreign affiliate that is legally a part of the parent firm. In the U.S. tax code, foreign branch income is taxed as it is earned in the foreign country.

Foreign Exchange[b] — Any type of financial instrument that is used to make payments between countries is considered foreign exchange. Examples of foreign exchange assets include foreign currency notes, deposits held in foreign banks, debt obligations of foreign governments and foreign banks, monetary gold, and SDRs.

Foreign Freight Forwarder — A person engaged in the business of assembling, collection, consolidation, shipping and distributing less than carload or less than truckload freight. Also, a person acting as agent in the trans shipping of freight to or from foreign countries and the clearing of freight through customs, including full preparation of documents, arranging for shipping, warehousing, delivery and export clearance.

Foreign Sales Representatives — Generally, a representative or agent refers to a person who is responsible for closing the sale and taking orders on a commission basis. They do not take financial responsibility or collect payment for the goods sold, and they assume no risk or responsibility for the product. A foreign sales representative is a person taking on this description, but is operating out of a foreign country.

Forward vertical integration — A strategy that involves a supplier entering the industry that it supplies inputs to.

Franchising — A parent company grants another independent entity the privilege to do business in a pre-specified manner, including manufacturing, selling products, marketing technology and other business approach.

Free Trade Zones — A generic term referring to special commercial and industrial areas at which special customs procedures allow the importation of foreign merchandise without the requirement that duties be paid immediately.

Free-rider[a] — A casual term used to infer that a country which does not make any trade concessions, profits, nonetheless, from tariff cuts and concessions made by other countries in negotiations under the most-favoured-nation principle.

G

G15[a] — Group of 15 developing countries acting as the main political organ for the Non-Aligned Movement.

G7[a] — Group of seven leading industrial countries: Canada, France, Germany, Italy, Japan, United Kingdom, United States.

G8[a] — G7 plus Russia.

GATS[a] — The WTO's General Agreement on Trade in Services.

GATT[a] — General Agreement on Tariffs and Trade, which has been superseded as an international organization by the WTO. An updated General Agreement is now the WTO agreement governing trade in goods. GATT 1947: The official legal term for the old (pre-1994) version of the GATT. GATT 1994: The official legal term for new version of the General Agreement, incorporated into the WTO, and including GATT 1947.

General obligations[a] — Obligations which should be applied to all services sectors at the entry into force of the GATS agreement.

Generic[a] — Copies of a patented drug, or of a drug whose patent has expired (sometimes also related to trademarks).

Geographical indications[a] — Place names (or words associated with a place) used to identify products (for example, "Champagne", "Tequila" or "Roquefort") which have a particular quality, reputation or other characteristic because they come from that place.

Global Involvement — Refers to the level and/or degree of commitment the company has made to the international marketplace. The company's involvement increases as the company evolves from being an exporter to becoming a global company. The levels of involvement are: Accidental (casual) exporting, active exporting, licensing/franchising, foreign based branch, foreign based marketing subsidiary, and foreign production.

Global Marketing — A marketing strategy that consciously addresses global customers, markets, and competition in formulating a business strategy.

Global Marketing Information Systems — A system designed to acquire, store, catalogue, analyze, and make available to decision makers information from global sources within and external to the firm for use as the basis for planning and decision making.

Global Strategy — A strategy that seeks competitive advantage with strategic moves that are highly interdependent across countries. These moves include most or all of the following: a standardized core product that exploits or creates homogenous tastes or performance requirements, significant participation in all major country markets to build volume, a concentration of value creating activities such as R&D and manufacturing in a few countries, and a coherent competitive strategy that pits the worldwide capabilities of the business against the competition.

GPA[a] — Government Procurement Agreement: a "plurilateral" agreement (ie, signed by only some WTO members) covering the procurement of goods, services and capital infrastructure by governments and other public authorities.

Gross Cost of Merchandise Sold — The gross cost of merchandise handled less the closing inventory cost. The gross cost of merchandise sold is subtracted from net sales to calculate maintained mark-up. Maintained mark-up is then adjusted by cash discounts and workroom costs to determine gross margin of profit.

Gross Domestic Product (GDP)[a] — An estimate of the total national output of goods and services produced in a single country in a given time period and valued at market price. 2. GDP equals gross national product less net property income from abroad.

Gross Margin — The difference between net sales and total cost of goods sold.

Gross National Product — A measure of the market value of goods and services produced by the labor and property of a nation. Includes receipts from that nation's business operation in foreign countries, as well as the share of reinvested earnings in foreign affiliates of domestic competition.

Gross National Product (GNP)[b] — Gross national product was formerly used as a measure of a country's overall economic activity, equal to GDP less compensation of employees and property income payable to the rest of the world plus the corresponding items receivable from the rest of the world; GNP has been renamed gross national income (GNI) in the System of National Accounts.

GRULAC[a] — Informal group of Latin-American members of the WTO.

GSP[a] — Generalized System of Preferences — programmes by developed countries granting preferential tariffs to imports from developing countries.

H

Harbor Maintenance Fee — Is an ad valorem fee assessed on cargo imports and admissions into foreign trade zones. The fee is 0.125 percent of the value of the cargo and is paid quarterly, except for imports which are paid at the time of entry. Customs deposits the harbor maintenance fee collections into the Harbor Maintenance Trust Fund. The funds are available, subject to appropriation, to the Army Corps of Engineers for the improvement and maintenance of U.S. ports and harbors.

Hard Currency — The currency of a nation which may be exchanged for that of another nation without restriction. Sometimes referred to as convertible currency. Hard currency countries typically have sizeable exchange reserves and surpluses in their balance of payments.

Harmonized System[a] — An international nomenclature developed by the World Customs Organization, which is arranged in six-digit codes allowing all participating countries to classify traded goods on a common basis. Beyond the six-digit level, countries are free to introduce national distinctions for tariffs and many other purposes.

Harmonizing formula[a] — Used in tariff negotiations for much steeper reductions in higher tariffs than in lower tariffs, the final rates being "harmonized" i.e. closer together.

HS 6-digit[a] — The World Customs Organization's Harmonized System (HS) uses code numbers to define products. A code with a low number of digits defines broad categories of products; additional digits indicate sub-divisions into more detailed definitions. Six-digit codes are the most detailed definitions that are used as standard. Countries can add more digits for their own coding to subdivide the definitions further according to their own needs. Products defined at the most detailed level are "tariff lines".

I

Import duties — The same as customs duty. Tax levied on imports (and, sometimes, on exports) by the customs authorities of a country to raise state revenue, and/or to protect domestic industries from more efficient or predatory competitors from abroad. Also called tariff, duty is based generally on the value of goods (called ad valorem duty) or upon the weight, dimensions, or some other criteria of the item (such as the size of the engine, in case of automobiles).

Import licensing[a] — the need to obtain a permit for importing a product; administrative procedures for obtaining an import licence.

Indirect Exporting — Using the services of independent marketing organizations, or cooperative organizations, located within the home country in exporting.

Industrial Goods — Goods or components produced for use primarily in the production of other goods.

Industrialized Countries (IC) — (Developed Countries) A term used to distinguish the more industrialized nations — including most OECD member countries — from developing or less developed countries. The developed countries are sometimes collectively designated as the Group B countries or the North, because most of them are in the Northern Hemisphere.

Industry Concentration — The extent to which a small number of firms dominate an industry.

Inflation[b] — A sustained increase in the general price level, often measured by an index of consumer prices. The rate of inflation is the percentage change in the price level in a given period.

Insurance Certificate — A document indicating the type and amount of insurance coverage in force on a particular shipment. Used to assure the consignee that insurance is provided to cover loss of or damage to the cargo while in transit.

Intellectual Property Rights (IPR)[a] — Ownership of ideas, including literary and artistic works (protected by copyright), inventions (protected by patents), signs for distinguishing goods of an enterprise (protected by trademarks) and other elements of industrial property.

Intensive Distribution — As many outlets as possible are used at each level of the marketing channel.

International Court of Justice (ICJ) — The principal judicial organ of the United Nations. It settles disputes between the sovereign nations of the world but not between private citizens.

International market due diligence — Involves analyzing foreign markets for their potential size, accessibility, cost of operations, and buyer needs and practices to aid the company in deciding whether to invest in entering that market.

International Monetary Fund (IMF) — A multinational organization whose objective is to promote international financial cooperation and to coordinate the stabilization of exchange rates and the establishment of freely convertible currencies.

International Product Cycle — A model developed by Professor Raymond Vernon that shows the relationship of production, consumption, and trade over the life cycle of a product. Based on empirical data for pre 1967 era, the model showed how the location of production shifted from the United States to other advanced countries and then to less developed countries.

International Trade Product Life Cycle — A trade cycle model that suggests that many products go through a cycle in which high income, mass consumption countries are initially exporters, then lose their export markets, and finally become importers of the product.

ISO 9000 — The general name for the quality standard accepted throughout the European Economic Community. It was initially adopted in 1987. ISO is a series of documents on quality assurance published by the Geneva based International Standards Organization. The five documents outline standards for developing Total Quality Management and a Quality Improvement Process. 9000 consists of guidelines for the selection and use of the quality systems contained in 9001 9003. 9001 outlines model of quality assurance in design, development, production, installation, and servicing. 9002, outlines a model for quality assurance in production and installation. 9003 outlines model for quality assurance for final inspection and testing. 9004 is not a standard but contains guidelines for quality management and quality system elements.

J

Joint Venture — A partnership between a domestic firm and a foreign firm and/or government.

Joint Venture (Manufacturing) — A partnership between a domestic manufacturing firm and a foreign manufacturing firm.

Joint Venture (Marketing) — A partnership between a domestic marketing firm and a foreign marketing firm.

L

Less Developed Country (LDC) — A country showing: (1) a poverty level of income, (2) a high rate of population increase, (3) a substantial portion of its workers employed in agriculture, (4) a low proportion of adult literacy, (5) high unemployment, and (6) a significant reliance on a few items for export. Terms such as third world, poor, developing nations, and underdeveloped have also been used to describe less developed countries.

Letter of Credit — A written commitment to pay, by a buyer's or importer's bank to the seller's or exporter's bank. A letter of credit guarantees payment of a specified sum in a specified currency, provided the seller meets precisely-defined conditions and submits the prescribed documents within a fixed timeframe.

Licensing — A contractual transaction where the firm (licensor) offers some proprietary assets to a foreign company (licensee) in exchange for royalty fees.

Lingua Franca — English has emerged as the predominate common language, or lingua franca, of international business. (i.e. countries that have many linguistic groups, such as India and Singapore, have adopted English as an official language to facilitate communication among diverse groups.

Lisbon Agreement[a] — Treaty, administered by the World Intellectual Property Organization (WIPO), for the protection of geographical indications and their international registration.

Local-content measure[a] — Requirement that the investor purchase a certain amount of local materials for incorporation in the investor's product.

M

Madrid Agreement[a] — Treaty, administered by the World Intellectual Property Organization (WIPO), for the repression of false or deceptive indications of source on goods.

Management Contracts — Strategic alliance where a foreign based company operates a company in a local market for a local investor.

Marginal - Cost Pricing — A method of determining the sales price by adding a profit margin onto either marginal cost of production or marginal cost of sales.

Markets — Collection of buyers and sellers that, through actual or potential interactions, determine the price of a product.[1]

Market Channel Structure — The group of channel members to which a set of distribution tasks has been allocated.

Market Penetration — A growth strategy designed to enhance competitive advantage by developing low risk improvement or revisions to the percent product range. These are proactive moves designed to identify and target changing customer requirements, or reactive moves for market defense triggered by competitive actions.

Market Positioning — Positioning refers to the customer's perceptions of the place a product or brand occupies in a market segment. In some markets a position is achieved by associating the benefits of a brand with the needs of life style of the segments. More often, positioning involves the differentiated company's offering from the competition by making or implying a comparison of the specific attributes.

---

[1]Ernst Berndt, Joseph Doyle, Michael Chapman, and Thomas Stoker.*15.010 Economic Analysis for Business Decisions, Fall 2004.* (Massachusetts Institute of Technology: MIT OpenCourseWare), http://ocw.mit.edu (Accessed). License: Creative Commons BY-NC-SA

Market Potential — The total amount of a product for all firms in an industry that customers will purchase within a specified period at a specific level of industry wide marketing activity.

Market Profile — A breakdown of a facility's market area according to income, demography, and lifestyle.

Market Segmentation — The process of subdividing a market into distinct subsets of customers that behave in the same way or have similar needs. Each subset may conceivably be chosen as a market to be reached with a distinct marketing strategy.

Market Share — The company's total sales of the product or service divided by total market sales.

Market Structure — The pattern formed by the number, size, and distribution of buyers and sellers in a market.

Marketing Channel — The system composed of marketing organizations that connect a manufacturer to the final users in a foreign market.

MEA[a] — Multilateral environmental agreement.

Merchandise Processing Fee — Sets a fee schedule for formal entries (generally, those valued over US$1,250) at a minimum of US$21 per entry and a maximum of US$400 per entry, with an ad valorem rate of 0.17 percent. The fee for informal entries (those valued at under US$1,250) is US$2 for automated entries, US$5 for manual entries not prepared by Customs, and US$8 for manual entries prepared by Customs.

MERCOSUR[a] — Argentina, Brazil, Paraguay and Uruguay.

MFA[a] — Multifibre Arrangement (1974-94) under which countries whose markets are disrupted by increased imports of textiles and clothing from another country were able to negotiate quota restrictions.

MFN[a] — Most-favoured-nation treatment (GATT Article I, GATS Article II and TRIPS Article 4), the principle of not discriminating between one's trading partners.

Mission Statement — An expression of a company's history, managerial preferences, environmental concerns, available resources, and distinctive competencies to serve selected publics. It is used to guide the company's decision making and strategic planning.

Modes of delivery[a] — How international trade in services is supplied and consumed. Mode 1: cross border supply; mode 2: consumption abroad; mode 3: foreign commercial presence; and mode 4: movement of natural persons.

Money[b] — Anything that is generally accepted in exchange as payment for goods and services. While the key function of money is to act as a medium of exchange, money also serves as a store of value, unit of account, and standard of deferred payment.

Monopolistic Competition — A market structure in which several or many sellers each produce similar, but slightly differentiated products. Each producer can set its price and quantity without affecting the marketplace as a whole.

Monopoly — A situation in which a single company owns all or nearly all of the market for a given type of product or service. This would happen in the case that there is a barrier to entry into the industry that allows the single company to operate without competition. In such an industry structure, the producer will often produce a volume that is less than the amount which would maximize social welfare.

Montreal Protocol1 — A multilateral environmental agreement dealing with the depletion of the earth's ozone layer.

Multilateral[a] — In the WTO, involving all members.

Multi-modal[a] — Transportation using more than one mode. In the GATS negotiations, essentially door-to-door services that include international shipping.

N

NAFTA — The North American Free Trade Agreement (NAFTA) is an agreement creating a free trade area among the United States, Canada, and Mexico, with a total population of more than 380 million and a combined GDP of U.S. $7.5 trillion. NAFTA went into effect on January 1, 1994.

Negotiated Price — A price that is the result of negotiations between the buyer and the seller.

New Entrants — Firms that do not currently compete in an industry but might join the industry in the future.

Newly Industrializing Countries (NICs) — Relatively advanced developing countries whose industrial production and exports have grown rapidly in recent years. Examples include Brazil, Hong Kong, Korea, Mexico, Singapore, and Taiwan. The term was originated by the Organization for Economic Cooperation and Development (OECD).

Non-Tariff Barriers (NTBs) — The ongoing administrative, discriminatory, and ad hoc safeguard actions and practices to protect home industries. Typical NTBs include exclusion orders, standards, exclusionary distribution, and administrative delays.

O

Ocean Bill (Ocean Bill of Lading (B/L)) — A receipt for the cargo and a contract for transportation between a shipper and the ocean carrier. It may also be used as an instrument of ownership (negotiable bill of lading) which can be bought, sold, or traded while the goods are in transit. To be used in this manner, it must be a nego-tiable "Order" Bill of Lading.

Offshore Sourcing — A company purchases major components from its foreign subsidiary and/or produces major components from independent suppliers overseas.

Oligopoly — A market dominated by a small number of partici-pants who are able to collectively exert control over supply and market prices.

Open account — A credit relationship in which the buyer pays upon the receipt of goods, or on deferred payment basis.

Overseas subsidiary — A partially or wholly owned company that is part of a larger corporation with headquarters in another coun-try. Foreign subsidiary companies are incorporated under the law's of the country it is located.

P

Packing Slip (Packing List) — A documents prepared by the ship-per listing the kinds and quantities of merchandise in a particular shipment. A copy is usually sent to the consignee to assist in check-ing the shipment when received. Also referred to as a bill of parcels.

Penetration Pricing — The strategy of setting a product's price relatively low in order to generate a high sales volume. This strat-egy is commonly associated with pricing new products that do not have identifiable price market segments.

Personal Tax — Government levy on the income, property, or wealth of an individual.

PESTEL analysis — An important and widely used tool that helps present the big picture of a firm's external environment in political, economic, sociocultural, technological, environmental, and legal contexts, particularly as related to foreign markets; analyses for market growth or decline and, therefore, the position, potential, and direction for a business.

Piggyback Marketing — An agreement whereby one manufacturer obtains distribution of products through another's distribution channels.

Porter's Five Forces — A framework that identifies and analyzes five competitive forces that shape every industry, and helps determine an industry's weaknesses and strengths. These forces are: Threat of new entrants, Threat of substitutes, Determinants of supplier power, Determinants of buyer power, Determinants of competitive rivalry.

Power of Attorney — A written legal document by which one person (principal) authorizes another person (agent) to perform stated acts on the principal's behalf. For example: to enter into contracts, to sign documents, to sign checks, and spend money, etc. A principal may execute a special power of attorney authorizing an agent to sign a specific contract or a general power of attorney authorizing the agent to sign all contracts for the principal.

Pro - forma Invoice — An invoice provided by a supplier prior to a sale or shipment of merchandise, informing the buyer of the kinds and quantities of goods to be sent, their value, and important specifications (weight, size, and similar characteristics). A pro forma invoice is used: (1) as a preliminary invoice together with a quotation; (2) for customs purposes in connection with shipments of samples, advertising materials, etc.

Product Attributes — The characteristics by which products are identified and differentiated. Product attributes usually comprise features, functions, benefits and uses.

Product Life Cycle (PLC) — The normal stages that a product passes through: research and development, growth, expansion, maturity, saturation, and decline. In the research stage, sales are slow and often need to be supplemented by heavy sales and advertising efforts. In the expansion stage, sales may grow more rapidly. In the maturity stage, sales start slowing down as most people who might want the product already have it, and there are few opportunities for increasing sales. In the decline stage, sales fall and the product eventually becomes obsolete.

Product Line — A group of closely related product items.

Promotion — The communication with individuals, groups, or organizations to directly or indirectly facilitate exchanges by influencing audience members to accept an organization's products.

Promotional Mix — Combination of different marketing promotion activities used by the export/international marketer.

Protective Tariffs — A duty or tax imposed on imported products for the purpose of making them more expensive in comparison to domestic products, thereby giving the domestic products a price advantage.

Psychographic Segmentation — The process of dividing markets into segments on the basis of consumer lifestyles.

Publicity — Non — personal communication in news story form, regarding an organization and/or its products that is transmitted through a mass medium at no charge.

Pull Strategy — A manufacturing strategy aimed at the end consumer of a product. The product is pulled through the channel by consumer demand initiated by promotional efforts, inventory stocking procedures, etc.

Purchasing Power Parity (PPP)[b] — A theory which relates changes in the nominal exchange rate between two countries' currencies to changes in the countries' price levels. The purchasing power parity theory predicts that an increase in a currency's domestic purchasing power will be associated with a proportional currency appreciation, and that a decrease will be associated with a proportional currency depreciation.

Push Strategy — A manufacturing strategy aimed at other channel members rather that the end consumer. The manufacturer attempts to entice other channel members to carry its product through trade allowances, inventory stocking procedures, pricing policies, etc.

Q

Quota — The quantity of goods of a specific kind that a country permits to be imported without restriction or imposition of additional duties.

R

Repatriation of Earnings — Capital flow from a foreign country to the country of origin. This usually refers to returning returns on a foreign investment in the case of a corporation, or transferring foreign earnings home in the case of an individual.

S

S.W.O.T. Analysis — An assessment of an organization's strengths, weaknesses, opportunities, and threats.

Sales Representative or Agent — Generally, a representative or agent refers to a person who is responsible for closing the sale and taking orders on a commission basis. They do not take financial responsibility or collect payment for the goods sold, and they assume no risk or responsibility for the product.

Selective distribution — Type of product distribution that lies between intensive distribution and exclusive distribution, and in which only a few retail outlets cover a specific geographical area. Considered more suitable for high-end items such as 'designer' or prestige goods.

Shipper's Export Declaration — From required for all U.S. export shipments by mail valued at more than $500 and for non-mail shipments with declared Value greater than $2,500. Also required for shipments requiring a U.S. Department of Commerce validated export license or U.S. Department of State license regardless of value of goods. Prepared by a shipper indicating the value, weight, destination, and other basic information about the shipment. The shipper's export declaration is used to control exports and compile trade statistics.

Shipper's Letter of Instructions — A form used by a shipper to authorize a carrier to issue a bill of lading or an air waybill on the shipper's behalf. The form contains all details of shipment and authorizes the carrier to sign the bill of lading in the name of the shipper.

Sight draft — A bill of exchange which is payable when it is presented.

Skimming Price Policy — A method of pricing that attempts to first reach those willing to buy at a high price before marketing to more price sensitive customers.

Special Documentation — Documents, other than the standard ones, the may be required by the government of the importing or exporting country.

Strategic Alliances — An agreement between two or more individuals or entities stating that the involved parties will act in a certain way in order to achieve a common goal. Strategic alliances usually make sense when parties involved have complementary strengths.

Strategic Business Unit — An autonomous division or organizational unit, small enough to be flexible and large enough to exercise control over most of the factors affecting its long-term performance.

Strategy — This describes the direction the business will pursue within its chosen environment and guides the allocation of resources and effort. It also provides the logic that integrates the perspectives of functional departments and operating units, and points them all in the same direction.

Substitute Products — The products that are viewed by the user as alternatives for other products. The substitution is rarely perfect, and varies from time to time depending on price, availability, etc.

Suppliers — Providers of inputs that the competitors in an industry need to create goods or services.

Sustained competitive advantage — A competitive advantage that will endure over time.

T

Tangible resources — Resources than can be readily seen, touched, and quantified, such as physical assets, property, plant, equipment, and cash. Physical assets such as a firm's property, plant, and equipment, as well as cash, are considered to be tangible resources.

Target Market — A specific group of customers on whose needs and wants a company focuses its marketing efforts.

Target Return Pricing — A method of pricing that attempts to cover all costs and achieve a target return.

Tariff — A tax assessed by a government in accordance with its tariff schedule on goods as they enter (or leave) a country. May be imposed to protect domestic industries from imported goods and/ or to generate revenue. Types include ad valorem, specific, variable, or some combination.

Terminal Charge — A charge made for services performed at terminals.

Time Draft — Bill of exchange payable at a fixed future date or a determinable future time such as 30 days after presentation (after sight). The purpose of a time draft is to allow the buyer some time to pay for goods bought. In contrast, a sight draft becomes payable at the time it is presented to the buyer. Also called usance draft.

Trade Discount — A discount from the list price of a commodity allowed by a manufacturer or wholesaler to a merchant.

Trade Show — A stage setting event in which firms present their products or services to prospective customers in a pre-formatted setting. The firms are generally in the same industry but not necessarily of the same nationality. A distinguishing factor between trade fairs and trade shows is size. A trade show is generally viewed as a smaller assembly of participants.

U

Uruguay Round — Multilateral trade negotiations launched at Punta del Este, Uruguay in September 1986 and concluded in Geneva in December 1993. Signed by Ministers in Marrakesh, Morocco, in April 1994.

V

Valuable Resources — Resources that help a firm create strategies that capitalize on opportunities and ward off threats.

Value - Added Tax (VAT) — An indirect tax on consumption that is assessed on the increased value of goods at each discrete point in the chain of production and distribution, from the raw material stage to final consumption. The tax on processors or merchants is levied on the amount by which they increase the value of items they purchase and resell.

W

Wharfage — A charge assessed by a pier or dock owner for handling incoming or outgoing cargo or the charge made for docking vessels at a wharf.

Wholly Owned Subsidiaries — A subsidiary in which the firm owns 100 percent of the stock.

World Trade Organization (WTO) — A multilateral organization that promotes free and fair trade among the nations of the world.

Other Glossary Sources

Alan Deardorffs' Glossary of International Economics — Available on: www.personal.umich.edu/~alandear/glossary/intro.html.

A printable PDF of terms can be accessed on https://texastrade. org/resources/import-export-glossary/

BIZMOVE GLOSSARY — Available on http://www.bizmove. com/export/m7q.htm

EXPORT GOV trade terms — Available on https://www.export. gov/article?id=Glossary-of-Trade-Terms

Global Edge Glossary of Terms — Available on: globaledge.msu. edu/Reference-Desk/Glossary.

Glossary of Export Terminology and Incoterms — Available on http://www.sthelenschamber.com/assets/0002/1282/Glossary_ of_Export_Terminology_and_Incocerms.pdf

The Asia-Pacific Economic Cooperation (APEC) glossary of Trade terms — Available on: statistics.apec.org.

The INTRACEN market access glossary — Available on: www.macmap.org/SupportMaterials/Glossary.aspx#Y.

The GLOBESTRATEGY glossary of terms — Available on: http://globestrategy.net/?page_id=1410

Endnotes

[a]From the WTO glossary of Terms. Henceforth referred to as WTO. Available on www.wto.org/english/thewto_e/glossary_e/glossary_e.htm
[b]*Source*: The Economist Magazine
[c]*Source*: IMF — Glossary of Terms. Available on http://www.imf.org/external/np/exr/glossary/showTerm.asp

Appendix B

GMMSO Survey Questionnaire

Please help us improve the GMMSO software by completing this questionnaire. Your opinion is highly valued. Thank you!

My major is: Place an **X** in the box as your answer for each statement below	
	Accounting
	Finance
	Human Resources
	Management
	Marketing
	International Business
	Other, please specify:

I am a: Place an **X** in the box as your answer for each statement below	
	Sophomore
	Junior
	Senior
	Graduate

Usability

Place an X in the box as your answer for each statement below	Strongly Disagree	Disagree	Neutral	Agree	Strongly Agree
A. The instructions provided were clear and helpful in completing the project.					
B. The web sites featured in the GMMSO were helpful in conducting research and completing the project					
C. The case samples were helpful in completing the project.					
D. The format of each phase was useful in completing the project.					
E. The GMMSO seemed to be laid out logically.					
F. The GMMSO should be completed individually (vs. groups).					
G. The instructor's level of involvement was adequate.					

The GMMSO based project should be completed: Place an X in the box as your answer for each statement below

	Entirely outside of class.
	During class time.
	In and outside of class.

Usefulness

Place an **X** in the box as your answer for each statement below	Strongly Disagree	Disagree	Neutral	Agree	Strongly Agree
A. The GMMSO enabled me to evaluate a company and the company's level of international involvement.					
B. The GMMSO provided me with the opportunity to use business concepts and practices I acquired in other business courses.					
C. The GMMSO enabled me to become familiar with a good number of useful web-based information sources.					
D. The GMMSO increased my understanding of international business.					
E. The GMMSO allowed me to determine a company's readiness to internationalize.					
F. The GMMSO increased my understanding of different countries around the world.					
G. The GMMSO enhanced my knowledge of cultural forces and its impact on business.					
H. The GMMSO increased my understanding and appreciation of the impact of a country's economic and political system on business.					

Table (*Continued*)

Place an **X** in the box as your answer for each statement below	Strongly Disagree	Disagree	Neutral	Agree	Strongly Agree
I. The GMMSO helped me identify high potential country markets for selected products or services.					
J. The system allowed for an in-depth analysis of high market potential countries.					
K. The system enabled me to determine market potential for my product/service.					
L. The system enabled me to perform a complete competitive analysis.					
M. GMMSO simplified selecting the best entry strategy.					
N. GMMSO was valuable in developing an effective marketing plan.					
O. GMMSO was useful in developing projected Profit & Loss statements					
P. The GMMSO increased my understanding of the importance certain environmental factors have in selecting best markets for a given product/service.					
Q. I feel more businesses classes should try to incorporate projects like the GMMSO.					
R. The GMMSO user fee charged was fair.					

Skills

Place an **X** in the box as your answer for each statement below	Strongly Disagree	Disagree	Neutral	Agree	Strongly Agree
A. The GMMSO provided me with the opportunity to make use of my critical thinking skills.					
B. The GMMSO improved my web-based research skills.					
C. The GMMSO improved my team working skills.					
D. The GMMSO improved my decision-making skills.					
E. The GMMSO was more challenging and beneficial than other non-web based business projects I have done.					

Suggestions

What would you do to improve the GMMSO? Please be specific.

What suggestions do you have for future users of the GMMSO? Please be specific.

Appendix C
Useful Databases in International Business

There are a multitude of sources of information and databases that a student of International Business can access in order to create realistic entry strategies for firms.

Disclaimer

All of these databases are correct at the time of going to press. The authors are not responsible for the content of these databases and may not be held responsible for the non-availability of these databases.

1. Business Contacts

UK Trade & Investment (UKTI) has a network of market specialists based in the U.K. and across the globe. Their contacts can be searched by countries.

The resource is available on: ☯ http://www.ukti.gov.uk/export/countries/contactus-selectcountry-export.html.

British Chambers of Commerce

A list of international contacts is provided by British Chambers of Commerce on: ☯ http://www.britishchambers.org.uk/business/trading-internationally/international-contacts.html.

2. Country Profiles

Globestrategy country business profiles
⑤ http://globestrategy.com/category/country-business-profiles/.

The International Trade Centre
The International Trade Centre offers country specific trade information and statistics. The resource is available on: ⑤ http://www.
intracen.org/.

INTRACEN online databases
The International Trade Centre offers country specific published
trade information on: ⑤ http://legacy.intracen.org/dbms/tirs/
TIR_Browse_EK.Asp?DS=MONOGRAPHS&TY=C.

IMF country profiles
The resource is available on: ⑤ http://www.imf.org/external/
country/index.htm.

US department of state Country Fact Sheets
The resource is available on: ⑤ http://www.state.gov/r/pa/ei/
bgn/.

US Commercial service country Commercial guides — the resource
is available on: ⑤ http://www.buyusainfo.net/z_body.cfm?dbf=
ccg1&search_type2=int&avar=19919&logic=and&loadnav=no.

Country Risk and Economic Research — the resource helps in
understanding country risks and is available on: ⑤ http://www.
coface.com/CofacePortal/COM_en_EN/pages/home/risks_home.

The Nations Online Project — a portal of gateways to the countries,
cultures and nations in the world and is available on: ⑤ http://
www.nationsonline.org/.

Doing Business — The Doing Business project provides objective
measures of business regulations for local firms in 185 economies

and selected cities at the subnational level. This is available on: ⑤ http://www.doingbusiness.org/.

3. Industry/ Business/Sectoral Analysis

UK sectors

U.K. Trade & Investment (UKTI) has a network of market specialists based in the U.K. and across the globe and has produced a sectoral analysis. Available on: ⑤ http://www.ukti.gov.uk/export/sectors.html.

UNIDO Statistical Country Briefs

Statistics for major indicators of industrial performance are presented by country to meet the needs of a wide range of data users. The country data are given in comparison with figures for the geographical region or development group it belongs to.

This is available on: ⑤ http://www.unido.org/index.php?id=1002110.

The International Trade centre

This organization offers a sector analysis of several key industries.

The resource is available on: ⑤ http://www.intracen.org/exporters/sectors/.

The Canadian Trade Commissioner

Sectoral reports on several key industries are available on: ⑤ http://www.tradecommissioner.gc.ca/eng/market-reports-sectors.jsp.

Tourism Industry Highlights

The resource is available on: ⑤ http://mkt.unwto.org/en/publication/unwto-tourism-highlights-2012-edition.

Tourism Market Trends

The resource is available on: ⑤ http://www.unwto.org/facts/eng/tmt.htm.

Tourism Indicators

The resource is available on: ⓣ http://www.unwto.org/facts/menu.html.

4. The Asia-Pacific Economic Cooperation (APEC) databases

The Asia-Pacific Economic Cooperation has several free databases. The statistics home page is at: www.statistics.apec.org.

Key Indicators Database
The Key Indicators Database has been developed to facilitate detailed analysis of trade, financial, and socio-economic trends in the Asia-Pacific region. Access to this database is free-of-charge and the data can be exported to Microsoft Excel.

The resource is available on: ⓣ http://statistics.apec.org/index.php/key_indicator/index.

Bilateral Linkages Database
The Bilateral Linkages Database has been developed to facilitate detailed analysis of the trade and investment flows within APEC and between APEC and the world

The resource is available on: ⓣ http://statistics.apec.org/index.php/bilateral_linkage/index.

5. Global Labor Market Statistics

Definition of Labor terms and Statistics
The resource is available on: ⓣ http://www.ilo.org/ilostat.

LABORSTA
View and download data and metadata for over 200 countries or territories from LABORSTA, an International Labor Office database on labor statistics operated by the ILO Department of Statistics.

Statistics include Labor Cost, Total and Economically Active Population, Employment, Unemployment, Hours of work, Wages, Consumer Price Indices amongst several other variables.

The resource is available on: ⓣ http://laborsta.ilo.org/.

Please note that LABORSTA is not being updated and gradually will be replaced with ILOSTAT. Data is available till 2008 on this database.

ILOSTAT Database

This new ILO database of labor statistics provides recent data for over 100 indicators and 165 economies. Annual data prior to 2008 and additional information, such as sources and methods, are still available in LABORSTA and gradually will be migrated to ILOSTAT.

The resource is available on: ⑤ http://www.ilo.org/ilostat.

ILO Thesaurus

The ILO Thesaurus is a compilation of more than 4,000 terms relating to the world of work, in English, French, and Spanish. Covers labor and employment policy, human resources planning, labor standards, labor administration and labor relations, vocational training, economic and social development, social security, working conditions, wages, occupational safety and health and enterprise promotion.

The resource is available on: ⑤ http://www.ilo.org//thesaurus/defaulten.asp.

CARIBLEX

This is the ILO's database of national labor legislation for the 13 ILO member States of the English — and Dutch-speaking Caribbean

The resource is available on: ⑤ http://www.ilocarib.org.tt/projects/cariblex/index.shtml.

Child Labor Statistics

The resource is available on: ⑤ http://www.ilo.org/dyn/clsurvey/lfsurvey.home.

Database of Conditions of Work and Employment Laws[1]

The TRAVAIL Database of Conditions of Work and Employment Laws provides a picture of the regulatory environment of working time, minimum wages, and maternity protection in more than 100 countries around the world.

The resource is available on: ⑨ http://www.ilo.org/dyn/travail/travmain.home.

CISDOC database
The CIS bibliographic database contains about 70,000 citations of documents that deal with occupational accidents and diseases as well as ways of preventing them.

The resource is available on: ⑨ http://www.ilo.org/dyn/cisdoc2/cismain.home?p_lang=en.

EPLex — Employment protection legislation database
EPLex provides information on all the key topics that are regularly examined in national and comparative studies on employment termination legislation.[1]

The resource is available on: ⑨ http://www.ilo.org/dyn/eplex/termmain.home.

Labor Force Surveys
The resource is available on: ⑨ http://www.ilo.org/dyn/lfsurvey/lfsurvey.home.

6. National Statistical Offices Websites[1]

You can find a list of country statistical databases on the UNSTATS website. The resource can be accessed through ⑨ http://unstats.un.org/unsd/methods/inter-natlinks/sd_natstat.asp.

7. Exporting guides

CANADA — *Step-by-Step Guide to Exporting* is available on: ⑨ http://www.tradecommissioner.gc.ca/eng/guide-exporting.jsp.

USA — *A Basic Guide to Exporting* is available on: ⑨ http://export.gov/basicguide/.

U.K. — guide to importing and exporting: Breaking down the barriers available on the HMRC website. Available on: ⑤ http://customs.hmrc.gov.uk/channelsPortalWebApp/channelsPortal WebApp.portal?_nfpb=true&_pageLabel=pageImport_InfoGuides &propertyType=document&id=HMCE_PROD_008051.

UK — Imports and exports available on: ⑤ https://www.gov.uk/browse/business/imports-exports

U.K. — UK Trade & Investment (UKTI) resources are available on: ⑤ http://www.ukti.gov.uk/export.html.

New Zealand — starting to export guides are available on: ⑤ http://www.nzte.govt.nz/get-ready-to-export/starting-to-export/pages/starting-to-export-guides.aspx.

Exporting from the EU — the Market Access Database (MADB) gives information to companies exporting from the EU about import conditions in third country markets. This is available on: ⑤ http://madb.europa.eu/madb/indexPubli.htm.

UK export finance and credit insurance — a Guide published in June 2012 which aims to provide insight into key aspects of how to finance export activities. This is available on: ⑤ http://www.icaew.com/~/media/Files/Technical/Business-and-financial-management/SMEs/5623-export-report-web-3-.pdf.

The British Exporters Association (BExA) — Guides. A series of useful information is available on: ⑤ online at http://www.bexa.co.uk/exportinfo.html.

Global Trader Guides from the British Chambers of Commerce
This site provides export guides on developed and emerging markets, key industry sectors, trade missions and events, thus providing an essential source for companies investigating commercial trading opportunities overseas. This is available on: ⑤ http://www.britishchambers.org.uk/business/trading-internationally/export-publications/#.UPKJ1B3ZaSp.

Research your export markets
Available on: ⑤ http://www.icaew.com/~/media/Files/Library/
collections/online-resources/briefings/directors-briefings/
EI2RESEA.pdf.

Export finance — a briefing on export finance. Available on:
⑤ http://www.icaew.com/~/media/Files/Library/collections/
online-resources/briefings/directors-briefings/EI3EXPOR.pdf.

Import finance Guide — Available on: ⑤ http://www.icaew.
com/~/media/Files/Library/collections/online-resources/
briefings/directors-briefings/EI4IMPO.pdf.

International Trade Guide — an accountant's guide to Trade.
Available on: ⑤ http://www.icaew.com/~/media/Files/Technical/
Business-and-financial-management/SMEs/ukti-accounts-guide-
accessible.pdf.

First steps to exporting — Available on: ⑤ http://www.icaew.
com/~/media/Files/Library/collections/online-resources/
briefings/directors-briefings/EI1FIRST.pdf.

The BIFA Good Practice Toolbox — a series of guides related
to international freight. Available on: ⑤ http://www.bifa.org/
content/Information-Pra.aspx.

8. Knowledge databases

These are a selection of online resources that can help the reader
with additional information and resources.

IMF — eLIBRARY — In-depth, independent analysis on the financial crisis, development, macroeconomics, poverty reduction,
trade, globalization, and much more .This is available on: ⑤
http://www.elibrary.imf.org/.

OECD Library — the OECD's global knowledge platform. This is
available on: ⑤ http://www.oecd-ilibrary.org/.

Open to Export is a community driven service for small and medium sized businesses, looking for support in exporting from the U.K. This is available on: ✪ http://opentoexport.com/.

British International Freight Association (BIFA) — the trade association for U.K.-registered companies engaged in international movement of freight by all modes of transport, air, road, rail, and sea. This is available on: ✪ http://www.bifa.org.

Austrade resources on exporting — this is available on: ✪ http://www.austrade.gov.au/How-to-export/default.aspx.

U.K. tradeinfo
This website is managed by HM Revenue & Customs (HMRC) Trade Statistics unit, and operates alongside the main HMRC website for the purpose of publishing and hosting U.K. trade statistics data. This is available on: ✪ https://www.uktradeinfo.com.

U.K. export finance — the U.K.'s export credit agency provides a range of services to support exporters. This is available on: ✪ http://www.ukexportfinance.gov.uk/.

Export Control Organisation — information from the Department for Business, Innovation and Skills on export licenses. This is available on: ✪ https://www.gov.uk/search?q=export+control.

GAPMINDER
Gapmider created by Hans Rosling is a tool that allows you to visualize data and statistics across several variables. A desktop version is also available. The resource is available on: ✪ http://www.gapminder.org/.

Peter Day's World of Business
The BBC's Insights into the business world with Peter Day features content from his Radio 4. In Business programs, and also Global Business from the BBC World Service has downloadable podcasts

and is available on: ⑨ http://www.bbc.co.uk/podcasts/series/worldbiz.

The International Trade Administration (ITA) — resources available on: ⑨ http://www.ita.doc.gov/data.asp.

Corruption Perceptions Index
The Corruption Perceptions Index ranks countries and territories based on how corrupt their public sector is perceived to be. A country or territory's score indicates the perceived level of public sector corruption on a scale of 0–100, where 0 means that a country is perceived as highly corrupt and 100 means it is perceived as very clean.

The resource is available on: ⑨ http://www.transparency.org/.

The EU doing Business portal
This portal provides information on taxes, importing and exporting goods, and financial support for businesses as well as other topics for business within the EU.

The resource is available on: ⑨ http://europa.eu/youreurope/business/.

World Bank Development Indicators
The primary World Bank collection of development indicators, compiled from officially-recognized international sources. It presents the most current and accurate global development data available, and includes national, regional, and global estimates.

The resource is available on: ⑨ http://data.worldbank.org/datacatalog/world-development-indicators

globalEDGE
Funded in part by the U.S. Department of Education Title VI B grant, globalEDGE delivers a comprehensive research tool for academics, students, and business people. Connect with over 47,000 people using the gE Network while tapping into a directory of over

5,000 quality resources. globalEDGE provides tools and resources to efficiently research nearly any international business question you may have.

The resource can be accessed through ⊕ http://globaledge.msu.edu/.

The resource offers the following information:

- **Research by Trade Bloc** — data about the 11 major trading blocs and the participating countries.
- **Industry Insights** that provide news, events, and statistical data for any of twenty distinct industry sectors.
- The **Global Resource Directory** that offers a rich collection of thousands of international business- and trade-related resources and is available on: ⊕ http://globaledge.msu.edu/Global-Resources.
- **Market Potential Index** (MPI) for Emerging Markets ⊕ http://globaledge.msu.edu/Knowledge-Tools/mpi.
- **Country Comparator** which helps to compare countries across a variety of economic indicators including GDP, inflation, and exports and is available on: ⊕ http://globaledge.msu.edu/Comparator.
- globalEDGE Database of International Business Statistics™. This is a free database of statistics and is available on: ⊕ http://globaledge.msu.edu/Knowledge-Tools/dibs. A free registration is required to access this database.

9. United Nations Databases[1]

International Standard Industrial Classification of All Economic Activities

The International Standard Industrial Classification of All Economic Activities (ISIC) is the international reference classification of productive activities. Its main purpose is to provide a set of activity categories that can be utilized for the collection and reporting of statistics according to such activities.

The resource is available on: ⑤ http://unstats.un.org/unsd/publication/seriesM/seriesm_4rev4e.pdf.

The United Nations Statistics Division Resources

This division of the UN compiles and disseminates global statistical information, develops standards and norms for statistical activities, and supports countries' efforts to strengthen their national statistical system

UN Comtrade Yearbook

The *International Trade Statistics Yearbook, Volume II — Trade by Commodity* provides information on the world trade of individual commodities (3-digit SITC groups) and 11 world trade tables covering trade values and indices.

The resource is available on: ⑤ http://comtrade.un.org/pb/.

Sectoral Classification List (W/120)

The services sectoral classification list (W/120) is a comprehensive list of services sectors and sub-sectors covered under the GATS.

The resource is available on: ⑤ http://tsdb.wto.org/Includes/docs/W120_E.doc.

Analytical trade tables of the International Merchandise Trade Statistics Section (IMTSS)

The International Merchandise Trade Statistics Section (IMTSS) of the United Nations Statistics Division (UNSD), Department of Economic and Social Affairs produces analytical trade tables containing trade values and indices for countries (areas) and regions.

The resource is available on: ⑤ http://unstats.un.org/unsd/trade/imts/analyticaltradetables.htm.

Specific country profiles on IMTSS

The resource is available on: ⑨ http://comtrade.un.org/pb/
CountryPagesNew.aspx?y=2011.

UNDATA
UNdata is an internet-based data service which brings UN statistical
databases within easy reach of users through a single entry point.
The resource is available on: ⑨ http://data.un.org/.

Energy Statistics Database
The Energy Statistics Database contains comprehensive energy statistics on the production, trade, conversion, and final consumption
of primary and secondary; conventional and non-conventional; and
new and renewable sources of energy. The Energy Statistics dataset,
covering the period from 1990 onwards, is available at UNdata.
For data prior to 1990, please refer to ⑨ *http://unstats.un.org/unsd/
energy/edbase.htm which needs subscription.*

FAOSTAT
FAOSTAT provides access to over 3 million time series and cross-
sectional data relating to food and agriculture. FAOSTAT contains
data for 200 countries and more than 200 primary products and
inputs in its core data set
The resource is available on: ⑨ http://faostat.fao.org/.

Global Indicator Database
The Global Indicator Database is comprised of a wide range of
important statistics and metadata drawn from the United Nations,
UN agencies and other international sources. It covers key economic, social, financial, and development topics, broadly based on
the structure of the UN Statistical Yearbook (SYB).
The resource is available on: ⑨ http://unstats.un.org.

Human Development Report

The Human Development Report is a reliable source and an alternative perspective on critical issues for human development worldwide.

The resource is available on: 🌐 http://hdr.undp.org/en/statistics/data/.

International Financial Statistics
International Financial Statistics (IFS) is a standard source of international statistics on all aspects of international and domestic finance.

The resource is available on: 🌐 http://elibrary-data.imf.org/FindDataReports.aspx?d=33061&e=169393.

UNESCO Data Centre
The Data Centre contains over 1,000 types of indicators and raw data on education, literacy, science and technology, culture and communication.

The resource is available on: 🌐 http://stats.uis.unesco.org/unesco/

UNSD Demographic Statistics
The United Nations Demographic Yearbook collects, compiles, and disseminates official statistics on a wide range of topics.

The resource is available on: 🌐 http://unstats.un.org/unsd/demographic/.

World Health Statistics
World Health Statistics presents the most recent health statistics for WHO's 193 Member States.

The resource is available on: 🌐 http://apps.who.int/whosis/data/.

10. UNCTAD resources

UNCTAD promotes the development-friendly integration of developing countries into the world economy. Several of its statistics are freely available online and are useful in understanding the world of International business.

UNCTAD Statistics[1]

Being the United Nations' focal point for the integrated treatment of trade and development and the interrelated issues in the areas of finance, technology, investment, and sustainable development, UNCTAD compiles, validates, and processes a wide range of data collected from national and international sources.

UNCTAD produces more than 150 indicators and statistical time series essential for the analysis of:

- International trade.
- Economic trends.
- Foreign direct investment.
- External financial resources.
- Population and labor force.
- Commodities.
- Information economy.
- Creative economy.
- Maritime transport.

The resource is available on: ☞ http://unctad.org/en/Pages/Statistics.aspx.

Trade Analysis Branch[1]

The Trade Analysis Branch (TAB) of the Division on International Trade in Goods and Services, and Commodities undertakes policy-oriented analytical work aimed at improving the understanding of relevant and emerging issues in international trade.

The resource is available on: ☞ http://www.unctad-trains.org/.

United Nations Multilingual Terminology Database

This database was compiled over the years in response to diverse and wide-ranging demands of United Nations language staff for terminology and nomenclature.[1]

The resource is available on: ☞ http://unterm.un.org/.

UNCTAD Handbook of Statistics
The UNCTAD Handbook of Statistics provides essential data for analyzing and measuring world trade, investment, international financial flows and development.
The resource is available on: 🕏 http://unctad.org/en/PublicationsLibrary/tdstat37_en.pdf.

World Statistics Pocketbook
A downloadable compilations of key statistical indicators prepared by the United Nations Statistics Division
The resource is available on: 🕏 http://unstats.un.org/unsd/pocketbook/.

11. World Telecommunication/ICT Indicators Database

World Telecommunication/ICT Indicators Database
The resource is available on: 🕏 http://www.itu.int/ITU-D/ict/statistics/.

Global ICT trends
The resource is available on: 🕏 http://www.itu.int/ITU-D/ict/statistics/.

Fixed telephony
The resource is available on: 🕏 http://www.itu.int/ITU-D/ict/statistics/.

Internet users
The resource is available on: 🕏 http://www.itu.int/ITU-D/ict/statistics/.

Gender Statistics
The resource is available on: 🕏 http://www.itu.int/ITU-D/ict/statistics/Gender/index.html.

12. WTO Resources

The World Trade Organization (WTO) is the only global international organization dealing with the rules of trade between nations. Several of the WTO statistics are freely available online and are useful in understanding the world of International business.

Short-term merchandise trade statistics
The WTO Secretariat makes available a number of different types of short-term merchandise trade data.

The resource is available on: ⊛ http://www.wto.org/english/res_e/statis_e/quarterly_world_exp_e.htm.

Trade and tariff indicators
The resource is available on: ⊛ http://www.wto.org/english/res_e/statis_e/statis_maps_e.htm.

Participation in Regional Trade Agreements
A country wise resource showing RTA details. The resource is available on: ⊛ http://www.wto.org/english/tratop_e/region_e/rta_participation_map_e.htm?country_selected=ALB&sense=b.

WTO trade topics
A wealth of information is available on: the trade topics. The resource is available on: ⊛ http://www.wto.org/english/tratop_e/tratop_e.htm.

International trade and market access data
The WTO's databases and publications provide extensive access to trade and tariff data. This information includes Tariff profiles, Trade profiles, Services profiles , World merchandise exports by main product, origin and destination, and many more useful statistics

The resource is available on: ⊛ http://www.wto.org/english/res_e/statis_e/looking4_e.htm#summary.

13. World Customs Union

The resource is available on: ⑨ http://www.wcoomd.org/.
International Customs Tariffs Bureau — downloadable customs profiles for all member countries
   The resource is available on: ⑨ http://www.bitd.org/

14. World Bank

World Development Indicators[1]
The World Development Indicators (WDI) is the statistical benchmark that helps measure the progress of development.
   The resource is available on: ⑨ http://databank.worldbank.org/data/home.aspx.

New

UK Tariff Codes
A complete list of the commodity codes required to classify goods for import or export. These codes are used to find import duties, taxes, rebates, reliefs, licenses and special conditions that apply to particular goods:
   ⑨ http://data.gov.uk/dataset/uk-tariff-codes-2009-2010.

Code-Point Open
Code-Point Open contains a list of all the current postcode units in Great Britain, each of which has a precise geographic location at a resolution of one meter
   ⑨ http://data.ordnancesurvey.co.uk/datasets/code-point-open.

DataViva
DataViva is a Data Visualization Engine created by the Strategic Priorities Office of the government of Minas Gerais. DataViva makes available official data about exports, industries, locations, and occupations for the entirety of Brazil through eight apps and more than 100 million possible visualizations.
   ⑨ http://dataviva.info/.
Africa Open Data

Africa's largest central repository for Government, Civil Society, Corporate, and Donor Agency Data.
⊛ http://africaopendata.org/.

Data South Australia
data.sa helps you locate openly licensed data so you can transform that data, creating new ideas and application.
⊛ http://data.sa.gov.au/.
data.norge.no.
Norway's official government open data catalogue.
⊛ http://data.norge.no/.

Appendix D

Company Profile Questionnaire

Please take a few minutes and complete this questionnaire, which is designed to provide us with a profile of your company's product(s)/ service(s) and your level of involvement in international business. Your responses will be used by our project team to address your needs. Please complete and return the questionnaire along with (4) sets of product literature and (1) set of company information at your earliest convenience. Your cooperation is greatly appreciated. All information will be kept strictly confidential.

_____ YES, My Company wants to participate in the Global Marketing Management Program.

Contact Person _____ Title _____
Telephone _____ Fax _____
Company Name _____
Street Address _____
City/State/Zip _____
Telephone/Fax(If different from above)_____

1) Describe your principle product/service. (Please provide four sets of product literature.)

2) Describe your company's mission and objective(s).

3) Describe your company strategy for its principal product/ service.

4) How is your product/service unique, and/or what is its competitive advantage?

☐ less than $500,000   ☐ $5,000,000 to $10,000,000
☐ $500,000 to $999,999   ☐ over $10,000,000
☐ $1,000,000 to $4,999,999

5) Number of employees

☐ less than 10   ☐ 100 to 500
☐ 10 to 49   ☐ over 500
☐ 50 to 99

6) Total annual sales (U.S. and International)

7) How many years has your company been in operation?

8) What barriers has your company encountered? What problems are you currently experiencing in conducting international trade? (Check all that apply.)

☐ Lack of market information   ☐ Don't know how to get started
☐ Financing   ☐ Lack of trained personnel
☐ Price competition   ☐ Setting paid
☐ Product adaptability   ☐ Distributor identification and evaluation
☐ Servicing requirements   ☐ Foreign competition
☐ Distribution channels   ☐ Language and cultural differences
☐ Trade or legal restrictions   ☐ Other (please specify)

9) Please rank the export needs of your company in order of preference.
(1 = Most Preferred 9 = Least Preferred)

☐ Assess company export potential
☐ Distributor identification and evaluation
☐ Identify key foreign markets

□ Export financing and insurance
□ Individual country market analysis
□ Export shipping and documentation
□ Market entry conditions and terms of access
□ Other (please specify)

10) Please list specific questions that you would like your project team to address during this project.

11) Is your company currently involved in international trade?

□ Yes (if yes, please answer questions 12–20)
□ No (if no, stop here)

12) What is your company's level of involvement in international business? (Check all that apply.)

□ Filling orders   □ Contract manufacturing
□ Actively seeking export sales   □ Licensing agreements
□ Overseas subsidiary (sales/   □ Importing
  marketing)   □ Other (please specify)
□ Foreign production (joint
  venture)
□ Foreign production (wholly
  owned)

13) How many years has your company been involved in international business?

14) Does your company have a written international marketing plan?

□ Yes
□ No

15) What percentage of your sales are:
exports _____ percent   imports _____ percent

16) What products/services do you sell internationally?

17) List your top 3 export country markets based on sales volume.

1 _____

2 _____

3 _____

18) How do you distribute abroad? (Check all that apply)

Indirect exporting:

☐ Export management Co.
☐ Export trading Co.
☐ Export agent
☐ Piggybacking
☐ Marketing Subsidiary
☐ Other (please specify)

Direct Exporting:

☐ Foreign based distributor
☐ Foreign based agents
☐ Direct to the end of the user
☐ Company's own sales/mktg. Subsidiary
☐ Other (please specify)

19) How is your international business function organized?

☐ Domestic sales/marketing department
☐ International headquarters company
☐ Export department
☐ Export management company
☐ International division
☐ Other (please specify)

20) The number of full- and part-time employees in international business are: _____ FT _____ PT

Appendix E

Product/Marketing Questionnaire

Please help us to identify target markets for your product/product line by completing this questionnaire. If the product/service being asked about is identical to your company's principal product/service and you have already offered the information on your PROFILE questionnaire, simply disregard the question. All responses will be kept confidential. Thank You.

Target Market

1) What is the product/product line you are interested in exporting?

2) Please describe the end user of your product.

3) Please describe the buyer of your product if different from (2).

4) If you currently export this product, please list all of your export markets in order of sales volume.

5) Are the characteristics of the foreign consumer different from those in the U.S.? If so, please describe them.

6) Is your product suited for (choose one):

   ☐ Industrialized countries
   ☐ Newly industrialized countries
   ☐ Less developed countries

Product

7) Is your product a consumer or industrial good? (please circle one)

8) What is/are the need(s) satisfied by your product?

9) What characteristics does your product have that give it an advantage or make it unique in the marketplace?

10) Are there any specific operating conditions or skills required in order to use your product (e.g., computer experience, electrical supply, large-scale operation, technical proficiency)?

11) Are the product-use conditions the same between the U.S. and foreign markets?

12) What training and after-sales service requirements does your product have?

13) What other products are used in conjunction with your product (related, complementary, or substitute)?

14) What type of patent and trademark protection does your product have? Is this type of protection important for your product?

15) Do you have product liability insurance for the U.S. market and/or foreign markets? If yes, please describe the extent of the coverage and the reason for being covered.

16) Does your product require a validated export license? If yes, explain why?

17) What country-specific factors could be used to determine sales potential for your product (e.g., number of food processing plants, computer sales, number of machine tool manufacturers, agricultural production and products)?

18) What factors could affect sales of your product to a particular country? Detail where appropriate (e.g., government regulations, economic conditions, culture, climatic and geographic conditions, educational level.)

Competition

19) Who are your major U.S. and foreign-based competitors in this product category?

20) How does their product compare to yours?

21) What is your market share?

U.S. Market	Foreign Market(s)	Country share
☐	_____	☐
	_____	☐
	_____	☐

Distribution

22) What are your main channels of distribution?

Domestic markets:

International markets:

23) Do you currently have foreign distributor agreements? If yes, list the countries:

Country	Exclusive ☐	Non-exclusive ☐
Country	Exclusive ☐	Non-exclusive ☐
Country	Exclusive ☐	Non-exclusive ☐
Country	Exclusive ☐	Non-exclusive ☐
Country	Exclusive ☐	Non-exclusive ☐

24) What are your methods of transportation?

    Domestic:

    International:

25) What is the company name of your foreign freight forwarder?

    Promotion

26) Please describe how you currently promote your product.

    Domestic markets:

    a) Promotion mix
    b) Media used
    c) Trade shows attended

    International markets:

    a) Promotion mix
    b) Media used
    c) Trade shows attended

    Price

27) What is the total unit cost of your product(s)?

28) What is your F.O.B. plant price?

29) Is your F.O.B. price for export the same as your domestic price? If not what is it?

30) What is the suggested U.S. selling price of your product(s)?

31) What are your trade discounts to channel members?

    U.S. _____ %

    Foreign _____ %

32) Are your products price above or below the competition? Why?

Appendix F

Bibliography

DeKanter, N. (2005). Gaming redefines interactivity for learning. *TechTrends: Linking Research and Practice to Improve Learning, 49*(3), 26–31.

Gomes, E., Janavaras, B., & Cheema, P. (2008). Improving decision making and critical thinking skills via web-based tools: The case of the global marketing management system online. *Journal of International Business and Economics, 8*(3), 132–142.

Hollensen, S. (2007). *Global Marketing — A Decision Oriented Approach.* Prentice Hall.

Janavaras, B., Gomes, E., Cheema, P., & George, S. (2008). International business strategy: an innovative teaching and learning approach. *Icfai Journal of Business Strategy, 5*(2), 24–35.

Janavaras, B. (1998). *Global Marketing Management System.* Pearson Education Inc.

Janavaras, B. (2007). Global business research and strategic planning tools. *Journal of International Business and Economy, 8*(1), 59–70.

Janavaras, B. J. (2012). Teaching and learning global marketing using the web. *AIB Insights, Modalities and Tools of International Business Education, 12*(1). ⊕ http://documents.aib.msu.edu/publications/insights/archive/insights_v012n01.pdf

Kotabe, M., & Helsen, K. (2001). *Global Marketing Management.* John Wiley and Sons.

Mintzberg, H. (1987). Crafting strategy. *Harvard Business Review, 65,* 66–75.

Shields, E. A. (2005). *A Guide to Project-based Learning.* McGraw-Hill On-Line Learning Center. ⊕ http://www.mhhe.com/business/management/PBL/.

Printed in the United States
By Bookmasters